C.S. LEWIS:
HIS LITERARY ACHIEVEMENT

COLIN MANLOVE

Originally published as *C. S. Lewis: His Literary Achievement*
Copyright © 1987 Colin Manlove
in Great Britain by Palgrave MacMillan
in the United States by St Martin's: New York

C. S. Lewis: His Literary Achievement
Copyright © 2010 Colin Manlove

Published by Winged Lion Press
Cheshire, CT

All rights reserved. Except in the case of quotations embodied in critical articles or reviews, no part of this book may be reproduced or transmitted in any form or by any means, electronic or mechanical, including photocopying, recording, or by any information storage or retrieval system, without written permission of the publisher.
For information, contact Winged Lion Press www.WingedLion.com

Winged Lion Press titles may be purchased for business or promotional use or special sales.

10-9-8-7-6-5-4-3-2-1

ISBN-13 978-1-935688-50-1

To Evelyn again,

wherever you are

Table of Contents

Chapter 1	Introduction	1
Chapter 2	*The Pilgrims Regress*	13
Chapter 3	*Out of the Silent Planet*	29
Chapter 4	*Perelandra*	49
Chapter 5	*That Hideous Strength*	79
Chapter 6	*The Great Divorce*	103
Chapter 7	*The Chronicles of Narnia*	123
Chapter 8	*Till We Have Faces*	195
Chapter 9	Conclusion	223
Bibliography		231
Index		237

Preface

This book first appeared in 1987, and the intention for this new appearance was that it should be reprinted. However, in the short time I left myself to check the typescript, I found numbers of things I wanted to change, and this to the best of my ability I have done. Among these have been a new Introduction, and new prefatory material to most of the chapters. The style and long paragraphs of the original have also received attention.

I still wish to acknowledge the stimulus I have received from certain books on Lewis – in particular Brian Murphy's *Out of the Silent Planet*, Peter Schakel's *Reading with the Heart: the Way into Narnia* and, since this book first appeared, Doris Myers's *C. S. Lewis in Context*. Even if they look at Lewis with prior themes in mind, their method is very fruitful.

I would like to thank Bob Trexler for his careful work on this book while he was busy setting up the new press that would publish it.

I also still wish to say how much this book owed on its first appearance to the care and encouragement of my late wife Evelyn.

C.N.M.

Chapter 1

Introduction

When this book first appeared in 1987, fifty books had been published on C. S. Lewis; now, in 2009, there are some two hundred. What can be the justification for the reappearance of this one? The answer has, with humility, to be that few of the others approach Lewis in quite the way that I do here.

In the first place there are very few analyses of Lewis's work as literature: that is, few that consider his style and technique in putting over his vision. This is a large claim, and I must pay tribute to the exceptions – to writers such as Clyde Kilby, Peter Schakel, Brian Murphy, Doris Myers and Lionel Adey. But even of these five, only Kilby and Adey are centrally concerned with assessing Lewis's literary skills; and Adey looks at Lewis in the light of one theme, that of the Mentor versus the Dreamer. Nevertheless these are the writers who have given me most, and who seem to me nearest to the heart of Lewis and his work.

My second claim to novelty is that I try to let the works dictate what I say, rather than putting ideas on to them. I find that many writers on C. S. Lewis tend to take one view and then trace it throughout his work. They argue generally from a position, assuming or trying to show that a belief or a theme is present in Lewis. Some suppose that because Lewis is a Christian he is their idea of a Christian. Others claim that because he read a certain book its ideas are to be found in his work. And all writers on Lewis tend to believe that he can never do wrong. Some of what these writers find is exciting and interesting, and can have the ring of truth: a recent example is Michael Ward's *Planet Narnia*, on the possible unity given to the Narnia books by the Renaissance picture of the seven planets. But when looking for one thing you tend to ignore everything else, and particularly what runs contrary to it.

For the *a priori* approach to Lewis's work I substitute an *a posteriori* one. That is, I try to let Lewis's books speak for themselves, and then draw the conclusions they suggest to me. This attempt at objectivity can never be perfect, for somewhere I will get in the way with my own ideas. However, it must be tried, not only because it may reach more of the truth about Lewis, but because that was the way he often thought and worked himself. He found out what he was doing by doing it.

One form of this *a posteriori* method I can introduce at the outset. I am not going to assume that Lewis is a better writer for being a Christian. Almost any writer, of whatever belief or lack of it, sometimes makes mistakes, reveals shortcomings or falls short of his or her aims. Lewis is certainly no exception to this. He is not a Dante, or a Spenser, or a Milton. He is a minor fiction writer of the twentieth century, employing a literary form we now call fantasy. As a Christian he may have inspired many, and his vision is often novel, exciting and moving, but this by itself does not make him a great writer.

If in America Lewis is sometimes seen as a literary saint, in Britain he and the kind of literature he writes have often been viewed in an opposite light by his peers. In many universities, fantasy is still regarded as a somewhat dubious genre, to be sponsored only to keep up student numbers. Many academics in the Oxford of Lewis's time saw Lewis as a sort of intellectual and spiritual prostitute who sold his talents to the *hoi polloi* and his soul to the Scripture Union. There are some in his native land who simply dislike Lewis's personality and literary approach, whether for his brisk heartiness, his supposed misogyny, his conservatism or his hostility to psychoanalysis. Some of these attitudes to Lewis we may reject, but from others we can learn something: and from all we can see that the uncritical view of Lewis will not do, that there are other possible views of him and his work, and that simply assuming he can do no wrong is inadequate both to the truth and to Lewis as a man.

There is another reason for not cutting Lewis off from this more critical world, which is that he did not do so himself. What is often forgotten about Lewis is that he was an atheist for fifteen years before becoming a Christian for the next thirty. And for much of that thirty he argued not just with unbelievers but with his unbelieving self. How else would his Christian apologetics continue to have such popularity almost fifty years after his death, unless it gave the impression of someone continually fighting for and renewing his faith through dispute? As far as he was concerned, one could never be a Christian, one could only try to be one. It is possible that Lewis remained a Christian because his faith could include his earlier atheism as debating partner. His faith was a live thing, a continual battle with a cunning enemy who knew his every strength and weakness, and could use his own weapons of reason and imagination against him. What might have appeared a quiet Oxford don's life was for him one where he stood stripped before God and tormented by doubt every day. People often marvel at his industry, but for him each book, each broadcast talk, each debate and even each letter, was a struggle to re-convince himself by convincing others. As for his daily life, one has only to read *The Screwtape Letters* (1942) to see how much he had to be vigilant against temptation. Indeed he seemed to his close friend Owen Barfield always like a 'spiritual alumnus taking his moral finals'.[1]

In a Britain steadily removing itself from Christian belief, Lewis was never one to preach only to the converted. During the war, for instance, he regularly addressed RAF pilots whose lives were an everyday gamble, and whose attitudes to Christianity might often be ribald or downright hostile. For years he was the central debater of the Oxford Socratic Club, doing battle with all comers. More than this, much of his work addresses the non-Christian. *The Problem of Pain* and *Miracles* are addressed to the ordinary thinking man – and there were such men then. Lewis writes with a point to prove, but he takes full account of the objections. One feels as one reads that this is not someone rehearsing a case, rather someone finding out a truth together with his reader. That immediacy made him very popular, and still does.

Most of all Lewis always began at the beginning. His apologetics assume nothing about his audience: he is no cleric supposing or demanding that his congregation come through the church door because they share his beliefs; he does not impose ideas *a priori*. This is largely because he too is beginning again, he is finding out with others and renewing his certainty through them. He always addressed people through the shared medium of reason and logic, so that if they agreed, it would be because they saw the sense in doing so. His audience might be well aware that he wanted to persuade them towards faith, but they knew that they were being guided on a visit rather than herded into a citadel. Lewis's view was that he could prove Christianity by argument, and this allowed any who heard him to argue back in the same terms. For Lewis the 'belief' element of Christianity was something given to you after argument had persuaded you to become one. That is why his Addison Walk argument with Tolkien and Hugo Dyson in 1929 converted him, but he did not come to believe until one day when he went on an outing to Whipsnade in 1931. (Indeed Lewis said that he had a still earlier conversion than this, because when he first read George MacDonald's *Phantastes* in 1916 his imagination was 'baptised'.)

Lewis's *Miracles: A Preliminary Study* (1947) reads like a manual, starting with basic terms, moving out to larger issues and then demonstrating how everything comes together. He builds a case like building a model, into a lattice of thought. And that is one of the first impulses behind his writing. He describes in *Surprised by Joy* how he inherited a defect in his thumb joints that made it impossible for him to make anything out of physical materials.

> It was this that forced me to write. I longed to make things, ships, houses, engines. Many sheets of cardboard and pairs of scissors I spoiled, only to turn from my hopeless failures in tears. As a last resort, as a *pis aller*, I was driven to write stories instead; little dreaming to what a world of happiness I was being admitted. You can do more with a castle in a story than with the best cardboard castle that ever stood on a nursery table.[2]

This is a key to Lewis's writing, as a mode of construction from pieces, as one might build a bridge or a crane from Meccano. Behind Lewis's work there is a pleasure in making, in assembling images or arguments into larger units that stand up to scrutiny. However deep the dispute or ugly the fictional environment, he is always enjoying himself. When in *The Great Divorce* he gives us an apparently vast hell that is then shown to be a tiny crack among the grass blades of heaven; when he gives us the thrust and counter-thrust of argument with the Lady in *Perelandra*; describes the stages by which Mark Studdock falls towards the devil in *That Hideous Strength*; or shows us the workings of a ministry of bureaucratic fiends in *The Screwtape Letters* – in all these Lewis is enjoying himself building something. There is always that side of his work where he is in love with the making itself. And always when he has finished he must go on to make something else, something different.

In Lewis's fiction, faith is learnt in new rather than traditional modes. He writes fantasy because it allows him to use the Christian supernatural in non-biblical ways. In his 'space trilogy' his hero Ransom goes out of this world and finds a divine universe. He discovers a new and very different Paradise on one planet, and a far different prohibition on its unfallen inhabitants than the apple-eating we know on Earth.[3] Not only this, he helps stop the Fall from happening. Lewis's writing counters the view that man and Earth are God's central concern, and that the Christian story is the only one of its kind. In his Narnia he gives us a world where a new pattern of death and salvation is carried out by a Lion God to save not just a human boy but a world of Talking Beasts. And in *Till We Have Faces* the usual patronage of 'virtuous pagans' and the idea that new truth only works forward in time are subverted in the pre-Christian world of Glome, where the god who loves Pyche is ultimately a form of Christ, and 'Bear ye one another's burdens' is a timeless supernatural principle.

All Lewis's protagonists develop towards a new spiritual awareness of the universe by a process of personal experience, moving often from ignorant agnosticism to belief. They discover things for themselves, without benefit of theology. John in *The Pilgrim's Regress*, led by a haunting desire through many misidentifications of it, eventually finds that his longing came from the very 'Landlord' from whom he has been trying to escape all his life. In the 'space trilogy', Dr Elwin Ransom of Cambridge grows out of his narrow fears to discover and become one with the divine basis of the universe: and Mark and Jane Studdock in *That Hideous Strength* learn faith through their mistakes. Orual in *Till We Have Faces* refuses to accept that her beloved Psyche is married to a god, and ruins Psyche's happiness and her own before eventually learning the truth. Thus all things in the fiction are dynamic, are in a state of flux and change. Even at the ends there is often no completion.

With Lewis's fiction, the pieces from which he built his work were initially images.

> In a certain sense, I have never exactly 'made' a story. With me the process is more like bird-watching than like either talking or building. I see pictures. Some of these pictures have a common flavour, almost a common smell, which groups them together. Keep quiet and watch and they will begin joining themselves up. If you were very lucky (I have never been as lucky as all that) a whole set might join themselves so consistently that there you had a complete story: without doing anything yourself. But more often (in my experience always) there are gaps. Then at last you have to do some deliberate inventing, have to contrive reasons why these characters should be in these various places doing these various things. I have no idea whether this is the usual way of writing stories, still less whether it is the best. It is the only one I know: images always come first.[4]

One may think this a little disingenuous – that 'keep quiet' may be true regarding the bird-watching analogy, but it is not true for what the brain and imagination are doing just as quietly. Lewis is claiming a little more of the 'given' in the process than is probably the case: but then he was never too fond of unconscious workings by the mind. He preferred mystery. 'Making up is a very mysterious thing. When you "have an idea" could you tell anyone exactly how you thought of it?'[5] But the point at issue here is that Lewis's stories did not start as connected chains but as free images that then linked up. What Lewis is attesting to is the power of the pictures in his work. This is a writer with a very strong visual sense. His books abound with striking and resonant images – the flight of the queen in the poem *The Queen of Drum*, the great ocean of Perelandra with its floating islands, the spire-like verticality and the colours of the Malacandrian forests and rocks in *Out of the Silent Planet*, the dreadful head in *That Hideous Strength*, the great lion on the sacrificial stone, the ship on the bright sea, the prince in the silver chair or the ascent to heaven in the Narnia books. Lewis has a cinematic ability to bring an image gradually into sharp focus, or to track away from an intense scene to the wider context around it. These images all form a major part of our experience of these books, for they are all highly vivid and individual while being fantastic.

'Then came the Form': as the images sorted themselves into the events of a story, they called for a form that would best express them. In the case of *Out of the Silent Planet* and *Perelandra* this was the popular genre of prose science fiction. With the Narnia books it was the fairy tale, or rather, Lewis's version of it. 'I fell in love with the form itself: its brevity, its severe restraints on description, its flexible traditionalism, its inflexible hostility to all analysis, digression, reflctions and 'gas'.[6] It is possible that Lewis came to the fairy tale because the earlier forms he had used, the pilgrimage allegory, the speculative novel and the posthumous vision had been too loose and baggy for him, and he felt he had talked too much.

Only at this point, Lewis says, did 'the Man' have his turn. Only at this point did he start to see that the story might be put to Christian use, which would be the more effective for being disguised as a fairy tale or a piece of science fiction. In a conversation with Brian Aldiss the science fiction writer and the novelist Kingsley Amis in 1962 Lewis said,

> The starting point of the second novel, *Perelandra*, was my mental picture of the floating islands. The whole of the rest of my labours consisted of building up a world in which floating islands

could exist. And then of course the story about an averted fall developed. This is because, as you know, having got your people to this exciting country, something must happen.[7]

Here he rates the initial image so highly as to say that it is the real subject of his work. But to this claim Aldiss replies, 'I am surprised you put it this way round. I would have thought that you constructed Perelandra for the didactic purpose.' To which Lewis responds, rather glibly, 'Yes, everyone thinks that. They are quite wrong.' This raises the possibility that what Lewis thinks he is doing in his work is not what he does – or at least, is not for many the effect he produces.

The likely gap between an author's intention and his achievement is now a critical commonplace, which states that what an author says and what he or she does should not simply be identified, but at best compared. However in Lewis's case the image is indeed primary, but what happens is that he sometimes mixes in an amount of theology, morality and argument that clouds this and makes us think it more important. Lionel Adey has portrayed in Lewis a continual struggle between the 'Dreamer' and the 'Mentor', the one concerned with imagery and fiction, the other with making significance out of them.[8] The Mentor had in *That Hideous Strength* got the upper hand. And as we have seen, that is part of the reason for Lewis's move to the form of the fairy tale, which severely limits analysis.

Clearly Lewis thinks of himself as making his fictions in an *a posteriori* manner. He says that he did not start writing the Narnia books with a series of Christian truths he wanted to push into the minds of his readers, but that 'Everything began with images; a faun carrying an umbrella, a queen on a sledge, a magnificent lion. At first there wasn't even anything Christian about them; that element pushed itself in of its own accord.'[9] He started from pieces, and then the whole was gradually built up. In *The Pilgrim's Regress* he begins with a dark mountain and a desired image of an island, and then portrays a man leaving the mountain in search of the island, and what he finds on his journey. In *Out of the Silent Planet* he starts from the idea of travel to Mars, and then describes a character finding out about it and a wider and supernatural cosmos beyond it. *That Hideous Strength* opens with a weak university don who compromises himself to join a circle of what he thinks are progressive scientific people, and then finds the implications of what he has done steadily widening until he is being asked to ally himself with the devil. *The Lion, the Witch and the Wardrobe* imagines a strange country entered by a group of children through a wardrobe in an eccentric professor's house.

Broadly there is nothing extraordinary in this. Many writers, particularly on the fantastic side, start with a single image, landscape or relationship and work out from that. Brian Aldiss in his *Cryptozoic!* (1967) imagines that one might be able to travel back to the Cretaceous period and then describes the world to be found there; E.A. Abbott's *Flatland* (1884) invents a world where everything is in two dimensions; Mary Shelley's *Frankenstein* (1818) gives us an inventor who creates a crudely-formed living man of human sensibility, then follows how that man is treated in the world. They all start from a single image or idea. And therefore all might expect that anyone writing about their work will take account of this and see how well they put their worlds together – in other words, will work from single data outwards to the formation of generalities and conclusions.

But in Lewis's case this is made particularly necessary by the special emphasis he gives to the single image that starts his work. We have seen how he begins from individual pictures to build up a whole fiction. But these images are often not simply the inspiration of literary creation, but something deeper. In his essay 'On Stories' he says that the excitement one derives from imaginative stories is for him not separable from the image that creates it. If he reads the story of *Jack the Giant Killer* the excitement is not simply that of a man surmounting danger but of a man '"surmounting *danger from giants*"....The whole quality of the imaginative response is determined by the fact that the enemies are giants. That heaviness, that monstrosity, that uncouthness, hangs over the whole thing.'[10] It is the particular source of the danger, not danger generally, that is for him thrilling. And stories, for him, exist to give such imaginative excitement.

Furthermore, when the source of the thrill is marvellous or mysterious, it is at its most potent. Lewis praises David Lindsay, author of *A Voyage to Arcturus*, (1920), as 'the first writer to understand what "other planets" are really good for in fiction':

> His Tormance is a region of the spirit....No merely physical strangeness or merely spatial distance will realise that idea of otherness which is what we are always trying to grasp in a story about voyaging through space: you must go into another dimension. To construct plausible and moving 'other worlds' you must draw on the only real 'other world' we know, that of the spirit.[11]

What Lewis is saying is that, in his preferred kind of fantasy, the whole story is about the image that prompted it. The being and end of such an imaginative fiction is a single quality, often coming through a single image that both inspires and is radiated from the work. Stories have to be a series of events, 'but it must be understood that this series – the plot, as we call it – is only really a net by which to catch something else.' The real subject 'has no sequence in it' and is more like a state or quality. 'Giantship, otherness, the desolation of space, are examples.'[12] These images awake both wonder and desire in the reader, Lewis believes, because they come ultimately from a source we cannot define.

That is part of it: yet it is not quite all. Were it so, we might admire, but we need not love. What runs through all Lewis's fiction is a strange current of what he called 'joy', a feeling of intense desire or *Sehnsucht* which has no identifiable object save Heaven. Lewis believed we are each born with it and that most of us ignore or dismiss it. He, perhaps because it came to him more strongly, nurtured it from the first.[13] It is what binds the universe to him and his universe to us. Its very 'vagueness' thrives and becomes more poignant amid the precision and definiteness of Lewis's portraits, not because it is inherently unclear, but because we have not the spiritual sight to perceive its definiteness.

This 'joy' changes throughout Lewis's fiction. In *The Pilgrim's Regress* it is a kind of talisman that leads John forth, a golden key looking for a door, a spiritual litmus paper he has to dip into every area of life. In the 'space trilogy' it has become more pervasive, has spread across the planets and even the supposed 'void' of space itself to reach the Creator Maleldil who sustains all things. In *The Great Divorce* it is the proffered bliss of heaven that the damned refuse. In the 'Narnia' books a touch of it sits on Narnia, and it grows as the children later journey over the sea to the world's end, or as Narnia finally fades and they travel beyond it to Aslan's country. In *Till We Have Faces* 'joy' appears as a vision refused, a vision that torments and finally breaks down the soul that tries to resist it.

Yet always it is that which awakens a desire at the bottom of the soul, the desire so private that we are, as Lewis puts it, unwilling to speak about it, the desire which by being so private is also supremely 'public' in the sense of being sent by the most 'public' fact of the universe. And in whatever form that desire appears, tantalising, touching, punishing, it is the spiritual 'glue' that binds Lewis's fiction to us. Like so much else in his works – intellectual or spiritual – it is his own experience; and yet strangely, the more it has been his, the more he has been able to make it ours.

Lewis has a very strong sense of the numinous – a numinous he makes the foundation of his argument in *The Problem of Pain* – and he can find it in the meanest grain as in the greatest angel. There is scarcely one of his books where he does not whet our appetites enormously with the sense of its impending presence. Where does John's desire come from? What will Oyarsa be like at Meldilorn? What kind of divinely-appointed mission will Ransom be performing in Perelandra? We feel its approach in the angelic Oyéresu of *That Hideous Strength*, in the God of *Till We Have Faces*, in the soft yet mighty paces of Aslan in the 'Narnia' books. And every pattern, every spiritual subtlety, every movement and balance in each work is dipped in and pervaded by it. How could Orual's experience in *Till We Have Faces* mean so much to us did it not involve the most intimate and profound desires and repugnances of the human spirit? These are things literary criticism is reluctant to speak about, because they are personal, unquantifiable and somehow immodest. But the usual literary criticism will not suffice here. God is not concerned with modesty. To tell of Lewis's work without founding such talk on the 'dialectic of Desire' that runs through it is to lose as much of its essential nature as to talk of his books as though they could be reduced to spiritual formulae and lessons. We need to get as much of Lewis in as we can, not just to do him justice, but because through him we have to get in as much of his universe as we can. And having done so, perhaps we can begin.

Endnotes

1. Barfield, 'Introduction', Jocelyn Gibb, ed., *Light on C.S. Lewis* (London: Geoffrey Bles, 1965), xvi.
2. Lewis, *Surprised by Joy: the Shape of my Early Life* (London: Bles, 1955), 16.
3. Lewis believed that 'If there are other rational species than man, existing in some other part of the actual universe, then it is not necessary to suppose that they also have fallen' (*The Problem of Pain*, 73; see also *Miracles*, 55-6, 128).
4. Lewis, 'On Three Ways of Writing for Children' (1952)', in Lewis, *Of Other Worlds: Essays and Stories,* ed. Walter Hooper, 32-3.
5. Lewis, 'It All Began with a Picture' (1960), in *Of Other Worlds*, 42.
6. Lewis, 'On Three Ways of Writing for Children', 36-7.
7. Lewis, 'Unreal Estates' (1962), in *Of Other Worlds*, 87.
8. Adey, *C.S. Lewis, Writer, Dreamer and Mentor* (Grand Rapids, MI: Eerdmans, 1998).
9. Lewis, 'Sometimes Fairy Stories May Say Best What's To Be Said' (1956), in *Of Other Worlds*, 36
10. Lewis, 'On Stories' (1947), in *Of Other Worlds*, 8.
11. Ibid, 12.
12. Ibid, 18.
13. For Lewis's views on joy, see *The Pilgrim's Regress*, pp.5-10 and *passim; The Problem of Pain*, ch. X (on Heaven); 'The Weight of Glory', in *Transposition and Other Addresses;* and *Surprised by Joy:*

CHAPTER 2

The Pilgrim's Regress: An Allegorical Apology for Christianity, Reason and Romanticism (1933)

The Pilgrim's Regress, the first of Lewis's works of prose fiction, is cast as an allegory of the journey of a character named John through the world in search of an island of which he has had visions that have awakened his deepest longings. The book is called a 'regress' partly because John has in the end to return to the brook he left at the outset of the story. This is in contrast to the journey of Christian in Bunyan's *The Pilgrim's Progress*, who travels in a more or less straight line from the city of destruction to Zion.[1] In his book Lewis is putting into in schematic form his own journey to conversion, via humanism, idealism and theism and back to the Christianity he abandoned in adolescence – a journey later to be described in more direct and personal terms in *Surprised by Joy: The Shape of My Early Life* (1955).

In some ways *Pilgrim's Regress* is nearer to Bunyan's *Grace Abounding* than to his *Pilgrim's Progress*, for it describes how someone becomes a Christian, rather than how a Christian battles through life. Further, *Pilgrim's Regress* is engaged in a similar process of discrimination. In *Grace Abounding* Bunyan shows how he sought to find any certain sign in the Bible that he might be saved, or, if he had sinned, by how much his sin would be counted as unforgivable. So with Lewis in *Pilgrim's Regress*: is the Island real or an illusion? Are the rules of conscience attributable to God or to man? What is the true appearance of a man?

However *Pilgrim's Regress* is directed more at finding out the metaphysical roots of the world than at tracing spiritual development in its central character, and here it differs from both Bunyan works. The object in Lewis's book is to discover what a thing is rather than what it may become – and in this it is followed by the later space trilogy. It shows a man being gradually led to believe in God rather than a believer struggling to win God's acceptance or heaven, as in Bunyan. The hero John is rarely engaged in personal struggles with adversaries. He makes mistakes, and is reprimanded for them, but for most of the time he meets a series of personifications of different intellectual positions. These positions are supposed to be stages reached by John, but he is often insufficiently dramatised for them to come over as more than a series of standpoints – Humanism, Mr Sensible, Wisdom – which he visits in sequence and is told about.

Pilgrim's Regress has one other central concern that marks it off from Bunyan, and that is to show that one can come to belief in God by pursuing one of the images through which He calls to us in this life to its source. Bunyan's Christian goes on pilgrimage because he fears he may be damned otherwise. John's search for the source of his deep desire come through a range of misidentifications of it, whether as lust, escapism, Romanticism or illusion, until he realises that it is a desire for something that lies beyond earthly experience. His story shows how, as Lewis puts it, 'the dialectic of Desire, faithfully followed, would retrieve all mistakes, head you off from all false paths, and force you not to propound but to live through, a sort of ontological proof' (*The Pilgrim's Regress*, 5).

But that 'live through' is something of a problem so far as this first book is concerned. We live through the experience of Bunyan's Christian all right: there are hard roads to travel, ditches to fall into, hills to climb and dragons and giants to fight, and through all of them, however allegorical they are, Christian suffers literal enough effort and doubt and fear with which we can identify. Lewis's characters are much more inescapably allegorical, and John's feelings are often lost. Part of the reason for this is that Bunyan, for all his very specific theology, made his obstacle course for Christian one that is universally available. We can all respond to a Hill Difficulty or an Apollyon or a Doubting Castle: we absorb the meanings almost without noticing. But Lewis has presented a very specific intellectual process without always making it readily accessible to a general audience.

Looking back on the book after ten years, in his preface to the third edition, Lewis felt disappointed, finding its chief faults to be 'needless obscurity, and an uncharitable temper' (5). One explanation he gives for the obscurity is that he assumed his own journey towards becoming a Christian to be a typical one, when in retrospect he saw it to be 'a road very rarely trodden'. He felt it therefore requisite to add explanatory headnotes to the pages of the original. Sometimes these are unnecessary, sometimes rather reductive (the fine account of Uncle George's going over the brook at the beginning is rendered as 'An uncomfortable funeral, lacking both Pagan fortitude and Christian hope' (26)). Sometimes they add an 'ism' to what we have been seeing in quite immediate terms – Vertue's wish to punish his body so that his spirit may come nearer to God is labelled 'Oriental pessimism' compared to the 'Hegelian optimism' John shows in his trust in the divine base of the flesh; and John's realisation that the images he has been following are only images becomes 'From Pantheism to Theism' (140, 139, 144). The effect is rather like that of the marginal annotations Coleridge gave to his later edition of *The Ancient Mariner*: interesting, sometimes helpful, often obscure, always beside the point.

The problem however is not only the untypical character of the experience but the issue of how well it is put over and realised. Lewis's own feeling of *Sehnsucht* through haunting images of joy may be special to him, but it is possible to make it vivid to others – as he does in much of his fiction and in *Surprised by Joy*. That he feels called upon to give an elaborate account of its working in the preface to the 1943 edition shows not that he cannot try too hard to get a difficult concept over, but that he feels he has not done the job well in the first place. And we are quite prepared to read of odd journeys to faith – that of Traherne, a Law, a Simone Weil – provided they are well told.

Yet there are many fine things in the book, not least the opening description of John's upbringing in the land of Puritania and his delight in the natural surroundings about his parents' garden. We might be in something of the Ulster setting that Lewis knew as a child. John is stopped one day from aiming a stone at a bird, and told that 'the Steward' would not like it. When he asks who the Steward is, he is told that he is appointed by 'the Landlord' to make the rules for the country; when he asks who the Landlord is, he is told that he owns all the country; and when he asks why, he is taken to see the Steward. This meeting is vividly rendered. John is dressed in tight-fitting, starchy clothes and taken to a big dark house where he is sat on a chair in the hall so high that his feet dangle off the ground (Lewis perhaps got this idea from E. Nesbit's story 'The Cockatoucan' where a girl similarly harshly dressed is also left on a high chair before being taken to visit her aunt).

Then there is the extraordinary scene that follows between John and the Steward. John's parents come out grim faced, and John is sent in to meet what turns out to be a jolly, red-faced man, kind and full of ideas, with whom he has 'a good talk about fishing tackle and bicycles' (21). All of a sudden, this man takes down from the wall a mask with a white beard attached to it and then puts it on his face 'so that his appearance was awful'. That is, we later interpret, he turns from his 'jolly fellow' self to his Presbyterian minister self. He then tells John he is going to tell him about the Landlord of that country (God). He says how the Landlord is most kind to suffer the existence of tenants on his land, and that the Landlord has made a list of all the things one must not do, a copy of which he gives John to read.

By now, thanks not least to the queer, sing-song voice in which the Steward has repeated the words 'very kind' of the Landlord, John has begun to be frightened. The rules are so many and cover so many things John does every day, and other things he knows nothing about, that he feels he could never remember them all. The Steward says he hopes John has not broken any of them, and John is at a loss as to what to say. Then suddenly the Steward whips off his mask and says, '"Better tell a lie, old chap, better tell a lie. Easiest for all concerned,"' before he snaps it back on again. John duly lies, and the Steward, with his eyes seeming to twinkle through the mask, tells him that that is just as well, because if he did break any of the rules and the Landlord got hold of him, he would shut him in a black hole full of snakes and huge scorpions forever. He then proceeds to say how kind the Landlord is, and how he should therefore be obeyed.

When John asks whether he might not be forgiven if the Landlord caught him in breach of any one of the rules, the Steward goes into a long and incomprehensible discourse which ends by him saying 'that the Landlord was quite extraordinarily kind and good to his tenants, and would certainly torture most of them to death the moment he had the slightest pretext' (22). Nor can the Landlord be blamed when it is so good of him to let people live there at all, '"people like us, you know"'. After this the Steward takes off his mask, has a nice chat with John, gives him a cake and takes him out to his father and mother: 'But just as they were going he bent down and whispered in John's ear, "I shouldn't bother about it all too much if I were you." At the same time he slipped the card of the rules into John's hand and told him he could keep it for his own use' (22).

This scene is a wonderful start to the book. Its strength lies in the way that Lewis has recaptured the child's point of view, where everything in the world seems strange and abrupt. Here it is a way of highlighting the behaviour of adult human authorities whose inconsistencies show how inadequate is their world-view. But much more Lewis has caught that sudden sense of there being layers and layers beneath apparent reality, of which we could not have dreamed. Such is to be John's and our journey through the book. The child here is forced to see much more meaning behind life than he ever supposed. For us, the story has abruptly shifted from a semi-realistic one of a boy's development, to a sudden allegorical account where 'normal' causality and motivation disappear, and a man can switch from the avuncular to the threatening, and from his own face to a mask, without warning or evident reason.

The child's position is one of being totally in the power of the adult (as the adults say they are in that of the Landlord), pushed from one place to another, constantly having things done to him, reduced to the threat of having horrible things done to him in a place from which he cannot move for eternity. And he is bound as he sees it to fail: the Landlord's 'kindness' and the impossibility of keeping the rules ensure this. Then there are those terrifying removals of certainty for a young person (reminiscent of another and different Irish childhood described in James Joyce's *A Portrait of the Artist as a Young Man* (1916)) when the world and especially those people one thinks of as protective – one's parents, the minister, God Himself – can become in a moment somehow threatening and remote.

At the same time we know there is allegory here, even if we have to work at it. John is being given his first religious instruction in Puritanical society where the belief is that man's depravity makes him scarcely able to keep the commandments and hardly fit for salvation. It is a Puritanism which can as readily cover the sort of pugilistic Roman Catholicism with its insistence on the power of Hell that we see in Joyce's *Portrait*, as the starched Calvinism that holds to a notion of total human corruption; and the Rules are as much directed at the multitude of sins great and small interdicted by the Catholic church and subject to confession. Nothing too particular or peculiar here at the allegorical level; and yet the scene itself is very individual.

Indeed it is precisely the fact that this is so forceful – even hallucinatory – a rendering of a child's experience and point of view that make the allegory come over strongly. What mystifies John has to be interpreted by us. What is the significance of the frightening mask? We can understand it as an image of hypocrisy. The Steward puts it on to appear other than he naturally is; it is a form of concealment, even though it is meant to be an expression of 'the way things really are'. Later we see masks worn by the people surrounding John's Uncle George at his death. This is a society of people pretending to be what they are not.

At first it seems frighteningly inconsistent for the Steward to whip off the mask and tell John to lie or not to bother about any of it; just as later when John looks at the card of rules he finds that on its back it tells him not to trouble about any of what he is ordered to do on the front (23). But we can just see that this points to a duality in human nature that is forced into relief in Puritania, a duality between the self to be overcome and the self that will not be overcome. And already we are beginning to 'see feelingly' the limitations of the Rules or 'Law'. Yet none of this reduces the strangeness of the scene itself. A similar strange power is present in the account of Uncle George's death, when the dying uncle cannot wear a proffered mask but goes naked of feature, with the result that 'his face became so dreadful that everyone looked in a different direction and pretended not to see it' (26).

In this way Lewis starts the book brilliantly, with a child's trauma about masks, rules and a black hole so profoundly stamped on his personality that they will colour his experience throughout his life. For long he will see the Landlord as grim and terrible and will seek to escape him. The pity of it as far as the book is concerned is that the vivid humanity and terror of these childhood scenes disappear later in the narrative, and we move to a thinner and more exclusively spiritual and allegorical air. The freedom of lived (but no less potentially allegorical) experience is abandoned for a grid, a rule-card even, of experience made nothing but significant.

Nevertheless the power of these opening pages is thematically appropriate. For the strength of their reality exerts a literary force over the rest of the book that is matched by John's coming back at the end of his story to where he started. There it is to find the Landlord and his old home transformed, because he no longer sees them in his former terrified way: but still the gravitational pull exerted by those early experiences has served somehow to pull him back to them, to make his progress not so much linear as spiral.

There is one other childhood experience that drives and draws John through his life, and it is one that comes from a vision rather than from present experience. It is one that, in contrast to the schematised nature of the allegory, keeps a certain amount of 'wildness' and unpredictability in the story. Significantly it comes as an image of wild nature. John's first sensation of it is as, one day, he wanders down the road by his home further than ever before, and finds a wall with a strange window in it. From this window he hears a far voice that says 'Come,' and then, as he looks through it he sees a green wood full of primroses beyond, a wood that he seems to recall from long ago. And while he tries to place it in his memory,

> There came to him from beyond the wood a sweetness and a pang so piercing that instantly he forgot his father's house, and his mother, and the fear of the Landlord, and the burden of the rules. All the furniture of his mind was taken away. A moment later he found that he was sobbing, and the sun had gone in. (24)

It seems to him in retrospect that a mist over the woods had parted for an instant, and that he saw a beautiful green island in a calm sea, with Oreads and enchanters in its woods. He is filled with longing for this island. Yet he knows at the same time with one part of his mind that his desire for the island is not the same as the desire awakened by the original piercing pang, and that it is only his image of it. Still, he is too young to make anything of this, and he sets out from home that night to find the island.

John's journey away from home is driven no less by his fear of the Landlord than by his longing for the mystic island. These two motives may seem quite different, but they are ultimately to come together. For at the beginning the Landlord's castle is presented as being on a dark moorland mountain to the east of the country of Puritania in which John is brought up. When John runs away from the Landlord and towards his island desire, he goes west, where he thinks the island lies. But when he arrives in the far west, it is to come to a strait across which he can see the Landlord's mountain again. The world is round, and to go to the west is also in the end to go to the east. The island of John's desires becomes one with the Landlord: what he really sought was the Landlord's castle all the time. The threatening Landlord John left behind is actually the source of all his desire, and in running away from him he is also running towards him.

Heaven is various, and goodness can be terrible: no simple image of beauty in the form of the island or terror in the form of the Landlord will suffice; the truth exists in dreadful beauty. The circularity of the earth, far from disproving the existence of God, as in his ill-thought way the character Mr Enlightenment is later to claim (36), is actually an image of Heaven itself, the circle being an old symbol of perfection. And the place of sunset (Christ's Crucifixion?) is that of sunrise (or Resurrection). As the wished-for island becomes the Landlord's castle, so beauty exchanges its nature with 'ugliness'. (This exchange we will see again in Lewis's last published fiction, *Till We Have Faces* (1956).) At the same time the dark view of the Landlord's castle with which we began has changed to a bright one. Yet both views remain ultimately true. God is as dreadful as He is loving. While the neurotic terror of Him in the early pages is dismissed, the fear and trembling of which it was a distorted image remain true. So, just as John's story reveals to him the true nature of his desire, it shows also him the true source of his fear.

So far as the narrative is concerned, there was everywhere and nowhere to go. John, had he been able to see aright, might have understood the Landlord's nature without having to move away from his home. Such is the nature of earthly experience, the book seems to tell us: Heaven is as near to us as our hands, but we often have to journey far out of the way to realise the fact.

And yet, at the merely human level of experience, to travel mentally is better than to stay still. The character History tells John that the Tough-Minded people of the Tableland "'*know* very little. They never travel and consequently never learn anything'" (150); and that "'a little travel would soon blow to pieces'" the fixed notions of the Pale Men (159). Most of the antagonistic allegorical figures of the story stay in or have one place – the Halfways in Thrill, the Clevers and Mr Enlightenment in Eschropolis, the giant Spirit of the Age as a mountain, Mr Sensible in his house, the three Pale Men in their hut, Mr Savage in his cave, Mr Broad at home, even Mr Wisdom in his pillared house, all along the near side of a great canyon in the middle of the world. (And there are many more scattered about, mentioned on the map of this world.) Each of these personages offers John a world-view, either wrong or only partly true, as he passes: each has its little fixed nugget of information to provide and no more.

But John is moving through all this information and developing it as he goes. Accompanying him for much of the way are Reason, with her sharp sword, and Vertue with his struggle to improve himself; and later Contemplation with her insight and Mother Church who comes to John when he needs her to cross the canyon of original sin. If others move at all, the move is no development or progress on their part. Mr Broad has to leave his house before erosion causes it to collapse into the canyon: his servant Drudge goes with the travellers, but only to find his natural home among the dwarves of Mr Savage in the north. Mr Savage is going to invade the south, but will return north again afterwards: he prides himself in being the farthest north of all the inhabitants of this world. Gus Halfways takes John 'home' to Eschropolis with him in his car. The later figures, particularly Wisdom, are nearer the truth, though they cannot move into it.

The layered landscape of the great canyon is an image of that piercing through to deeper layers of understanding that John follows through the story. At first he is often surrounded by others – by the brown girls, the Clevers, the prisoners in the jail of the Spirit of the Age. But later he is more alone, with only Reason or Virtue for company, and when he comes upon society, he is more able to move on from it. He finds that neither Mr. Sensible, Mr. Angular, Mr. Humanist nor Mr. Broad can help in his search for his island, and even Mr. Wisdom is too world-renouncing for his desire. The shift from 'society' to isolation shows John's refusal of the codes of conduct by which societies live – those of Enlightenment, self-indulgence, Mammon and others. He moves to figures that live in alienation or retirement from society – Mr Neo-Angular, Mr Sensible, Mr Broad, Mr Wisdom, History – and then to total isolation, when he climbs down into the canyon on his own. All this mirrors his increasing exposure to truth: it is a kind of stripping away, as well as a growth of independent will. And at the same time as John develops in the narrative, he grows from a child to a man, no longer so subject to external influences as he has been.

The pattern of moral development in the book could be called 'Hegelian': it proceeds via thesis and antithesis to synthesis. At first John is with people wholly involved with the world and its pleasures or corruptions – the brown girls, old Mr Enlightenment with his reason, Mr Halfways and Media, the Clevers, Sigismund Enlightenment (Freud, and his theory of all images and urges being ultimately sex-based), Mr Sensible with his Horatian life. Then he is with world-renouncers such as Neo-Angular, world-destroyers such as Mr Savage, or people who live the life of the mind (with progressively more insight) such as Classicist, Humanist, Wisdom and History.

Those who wallow in the flesh and the physical lie to the south of the world, and John spends most of his travels – as befits a furtive Puritan – a little way to the north, among people who offer some intellectual justification, however poor, for their own sensual pleasures. Indeed all the characters John meets represent some intellectual or philosophical position, and John debates with them before following a course of action. Old Mr Enlightenment, for instance, provides at least some battered reasoning[2] for John's abandoning all belief in the Landlord's existence:

he is an emblem of the half-baked atheism that an adolescent (as John then is) can so readily fall into.

Nevertheless Mr Enlightenment's views all come down to an introduction to the bodily pleasures John is to enjoy with Media Halfways, and to his sensual interlude in the southern town of Thrill. Then John meets, as a young man, the Clevers, who soon reduce the Island to weird music, art to brutality and polite society to sexual perversity. Sigismund Enlightenment, whom John next encounters, tells him that his Island is a mask for his lusts and reduces him to disgust at the body and its secretions: Reason, who saves him, argues him out of the dungeon of the Spirit of the Age. Mr Sensible, a mass of clichés, tags and evasions, is a picture of the mind gone diseased: but what he really lives for are the pleasures of the table (dubious in his case), idle chat and graceful elegiac posturing – "'I defy system. I love to explore your minds *en deshabille*'" (84). With all these characters, whatever discussion there is is accompanied or followed by some physical action or inaction.

With later characters there is generally only discussion, after which John leaves – with Mr Neo-Angular, Mr Wisdom and History. Several commentators have objected to the lengthy and untransmuted passages of direct philosophy and theology that occur in these sections,[3] and certainly they sometimes seem better to belong in some text of apologetics than in a story: but they can also be seen as functional in a larger design. John moves out of a context in which minds are bogged down in body to one where mind is quite free of the senses, and can become bogged down in itself. The movement is part evolutionary, part 'the other side of the coin'; certainly the atmosphere becomes more rarified. We are much more aware of John being among cliffs and high places; previously, the land was relatively flat.

In these contexts the separation of 'body' from 'mind' becomes the danger, where earlier it was their near-identification. We see this in the conversation of John and Vertue after they have heard the idealist counsels of Mr Wisdom that all things are 'neither wholly real nor wholly illusion' (124). Vertue rejects the body entirely, where John extends it to all eternity. Vertue says that if our real good is elsewhere, what are we doing calling anything in this world 'innocent pleasure'? To John this is "'a very strange view,'" and he says he has taken from Wisdom's lessons precisely the opposite view. He believes that only a remnant of Puritanism in him has till now kept him from "'the blameless generosity of nature's breasts'" which he now gladly embraces. He asks Vertue if pleasure is not '"as necessary to the perfection of the whole as the most heroic sacrifice?"' The conversation continues like a shuttlecock:

> 'I am assured that, in the Absolute, every flame even of carnal passion burns on - '
>
> 'Can even eating, even the coarsest food and the barest pittance, be justified? 'The flesh is but a living corruption – '
>
> 'There was a great deal to be said for Media after all – '
>
> 'I see that Savage was wiser than he knew – '
>
> 'It is true she had a dark complexion. And yet – is not brown as necessary to the spectrum as any colour?'
>
> 'Is not every colour equally a corruption of the white radiance?' (139-40)

There is the opposition, like a canyon. But now there is a sense in this interplay that both are parts of the truth, and must be brought together in a living dialectic rather than left in antagonism like this.

John has indeed been brought to something of such a resolution through his own experience of the image of the Island. Does it come from God, or is it a delusion of his own or even sent from some other source (160)? Is the Island what he desires, or is it only an image of the desirable? History teaches John that the Landlord has through time sent man several different images to awaken his longing, suggesting that the Island is not the source of the desire. Through the story John has swayed between one and the other view, now dismissing the Island as an illusion of one form or another, now identifying it wholly with the Real. Yet the truth lies in the interplay of both. When Wisdom comes to John in a vision while he is crossing the canyon, to tell him that 'all his adventures were but figurative... [and] mythology', a voice comes to him saying '"Child, if you will; it *is* mythology. It is but truth, not fact: an image, not the very real. But then it is My mythology... Have you not heard among the Pagans the story of Semele? Or was there any age in any land when men did not know that corn and wine were the blood and body of a dying and yet living God?"' (171). In the story of Christ we have myth made fact: in the incarnational fact we have the junction of flesh and spirit; in the dance of exchange that is Heaven we mortals experience images that both capture and miss the Real.

It is this more Christian reality that governs the story after John and Vertue cross the canyon of Man's original sin. The canyon is itself in part an image of duality and separation, overcome in crossing it (there is no difficulty in their re-traversing it on the way back (176)). And after it, Vertue and John keep constant company. But the marriage of opposites does not make them cease being opposites: Heaven itself delights in dialectic, and it is a 'dialectic of desire' that has brought John to where he is (10,157). Nor, on earth, and perhaps not in Heaven, is spiritual evolution ever done with. As Vertue and John pass back through a world now transformed to their cleansed visions, they encounter Superbia with her detestation of earth and the flesh, and we find that Vertue is still tempted by this; "'All said and done, there *is* something foul about all these natural processes'" (184). His Guide does not disagree, but bids him be careful to distinguish between Repentance and Disgust. Later we find John tempted by the witch of Luxuria (189-190). After this, Vertue and John each have to fight a dragon: John's is the cold male dragon of the North, and Vertue's is the hot female one of the South.[4] One might, given their positions, have expected it to be the other way round: but in fact it is part of the dialectical character of reality that John was led to lust by a northern coldness in his blood, and Vertue to asceticism and mortification by a native sensuality.

After this, the dance of truth continues in another form. As Vertue prepares to pass the brook he sees death as a loss of the individual self, a self never to be repeated; while John replies, "'I thought all those things when I was in the house of Wisdom but now I think better things. Be sure it is not for nothing that the Landlord has knit our hearts so closely to time and place – to one friend rather than another and to one shire more than all the land'" (197-8). What further interweavings of truth lie beyond this we do not know.

In one view the book has been a linear sequence, a journey from body to mind to Reality, a movement towards grasping the Other. And yet that Other was there all the time. John's story began with it in his awakened terror of the sheer otherness of the Landlord and his mountain, and with his initial, almost pure experience of joy through the Island: he apprehended terror and joy together from beyond the world. Then he lost them in the world, his terror of the Landlord reduced to nothing by the futilities of Mr Enlightenment, his joy translated to lust and illusion. But these first things were founded in truth: it is the mortal world that is itself an illusion, as John is to see on his journey back, when all that he saw before is revealed for what it truly is – or is not. The book as we have seen is both linear and circular. John had to develop and yet also in a sense had to stand still, and both are part of the heavenly interplay. When John concludes that "I have been wasting my labour all my life, and I have gone half-round the world to reach what Uncle George reached in a mile or so", his Guide replies, '"Who knows what your uncle has reached, except the Landlord? Who knows what you would have reached if you had crossed the brook without ever leaving home? You may be sure the Landlord has brought you the shortest way: though I confess it would look an odd journey on a map"' (173).

The Pilgrim's Regress can thus be seen to have a fair degree of patterning and 'organic' imagination behind it, giving it artistic strength. And the opening chapters, which dramatise ideas and feelings without explaining them directly, are an undoubted triumph. But it cannot be argued that this makes it a truly great success. Its main weaknesses have often been noted – a failure to individualise allegorical personages sufficiently, a tendency to put untransmuted essays into the mouths of spokesmen along the way, a disposition to become too personally involved in the subjects of attack. To that one might add a failure with the landscape. True, it is supposed to be only functional, in the sense that while John journeys through it, it testifies to an otherness beyond it that he will eventually meet: but still, Lewis can only describe it in rather perfunctory pastoral terms, without giving us a clear view of it.

These limitations can all be seen as the product of a form of inaccuracy – and accuracy is particularly needed in allegory. Lewis's style here does not have much of the clarity and bite that so characterises it in his later work. There are of course many exceptions to this. But often one feels that the many lengthy discourses could have been sharpened and made more immediate to us with the sort of well-turned epigram or illuminating image of which Lewis was to become so capable. Wisdom and History, old men though they are, mumble too much. Of course the book is about language in a sense, and how images can confuse, and it could perhaps be argued that it avoids clarity of statement for that reason. And we may also note that it is *about* inaccuracy, in the sense that John continually misinterprets the nature and source of his desire: the whole book describes a journey towards greater and greater precision. But one cannot really carry this argument too far. There is such a thing about being precise about imprecision, without at all being untrue to its nature. (Lewis does this well, for instance, in his short story 'The Shoddy Lands'.)

And try as we may, we will not be able to find much justification for this sort of thing:

> Then I dreamed that he led John into a big room rather like a bathroom: it was full of steel and glass and the walls were nearly all window, and there was a crowd of people there, drinking what looked like medicine and talking at the tops of their voices. They were all either young, or dressed up to look as if they were young. The girls had short hair and flat breasts and flat buttocks so that they looked like boys: but the boys had pale, egg-shaped faces and slender waists and big hips so that they looked like girls – except for a few of them who had long hair and beards (50).

This is a pet hate that Lewis has indulged, and the result is that it has turned into a stereotype. Physical appearance is being made to represent the moral without sufficient cause shown. What is *evil* about a room of steel and glass, or wrong about large windows? What are Lewis's many 'unfortunately' flat-chested, short-haired female readers going to make of this indictment of them? Of course the general theme is the unnatural – rooms are dominated by sterile phenomena, people drink nasty spirits instead of good beer, men and women have changed sex – but it is the loathing that comes over, not any really accurate and clear-headed analysis. And what of the men of long hair and beards? – doubtless beastly, pusillanimous socialists here, but Lewis is simply trotting out a blimp's hatreds. After all, most of our images of Christ are of a man with long hair and a beard.

The Pilgrim's Regress was not a popular book; and as we have seen Lewis himself came to have reservations about it. His later works have much less of the deliberate 'placing' one sees here, and much more fluency - doubtless the result of more facility and confidence in writing, and perhaps of less of an eye on an intellectual readership. All Lewis's later work, fiction and non-fiction alike, reads as though he were experiencing the stories or the thought-processes at the time of writing, and the result is much greater immediacy. It was an immediacy that he himself grew to regard as essential to stories at least, where the author must try to capture and share through his narratives an illusive joy or otherness.[5] Fidelity to experience, Lewis realised, was more likely to bring many meanings to life than standing back from it and pointing them out. For Lewis, as for his friend Charles Williams, inaccuracy was to become the mark of Hell: no inference should be made from this about the *The Pilgrim's Regress*, but the status of a precise manner in Lewis's work hereafter is increasingly more than a literary one.

Endnotes

1. For further comparisons between Lewis and Bunyan, see Gunnar Urang, *Shadows of Heaven: Religion and Fantasy in the Fiction of C. S. Lewis, Charles Williams and J. R. R. Tolkien*, 6-8.
2. Mr Enlightenment's reasoning is exposed in Chad Walsh, *The Literary Legacy of C. S. Lewis*, 65-6.
3. See e.g. Clyde S. Kilby, *The Christian World of C. S. Lewis*, 36; Walsh, 62-3, 68-9; Donald E. Glover, *C. S. Lewis: The Art of Enchantment*, 69, 70.
4. Edward J. Zogby, S. J., 'Triadic Patterns in Lewis's Life and Thought' in Peter Schakel (ed.), *The Longing for a Form: Essays on the Fiction of C. S. Lewis*, 21-2, sees this duality as part of a wider metaphoric use of masculine and feminine as 'gender-in-polarity' throughout Lewis's fiction, whereby 'the terms masculine and feminine [are]... the literary metaphors which Lewis uses to express the deepest relation of creature to Creator.'
5. Gilbert Meilaender, *The Taste for the Other; the Social and Ethical thought of C. S. Lewis*, sees this search for the 'other' as the key to all Lewis's work. See also Scott Oury, '"The Thing Itself": C. S. Lewis and the Value of Something Other', in Schakel (ed.), *The Longing for a Form*, 1-18.

CHAPTER 3

Out of the Silent Planet (1938)

In this book Lewis finds his natural fictional idiom – the portrayal of adventures in other worlds. His picture of Malacandra and his whole approach to the writing of *Out of the Silent Planet* derive in large part from the science-fictional idiom of H.G. Wells, Olaf Stapledon and David Lindsay (of *A Voyage to Arcturus*) – and also, in less serious vein, from Hugh Lofting's spoof of Wells, *Doctor Dolittle in the Moon* (1929).[1] It is true that in Lewis science fiction is turned to a more supernatural purpose, in that we deal not only with alien peoples on another planet, but with spirits, angels and God. But the hero, a Cambridge philologist, is throughout exploring and recording every area of the lives of the peoples of Malacandra, from their languages, customs and history to their body temperatures or even their excretory habits. Knowledge, *scientia*, is to the fore. Such knowledge, however, is seen in moral terms: it is seen as deriving from a selfless curiosity about the other. The acquisition of information under special dispensation can be seen as virtually the central theme of *Out of the Silent Planet*. It is knowledge gained from a journey out of self as much as out of a silent and uncommunicative planet.

The novel begins with a 'Pedestrian' on a walking tour. It is near evening, and he has found no lodging at one town, and is hoping to reach the next, Sterk, and a hospitable hotel by nightfall. The land is flat, mainly crop-fields, desolate, almost uninhabited, and after the birdsong ceases at evening, 'it grew more silent than an English landscape usually is.' As the Pedestrian passes a lone cottage, a woman rushes out and almost bumps into him. It turns out that she thought he was her son who has been working late for two gentlemen staying at a place nearby called The Rise. Ransom – for that is his name, he being a college don on holiday – resolves to call in and have her son sent home to her, and at the same time to ask the people at The Rise if he can stay the night.

He retraces his steps, but can see no sign of The Rise or of any light, only flat fields and 'a mass of darkness which he took to be a copse' (8). On closer inspection, however, he finds that this mass of darkness is actually divided from the road by a good hedge, in which is a white gate; and that the trees beyond form only a line behind which is an open space. The gate is locked. Ransom eventually, despite many misgivings, first throws his pack inside over the gate and then has to force his way through the hedge.

This and subsequent events may recall Wells's Traveller in *The Time Machine*; but we are also sensing allegory, as Lewis used it in *The Pilgrim's Regress*. For this landscape is suggestive of meaning. The Pedestrian's road over a lonely country from one inn to another, his pack, the mass of darkness, the wide fields before a concealed gate into an enclosure – these takes us back to Bunyan's *The Pilgrim's Progress*. Of course there are differences: the Pedestrian entering The Rise is not the same as Christian going through the wicket gate, for The Rise is to be simply an evil place, despite its suggestive name. And yet – in that one act of throwing his pack over the gate, has not Ransom taken a step of the spirit into a new dimension? It is the product of his pledge to the old woman and of his native courage and compassion, but hereafter – though there is one further act of commitment to come – he is in a dimension that contains strange other worlds, transformations of the spirit and encounters with planetary angels.[2]

The allegorical undertone continues after Ransom has got through the hedge and looked about him. At a distance over a neglected lawn he can make out a large stone house. The drive branches not far from him, the right-hand path sweeping round to the front door, while the left-hand one, which is heavily rutted, leads straight to the back. The house is dark, with some windows shuttered, others open and blank. Large volumes of smoke issue from a chimney at the rear, suggestive more of a factory or of a laundry than a kitchen (9-10).

It seems a perfectly ordinary, if depressing scene – but is it? The untidy and patchy lawn seems to continue something of the scrubby desolation of the landscape outside, suggesting life being crushed and worn down. We recall too that even before this the solitary old woman Ransom met on the heath emerged from a small and ugly brick cottage, and that she spoke in a monotonous, unemotional voice with limited vocabulary (6,7). Somehow the atmosphere of the story has become steadily more drained of life and joy. The branching of the drive is just a shade ominous, more so when we think of the left (sinister) and the right-handed paths, the left going straight ahead (like the road to hell in the old ballad) and the right not just running but *leading* the visitor in a gentle sweep; the one goes to the back parts of the house and the other to the front, where people are usually welcome. The path to the back is the one used, but has been torn up by machines: the neglected path to the front has been obliterated more naturally by moss. Of course we do not think of this at the time, but it makes its impression all the same.

The image of the house is a familiar one in literature: here one might think back to Spenser's Castle of Alma, for instance, image of the human body, or to Poe's House of Usher, symbol of mind. This house is abandoned – some of its 'eyes' gape, others are shuttered. The people Ransom is to meet do not live in it, do not really have any 'dwelling place' – they seem permanently in transit. They are to prove in fact centrally concerned with travel – in this book to Mars, though one of them has as his ultimate aim the perpetual expansion of man outwards from Earth. Ransom, by contrast, is travelling only while on holiday – he has a home, even if no one knows of his present whereabouts.

The house, lifeless, is in a sense like the people we are to meet, people who have lost their souls, who are empty vacancies inside themselves, without any love for others. When Ransom is brought into the house, he finds himself in a room without carpets or curtains, and only stains on the wallpaper to show where its original furniture and pictures were. There are packing cases scattered on the floor, two expensive armchairs, and tables covered with a litter of remains from a past meal. Everything is seen as chaos, the valuable thrown together with the worthless; nothing belongs, everything is temporary. Nothing is more or less important than anything else, which is to prove a hallmark of evil. It is all a landscape of the spirit, or rather a landscape of a certain absence of the spirit.[3]

It is the placing of the items that does it, this and the increasing sense of something not right. Were we to come on such a place ourselves, we might think little of it, and there might be nothing to think of it. But here we are responding to a psyche that is registering disquiet and picking out details on which to found it. It is an academic and a literary psyche, which may explain the hints of allegory in the scene; and it is a moral psyche, acutely sensitive to spiritual atmospheres. But at the same time it is to prove right. Subjective though it may seem, it is responding to what proves to be really there. Were it not so sensitive, it would not see the evil, would take the scene at face value, might also throw in its lot with what turn out to be two men intent on acquiring gold from another planet. But Ransom sees the devil beneath the detail. Clarity of vision and insight are to be two prime virtues in the book.

So, via Ransom's growing disquiet and hints of allegory that suggest a wider metaphysical context, the ordinary is gradually tapered into the extraordinary and the sinister. Here is this perfectly normal English countryside at dusk, with its perfectly normal walker looking for an inn for the night: yet is it really so unremarkable? Slowly the quite commonplace turns into something more than itself, and the landscape becomes as much a figurative and spiritual as an everyday one. It does not stop being everyday: the strength of the portrayal of the scene and the house is that it is exactly the sort of thing we might encounter ourselves. And yet, somehow, at the same time it is becoming alien.

In this way Lewis conveys that what we take for the normal can be really quite strange and interpenetrated with deeper forces than we know; just as in *The Screwtape Letters* he shows how the common life we assume to be the only reality is surrounded and acted on by the powers of Hell and Heaven. The 'allegorical' element here prepares the ground for Ransom's meeting not just with two rather nasty explorers about to set off to another planet, but with two representatives of the devil who are doing so.

Other significances are also latent. The novel is called 'Out of....': here Ransom has gone out of self; he has also gone out of the 'silent' world outside the grounds. True though, he has also gone into something, has invaded an 'enclosure'; and in a sense this act is repeated on a larger scale in the later invasion by the space-ship of the peace and innocence of Malacandra, a peace from which man must in the end be finally shut out by making sure that he will be unable to return. Yet in the whole journey Ransom is to go out of self further and further. That is what his interplanetary journey partly symbolises. The other men who go with him remain locked in their earthly selves and desires for gold. They learn nothing of the planet they go to, and make no effort to get to know its inhabitants. Because of this their whole journey is in the end futile and they are sent home.

Ransom's position, as against that of the two men he meets, is imagined in a dream he has when later they drug him in the house. He dreams that all three of them are in a brightly-lit garden surrounded by a wall beyond which is darkness. The other two want to go over the wall but Ransom does not, and warns them of the darkness; nevertheless on persuasion all three set about climbing over. But while the other two succeed and drop into the darkness, Ransom remains sitting astride the glass-covered top of the wall. Soon a door, which none of them had noticed, is opened in the wall and the 'queerest people' Ransom has ever seen appear, bringing the other two men back with them, before going out and locking the door behind them (19). Ransom is the man who will in a sense 'straddle both worlds' (or Earth and Malacandra) while the other two will be shut out of Malacandra after their attempted invasion.

Not all the details fit with this, however, for Ransom is to find Earth the dark place and Malacandra, and even the 'night' of space, the realm of brightness: the dream has to be seen as partly a reflection of Ransom's own present fears of the unknown, as well as a vision of what is to come. Still, as a vision, it is a way both of showing us the deeper meanings behind what is happening now, and of preparing us via symbols for the implications of later events.

The whole story thereafter is also one of growing strangeness. Ransom first learns that the two men in the house, a scientist called Professor Weston and a rich financier named Devine, are planning no earthly crime, but have actually built a space ship to go to Mars, or 'Malacandra' – indeed, that they have already made one prospecting journey there and have met an alien race and found abundant gold ore. These two have just kidnapped the son of the old woman Ransom met, with the purpose of offering him in sacrifice to the Malacandrians for access to the gold. Now they take Ransom instead on their long journey.

Eventually arrived on Mars, in one of the deep gorges beneath the surface in which many of the inhabitants live, Ransom manages to escape from his captors as the giant humanoid forms of the supposed Martian predators approach. As he wanders through the Malacandrian forests, Ransom meets a strange seal-like creature called a *hross*, which turns out to be rational. It takes him back to its community, where he stays for a while, learning more about this fantastic world. Then he is told that Oyarsa, the ruler of the planet, wishes to see him at a place called Meldilorn, and the *hrossa* direct him there via the high places of the *sorns*, who are the creatures to whom he was originally to be 'sacrificed'. These beings turn out, in the form of one Augray, to be in fact gentle and highly intelligent: Weston had entirely misunderstood what they said to him on his first journey. This *sorn* takes Ransom down to Meldilorn in the next gorge, an island in a lake. There he meets his third rational Malacandrian species, a frog-like creature called a *pfifltrigg*. But now he is to meet a creature that is more than alien: he is to meet an angel.

Since his meeting with the *hrossa*, Ransom has been told of creatures called *eldils*, which are made of light and are largely invisible and inaudible to him. The Oyarsa or guardian intelligence of the planet, which he finally meets on Meldilorn, turns out to be a sort of 'chief eldil'. Ransom, and eventually Weston and Devine, are brought to an interview with Oyarsa and asked to explain their reasons for coming, and why, either directly or indirectly, they have been responsible for the deaths of three *hrossa*. In the end, Oyarsa lets them return to Earth by their ship, under special conditions, and ensures the destruction of the ship when it reaches Earth, to prevent their ever returning.

But before they leave, Oyarsa tells Ransom much of the history of Malacandra. Malacandra is part of a 'celestial commonwealth' created and sustained by Maleldil (God). But in the far past the surface of Malacandra was laid waste by Satan, who was then overthrown and confined to Earth. Since then Earth has been the 'Silent Planet', no longer open to the universe, and under the sway of the 'Bent Eldil'. At the same time Oyarsa learns from Ransom something of conditions on Earth, so long cut off from commerce with the rest of the heavens. Ransom is then told that some great time of change is coming in the cosmos, and that he may well have a part of play in it.

This movement through the book from the strange to the alien, and from the alien to the awe-full, is accompanied on Malacandra by progress through a hierarchy. We move from the landscape to vegetation, and on to beasts (yellow giraffe-like creatures, that Ransom sees in the Malacandrian forest), rational beasts (the *hrossa*), reasoning, humanoid creatures of considerable intelligence (the *sorns*) and the angelic intelligence or Oyarsa, which lives in and is made of light. (Lewis is at pains to point out, however, that hierarchy includes equality: the three races of Malacandra live together with none superior. And though Ransom does traverse a hierarchy, it is not so regular that we do not find *eldila* among the *hrossa*, or meet the frog-like craftsmen, the *pfifltriggi*, in the heart of Meldilorn.)

During much of the story, Ransom's perspective literally expands. At first, when he is in contact with the evil, it is increasingly restricted: he enters the confines of the garden of The Rise, is shut in the house, and then in the steel ball of the space-ship. But that ship journeys out of the Earth, and in the wide reaches of space Ransom is able to view the burning of innumerable constellations. Then, after this prevision of eternity, he is shut in again as the space-ship enters the comparatively 'murky' atmosphere of Malacandra. In his bursting away from his captors and his flight through the forests towards the *hrossa*, Ransom's awareness of the planet extends to knowledge of the deep gorges or *handramits*. Then in his journey upwards to the home of the *sorn* Augray, he can see the canyon in which he has been become tiny, and can stand near the true, 'lifeless' Martian surface or *harandra*. Finally his meeting with Oyarsa expands his consciousness over the entire solar system.

Ransom's return journey on the space-ship, with its broken shutters now constantly open, lets him view the Malacandrian surface as it recedes, with the *handramits* turning to little threads on the great ochre of the desert surface; yet on that surface he sees great dark patches marking the homes of the *pfifltriggi* on the beds of the old Malacandrian oceans. He becomes overwhelmed by how little, despite all his travels, he has seen. 'His knowledge of Malacandra was minute, local, parochial. It was as if a *sorn* had journeyed forty million miles to the Earth and spent his stay there between Worthing and Brighton' (168). The world he has visited is far vaster than his experience of it.

In parallel, as Ransom begins to converse with the inhabitants of Malacandra, his knowledge literally widens. For they, unlike Weston with his space-ship (27-9), are only too willing to tell him about how they live. From the *hrossa* he learns more about the planet and its inward nature. They, in their relatively primitive lives, are perhaps closer to the planet than the other races, and that may be why we see the *eldila* with them and not with others; they are at one with their forests and lakes. From the *sorn* Augray, living high above the *handramits*, and of appropriately Olympian vision, Ransom learns more of the essential nature of *eldila*, and even of his own world. The *pfifltriggi*, who work in mines and in depths of the earth (79), have portrayed in stone the history of Malacandra, which his meeting with Oyarsa then unfolds to him. All these races – and Ransom's adventure – seem to follow an elemental sequence, from water (the lakes, the element of the *hrossa*) to 'air' in the bodies and location of the *sorns* (even if it is actually almost airless space where they are), to rock or 'earth' with the *pfifltriggi*, and in Meldilorn to fire, in the light of which Oyarsa is made, and in the sunlight that Ransom must endure in his return journey.

Throughout, Ransom's conceptions of reality are being continually overturned. At first he is in a house where all is not as it should be; then a drink of wine becomes a soporific; then the dubious behaviour of Weston and Devine turns to the unbelievable. The familiar becomes strange and remote: the strangely large moon that he sees when he wakes from the drug is in fact the Earth. Ransom is in a room where the ceiling seems far wider than the floor and he appears to be lying as if at the bottom of a very large wheelbarrow: and yet when inspected, every wall of the room is at right angles to the floor. This upset of the ordinary is explained when he finds that his room is a segment of a spherical space-ship, a segment seated on an inner sphere of the craft. If he walks from room to room around the craft, he finds apparent floors becoming walls as he approaches, and walls he has left turning to ceilings (30-1).

During the voyage Ransom also has an inverse experience, by which the previously remote becomes 'near': what he had taken to be the cold darkness and vacuity of space becomes to him a place blazing with light and excess of life, an 'empyrean ocean of radiance' that is 'the womb of worlds' (35). When the ship enters the atmosphere of Malacandra he experiences it not as a happy landfall, but as a dismal constriction into darkness and weight, a falling into, not out of a hole, 'a subtraction from the surrounding brightness' (44). He has had something like a religious experience.

On Malacandra the surroundings are so strange that he cannot at first take them in, and often finds that his first assumptions about them are wrong. First the planet is far more beautiful than he expected, full of colours and life where he thought to find nothing but rock and desert. There is water, but it bubbles with effervescence and is warm; instead of being made blue by the sky's refection it is actually blue; and the waves on a nearby lake are vertical spouts. Then what Ransom took to be heather-clad mountains turn out to be trees, and what look like brown clouds on the horizon are eventually found to be huge petrified forests on the Malacandrian surface. Further, Ransom assumes he is on that surface himself, when in fact he is at the bottom of one of the huge deep gorges or *handramits*.

When Ransom first meets a *hross*, he thinks of it as an animal until it begins to try to speak to him. And Oyarsa, whom Ransom finally meets, is an inversion of all that so powerful a being might be supposed to be. 'The merest whisper of light – no, less than that, the smallest diminution of shadow – was travelling along the uneven surface of the groundweed; or rather some difference in the look of the ground, too slight to be named in the language of the five senses, moved slowly towards [Ransom]' (138). At the end of the story Ransom has become so used to the ways of Malacandra that he cannot at first recognise Weston and Devine when they are brought before Oyarsa, but instead sees them as grotesque bipeds with fat legs, pear-shaped bodies and faces of puckered flesh with dark bristly fringes (145).

Out of the Silent Planet is a mixture of exciting narrative, long pastoral interlude and discussion. The element of story is prominent up to the point that Ransom escapes from Weston and Devine when they land on the planet, but thereafter sequential events rather drop away, as Ransom experiences the planet and meets its peoples. There is a brief reminder of Ransom's enemies when one of them shoots a *hross* from a distance, but that is all. He does not meet or speak with the men again till he arrives in Meldilorn. Meanwhile Ransom learns the ways of the *hrossa*, is told of the larger history of Malacandra by the *sorn* Augray, and meets the *pfifltriggi*, who are a practical people good at making and inventing things. Even when he meets Oyarsa, Ransom is still being told much about the planet and his fellow humans.

Narrative returns for a while at the end, when the space-ship with the three men in it is given just ninety days to return to Earth, which is now in a most unfavourable position for the journey, before Oyarsa will destroy or 'unbody' it. Weston has to cut inside the Earth's orbit nearer to the heat of the Sun to intercept the Earth and even then his schemes are nearly ruined by the Moon being in the way of the Earth in the direction of their travel. But the return just succeeds. The book closes with an account of how it came to be written, and with correspondence between 'Lewis' and Ransom, in which the latter gives more descriptions of life, languages and landscapes on Malacandra.

If we look over the whole book, action is largely confined to humans. They travel to Malacandra and back, they (Weston and Devine, that is), have plans and purposes: but on Malacandra nothing changes and there is no history. For history ended there when æons previously Satan blasted the planet so that life became confined to its deep gorges. No history, no becoming: though still on the planet life lived through individual change, growth, self-betterment and mortality. In a sense *Out of the Silent Planet* is about story itself.

Thus, much of the book is taken up with sojourning and with learning, so far as Ransom is concerned. And for him in a way that is the purpose of his adventures. He is a teacher on Earth, and here he has to learn, learn about himself, learn to accept the alien, learn that life is far vaster than any previous limit he set to it, learn too something of cosmic conditions and history, so that he will be prepared to act on Maleldil's behalf later. This is a story of preparation. Even Ransom's acts are preparation: his slaying of a *hnakra,* the monster of the Malacandrian lakes that the *hrossa* delight to hunt, is one touchstone to his own courage (though no more than throwing a pack over a gate), a courage that will be put to use in *Perelandra.*

Nor is any of the action, in a sense, necessary. Weston's and Devine's return to Earth from their original journey to Malacandra to procure a sacrifice for the *sorns* was a waste of time. They thought the *sorns*, who were sent by Oyarsa to converse with them and find out what they wanted, were dangerous, and when Oyarsa told them via the *sorns* that they would not be allowed to take any gold away with them as they proposed, until one of them came to speak with him, they refused to go themselves, misinterpreting the request as one for a human sacrifice. And thus, as Oyarsa says, "'If they had come a few miles to see me I would have received them honourably; now they have twice gone a voyage of millions of miles for nothing and will appear before me nonetheless'" (142).

The same is true of Ransom's flight from the *sorns* on Malacandra: it was quite unnecessary, as they posed no threat to him at all, rather the reverse. He too has gone the long way round, his 'narrative' in vain – at least at the level of narrative. The process is reminiscent of the circular journey in *The Pilgrim's Regress.* The futility of action in the book is (again as in *The Pilgrim's Regress*) an index to the stress on contemplation – to finding out what a thing essentially is rather than with what part it plays in a story. What real movement there is in the narrative is rather spiritual than physical.

This movement involves Ransom being brought out of himself, from seeing inaccurately with his emotions to seeing truly. For much of the story he exhibits various forms of fear and prejudice, which steadily diminish.[4] His fears of the *sorns* are natural enough since he has been told they want him for sacrifice, but they do stimulate his own obsessions. He is first terrified that they will be like the insect monsters of science-fiction horror stories; then, when he sees them, he thinks of them as ogres or ghosts; when he first meets Augray, this analogy sinks to 'goblins' or 'gawks' (106); and then as he comes to know them, changes to 'Titans' or 'Angels' (117). At first we ourselves cannot be sure that the *hrossa* will not pass him on to the *sorns* to be killed. Even at the end he is afraid of Oyarsa, though this fear is turned to a proper awe. All his fears are barriers between himself and an understanding of the true nature of the new world, though for most of the time they are not present enough to obscure his response.

Then there are Ransom's 'prejudices', which take several forms – most of them though, like his fears, relatively innocuous. He thinks of space as a void, but finds it full of life; he for long treats the *hrossa* as animals; he cannot understand at first how one race does not rule another on Malacandra, or why there are no wars; he has to be taught how for a *hross* a meeting is not one act but a developing process (84). He comes to learn that nothing in life is to be held on to or repeated, and that the self must be let go to become part of the larger unity to which it belongs, as a line to a poem, as the act of sex to the creation of a child, as Malacandra to the celestial commonwealth in which it swims, or as the body of a *hross* goes back to Maleldil (153).

Part of Ransom's disease is his imagination, which is to be the faculty attacked in the innocent Lady by the devil in *Perelandra*. But it is also his distance from phenomena. That is far worse with Weston and Devine. Their misconception of Oyarsa's wishes led them to express that distance in a journey of millions of miles back to Earth. They do not have any interest in the Malacandrians except as obstacles to the furtherance of their earthly wishes. Devine wants gold, and his object is to enjoy a variety of mundane pleasures with it: 'oceangoing yachts, the most expensive women and a big place on the Riviera figured largely in his plans' (33). Weston, less selfish for himself, wants human life to gain a foothold on other planets so that it can extend its survival. But this is not out of any love for humanity (he is prepared to kill anyone in the pursuit of his aims), nor even out of a desire that the race should survive in human form: he is concerned, as Oyarsa analyses it, only with the survival of the human seed, and beneath that with fear of death (156-63).

Devine's severance from reality is seen partly in the way that his character has hardly changed since his schooldays. (It turns out that Ransom and he were at the same school.) He still makes the same 'smart' jokes about school, still produces the same tricks, such as imitating the sound of a cork coming out of a bottle (14). And he smothers reality by talking in clichés: he scorns or pays so little attention to true facts that he wraps them in inert language – '"it's all straight stuff – the march of progress and the good of humanity and all that"' (18), '"there's always a native question in these things,"' '"you'll live up to the old school tie"' (33), '"Do your stuff"' (148). He always reduces the alien to his own vulgar level: when Ransom tries to describe to him how the light as they enter the atmosphere of Malacandra is altering in degree while staying the same in quality, "'Like thingummy's soap!" grinned Devine. "Pure soap to the last bubble, eh?"' (41). 'Things', 'stuff', 'thingummy': Devine does not really care to identify what he is talking about. Later when the corpses of the killed *hrossa* have been 'unbodied' or dissipated before Oyarsa, Devine can only remark, "'God! That would be a trick worth knowing on Earth... Solves the murderer's problem about the disposal of the body, eh?"' (154).

Neither Weston nor Devine can see Oyarsa. Ransom, whose eyes have been steadily opened to Reality during the narrative can see them, though still not quite with the clarity of Malacandrian eyes. Again, neither Weston nor Devine, unlike Ransom, has learned more than the crude rudiments of the common Malacandrian language (called 'Old Solar'). Had they done so, had Weston paid more attention to the 'human' subjects, including the study of language, that he despised, they might not have misunderstood Oyarsa's wishes. As it is, when Weston comes before Oyarsa he has to use pidgin Malacandrian (written as pidgin English in the book), which though intended by him as a condescension to dumb natives, is actually a picture of his own ignorance: "'Why you take our puff-bangs away? We very angry with you. We not afraid"'(147). In treating the Malacandrians as the children he thinks they are, he himself goes into a grotesque childish pantomime that causes all those watching him, including Oyarsa himself, to laugh. And because Weston cannot see Oyarsa, he thinks that the voice he hears is coming by ventriloquism through a *hross* he sees standing in what looks to him like a trance; but is in fact a catnap. He has no conception of conversation: he thinks people are to be shouted at, he cannot be bothered to explain things to Ransom on the space-ship. It is fitting that the exigencies of their journey should make it necessary for all three of them to go back in silence, for by then they have nothing to say to one another.

It is not for nothing that Ransom is a philologist in the story: he is a communicator with others.[5] His speed and interest in grasping the Malacandrian language and its dialects is an index to his desire to meet creatures outside himself. While Weston and Devine keep to their little self-rigged hut, Ransom is exploring the Malacandrian landscape, sleeping by hot streams, staying in the dwellings of the *hrossa* or the cave of a *sorn*. The emphasis on language is there from Ransom's first shattering encounter with a *hross*, when, on hearing it speak, he begins to think of the Malacandrian dictionary he might write; and so it continues to the very end, as we leave him still speculating on the origins of the Malacandrian tongue and of words in it. In this way, among other things, we are reminded that philology, the study of language, is as much a science as the physical science that Weston says has sole claim to the title.

Indeed, it has been argued, Ransom is much more of a scientist than Weston.[6] In his first reaction to hearing a *hross* speak we are told, 'The love of knowledge is a kind of madness' (62). This love, for its own sake, is a madness Ransom shows throughout. He cannot perhaps give chemical or physical explanations or analyses, but he tries to understand and give a full record of whatever he sees. And some of the truth concerning Malacandra is given to him, as a seeker after truth, by the *sorn* Augray and by Oyarsa. The book is packed full of facts – facts concerning Malacandrian geography, climate, history, flora, fauna, peoples, foods, languages, economy, occupations, religion, politics, biology, culture. Indeed in some sense the book is a celebration of the scientific impulse in its purest form. The world it describes is a wholly objective one, outside the perceiver, and sheerly different from anything Ransom has known; perfect material for detached (though not impersonal) investigation, and delight in its separateness. Lewis sees science at its best when its quest for knowledge is disinterested, when it is carried out for itself and not for human or selfish ends (the motives of Weston and Devine).[7]

At the end Ransom wishes that more could have been got in: he regrets that the account of the *hrossa* has had to be telescoped through the needs of the narrative. 'Those quiet weeks, the mere living among the *hrossa*, are to me, the main thing that happened. I *know* them ... that's what you can't get into a mere story' (181). But he also feels that his words are inadequate to the task. Although he knows many facts about the *hrossa*, he feels that he has been incapable of putting over the totality of his experience of them. 'I merely analyse them out of a whole living memory that can never be put into words, and no one in this world will be able to build up from such scraps quite the right picture' (181-2).[8] That of course is the problem of all language, that it can only be what T.S. Eliot called 'a raid on the inarticulate'. But here it is particularly problematic in that Ransom is describing what is entirely unknown to us.

Ransom keeps trying in a postscript, the very existence of which shows the desire to pack more into the record, to get across Malacandrian smells (181) or the precise nature of *eldila* and their speech, or the sound of a *hross* singing (183-4). And, to try to put over the totality of a Malacandrian experience, he ends with two scenes, one of a *hross* funeral on a Malacandrian morning, the other of a night time bathe with the *hrossa*. The impulse behind this scientific urge in Ransom is sheer delight in the diversity of being – there is one fine paragraph in this postscript where he describes the various kinds of *hross*, from the black *hrossa* he met, to the silver *hrossa*, and 'in some of the western *handramits* one finds the great crested *hross* – ten feet high, a dancer rather than a singer, and the noblest animal, after man, that I have ever seen' (182).

'The noblest animal, after man': Ransom is no over-passionate zealot, but keeps his feelings, like his intelligence, precise. And precision is seen as almost a moral value in this book.[9] Weston's doom is the imprecision of his motives, so clearly analysed and exposed by Oyarsa at the end to be based on mere terror of death, yet dressed in all the trappings of a great cause. Imprecision has taken Weston and Devine back to Earth on their fool's errand; and the blinding power of his imagination and its delusion keeps Ransom for long from plain facts. On Ransom's part, however, there is an increasing exposure of the self to truth. His meeting with Oyarsa, who is the essence of the planet Malacandra itself, occurs after he has progressively opened himself to various 'lesser' realities of that world. As Ransom so develops, he becomes in a sense more himself. In the interview at the end Oyarsa calls him by his name, Ransom, while Weston and Devine he calls only 'Thick One' and 'Thin One', mere abstractions (though dangerous ones).

The theme of removing vagueness is caught in Ransom's first arrival on Malacandra. As he looks out through the manhole of the spacecraft he can see only a piece of ground, 'a circle of pale pink, almost of white; whether very close and short vegetation or very wrinkled and granulated rock or soil he could not say'; but then when he slides out and gets his hands on the soil he finds that 'The pink stuff was soft and faintly resilient, like India-rubber: clearly vegetation' (45). When he looks around him,

> The very intensity of his desire to take in the new world at a glance defeated itself. He saw nothing but colours – colours that refused to form themselves into things. Moreover, he knew nothing yet well enough to see it: you cannot see things till you know roughly what they are. His first impression was of a bright, pale world – a watercolour world out of a child's paint-box; a moment later

he recognized the flat belt of light blue as a sheet of water, or of something like water, which came nearly to his feet. They were on the shore of a lake or river. (46)

That last short sentence has finally got us there, though we are still to find out whether it is lake or river. We find the same process in the description of the *sorns*, who at first seem like more of the tall plants of Malacandra, then like white statues, and then, as they move, Ransom realises something of what they are (50-1). Again, what seemed to be red, cauliflower-shaped clouds turn out to be the petrified forests of Malacandra; what seemed to be mountains are in fact the walls of the great gorges in which life on Malacandra dwells. Often, because Malacandra is so 'different', we can see Ransom straining to capture a phenomenon through multiple analogies, as when he says that a *hross* looked 'something like a penguin, something like an otter, something like a seal; the slenderness and flexibility of the body suggested a giant stoat' (61); or in the account of a *pfifltrigg* as 'rather like a grasshopper, rather like one of Arthur Rackham's dwarfs, rather like a frog, and rather like a little old taxidermist whom Ransom knew in London' (131). In a sense the very existence of the *eldila* on the planet is for Ransom a test of his exactness of sight. The *hrossa* can see them, but at first they are almost invisible to Ransom and almost inaudible (91); later he is better able to perceive them.

Often accuracy depends on achieving the right perspective. When Ransom looks at a *hross* he realises that there is a right and a wrong way to view the creature which depends on one's prior assumptions. If its rationality 'tempts' him (the word is perhaps significant) to think of it as a man, it becomes 'abominable – a man seven feet high, with a snaky body, covered, face and all, with thick black animal hair, and whiskered like a cat':

> But starting from the other end you had an animal with everything an animal ought to have – glossy coat, liquid eye, sweet breath and whitest teeth – and added to all of these, as though paradise had never been lost and earliest dreams were true, the charm of speech and reason. Nothing could be more disgusting than the one impression; nothing more delightful than the other. It all depended on the point of view (66).

But precision is not only a matter of plain sight or perspective – it also depends on how far one's 'eyes are opened' - on spiritual as much as physical vision. The *hrossa* can see *eldila* partly because they are innocent. Ransom's imprecisions are for long the product of his mind as much as his eyes. As we have seen his fears and fallen attitudes often blind him to the truth. The distance he puts between himself and the *sorns* is as much spiritual as material, and decreases. When finally he meets the *sorn* Augray, 'the spectre that had haunted him ever since he set foot on Malacandra', he feels 'a surprising indifference' (104). He at first patronises the *hrossa*, answering their questions 'by saying that he had come out of the sky', but receives a shock when they tell him that that is impossible because he cannot live without air, and therefore must have come from a planet (77). Among the *hrossa* he begins to learn emotional accuracy. When he starts imagining the fame he will have among them if he kills a *hnakra* or water-monster, he checks himself, 'he had had such dreams before, and he knew how they ended'; he imposes 'humility on the newly risen riot of his feelings' (91). When the *hross* Hyoi has been shot by Weston or Devine, Ransom looks for forgiveness for himself as one of same race as the killers; but he quickly realises that he must reject his 'whining impulse to renewed protestations and regrets, self-accusations that might elicit some word of pardon' (97).

As we have said, *Out of the Silent Planet* describes a progressive journey out of the self on Ransom's part. What he encounters is alien, but it is also a measure of Ransom's own alienation from true reality. The whole of his journey away from Earth and into closer understanding and acceptance of the other, is a progress towards his becoming capable of acting later as an agent of a larger purpose in the wider cosmic commonwealth. In a sense *Out of the Silent Planet* is at once a celebration of the strangeness of this new planet Malacandra, and 'only' a prolegomenon to the next book, *Perelandra*. It is part of the nature of the universe as it is to be portrayed at the end of *Perelandra* than anything in it is at once central and peripheral, supremely important and unimportant.[10]

In this book Lewis has taken considerable trouble to create a sense of credibility. Though the whole ultimately depends on a Christian and neo-Platonic view of the universe, that view is only gradually and steadily discovered by Ransom, in what almost seems a process of inevitability, the physically becoming the morally 'alien' (Malacandrian innocence) and then the supernaturally-accompanied alien. Much discussion occurs between Ransom and the *hrossa* and *sorns* concerning the physical make-up of *eldila* (183-4). Similarly a blend of the physical and the metaphysical is Ransom's experience of the vitalising power of 'space' on his spirit (34-5, 115, 171). Lewis wants to get rid of the terrestrial tendency for mind and body to be divided, not least by himself. Only gradually are we brought to make the transition from seeing the *hrossa* as peaceful creatures to seeing them as primally innocent beings, and with them all the races of Malacandra.

So too the larger supernatural dimension of Satan is not thrust into the narrative, but emerges only through discussion of how the physical surface of the planet is largely barren and life confined to the low places. Even then, it is not till the end, and even not fully then, that the implications of Weston's behaviour and the full 'supernatural' character of the universe are reached: like Ransom, the story grows into them. The pervasively scientific character of the book is functional to this end, since for Lewis the 'supernatural' emerges out of a heightened and fuller awareness of the natural.

But Ransom is not simply a developer towards the alienness of Malacandra. He too is an alien to them, even to the guardian intelligence Oyarsa, native of deep space. Earth is Thulcandra, the Silent Planet, cut off from the life all about it. Increasingly, as the story proceeds, we find that it is not just Ransom, but those he meets, who want to find things out or look at him (78, 80-1, 118-9, 126, 137-8). He finds out less from the *sorns* than they do from him. The interview with Oyarsa at the end is largely an interrogation. When we see Ransom meet a *hross* for the first time, and both leap apprehensively away from one another, our minds are with Ransom watching the *hross*: but the story takes us out of ourselves by reminding us, through Ransom, that we are to be 'looked at' too – indeed that in a way we are far more peculiar in our fallen state than any other creature or world in the universe.

Inversion seems to be one of the recurrent techniques of *Out of the Silent Planet*, as a way, as Dr Johnson put it, of making the new familiar and the familiar new. The whole book is presented not as fiction masquerading as fact as in some travellers' tales or Swift's *Gulliver's Travels*, but rather, because Ransom knows he will not otherwise be believed, scientific fact in the guise of fiction (177-80). Ransom's 'Malacandrian' view of Weston and Devine when they are brought before Oyarsa ironically undercuts his just previous objections to a grotesque distortion of his human form by a *pfifltrigg* in its stone carving of him (132). The alien becomes 'natural', the human grotesque, the Moon apparently seen from Earth turns into the Earth seen from space, empty and dark space becomes the home of life and light, and the planets are not 'islands of life and readily floating in a deadly void' but 'mere holes or gaps in the living heaven' (44). 'Out of' becomes 'into'; walls turn into ceilings and floors to walls; from the rocky observatory of the *sorn* the

Earth is seen upside down (111). Near the end, as the space-ship rises above Malacandra on its way back, Ransom sees a strange intrusion on the reddish-ochre of the planet, 'a curiously shaped patch with long arms or horns extended on each side and a sort of bay between them, like the concave side of a crescent...[that] grew and grew'. Suddenly he sees that this is not something on the planet but the encroaching darkness of space around it, which spreads like a claw until it closes and 'The whole disk, framed in darkness, was before him' (169).

We do not feel with this, 'Ah, it's only'; both impressions remain; Ransom feels fear, not relief, when he knows what it is. And that is the case throughout the book: the strange and the familiar go together. A much greater strangeness, and a much greater familiarity, are to meet Ransom on the next planet he visits, Perelandra.

Endnotes

1. *Doctor Dolittle in the Moon* has the idea of a harmonious society of different species under a ruling Moon Man; the Doctor and Stubbins are peaceful scientific observers; their behaviour is continually monitored by concealed moon people; and the Doctor has an obsession with languages very like that of Ransom. In Wells's *First Man on the Moon*, by contrast, the Selenites dominate in lunar society, and the concern is much more with a struggle by the earthmen to survive and with their often murderous battles with the moon people.

2. See also Thomas Howard, *The Achievement of C.S.Lewis: a Reading of his Fiction*, 65-6, and Brian Murphy, *C.S.Lewis*, 29-31, who see the act in moral terms, as a crucial move out of the self.

3. For another analysis of this and the next passage, in terms rather of the natural and humane versus the mechanical and inhuman, see Wayne Shumaker, 'The Cosmic Trilogy of C.S.Lewis' (1955), repr. in Schakel, *The Longing for a Form*, 59-60.

4. On the theme of fear, see Chad Walsh, 'The Reeducation of the Fearful Pilgrim', in Schakel, ed., *The Longing for a Form*, 66-71.

5. Compare Dabney Adams Hart, *Through the Open Door: a New Look at C. S. Lewis*, p.33: 'The metaphoric basis of language is a dominant theme in Lewis's first space-fiction novel, *Out of the Silent Planet*. The idea that our planet – controlled by evil – is silent, unable to communicate, is emphasized by the role of a philologist, Ransom, as spokesman, advocate, or intercessor for the human race. The Malacandrian way of life is revealed through Ransom's gradual comprehension of their language.'

6. Howard, 74, 75, 84; Murphy, 34.

7. That is why Lewis could say in his 'A Reply to Professor Haldane' (in Walter Hooper (ed.), *Of Other Worlds: Essays and Stories*) that he had never been opposed to science itself, either in *That Hideous Strength*, which Haldane had attacked, or elsewhere: 'The "good" scientist is put in precisely to show that "scientists" as such are not the target' (78). See also William Luther White, *The Image of Man in C. S. Lewis*, 81-3.

8. Compare also 168: 'He reflected that he would have very little to show for his amazing voyage if he survived it: a smattering of the language, a few landscapes, some half-understood physics – but where were the statistics, the history, the broad survey of extra-terrestrial conditions, which such a traveller ought to bring back?'

9. As in *Perelandra* – on which see C. N. Manlove, *Modern Fantasy: Five Studies*, 116-19, 281n.53. Lewis's 'precision' is to some extent linked to his conception of reality, and especially God, as defying in their sheer 'concreteness' any vagueness or abstraction

10. *Perelandra*, 199-201.

Chapter 4

Perelandra (1943)

Of all the books Lewis wrote this was the one he liked best, even if he thought *Till We Have Faces* his finest work.[1] Lewis felt he had succeeded better almost than anywhere else in creating an image of the desirable in Venus, so much so that he almost began to believe that Venus might in some reality be like that, and that the fiction had caught truth.[2] Here he came closest to catching a sense of that Reality which haunted him all his life and which he felt stories of the marvellous were best able to grasp: the mesh of their strange narratives might for a moment hold the bird of the soul's desire before it escaped once more to the far country from which it came.[3] Here we will try to assess how well Lewis does this.

In this novel Ransom is taken to Venus or Perelandra by angels for an unknown purpose. He finds that this planet, beneath an impenetrable cloud cover, is largely covered by ocean, on which are found numbers of floating islands. He meets on one island a green Lady who turns out, together with her Lord from whom she is at present parted, to make up the sole human pair on the planet. She is primally innocent. The scientist Weston, Ransom's captor in *Out of the Silent Planet*, now also arrives by space ship. Weston has gradually become an unwitting agent of the Bent Eldil or Satan, who has used Weston's interplanetary megalomania to escape his long confinement on Earth, and strike once more against the happy worlds created by Maleldil. On Perelandra, Satan takes Weston over to use him for this purpose, so that 'Weston' becomes 'the 'Un-man'. This Un-Man tries to tempt the Lady to disobey a prohibition that has been laid on her and her husband by Maleldil. For they have been forbidden to sleep on the 'Fixed Land', the land fastened to the bedrock of the planet.

Ransom opposes as best he can the Un-man's arguments that she should do this, and the Lady uses her own reason to try to determine the truth. But gradually the Un-man shifts his attack away from argument to a kind of hypnotism, by filling the Lady's imagination with stories of heroic women of earth who have advanced civilisation by refusing to bow to outworn commands. Ransom feels that these are 'Third-Degree methods'; but is powerless to stop them, until one night Maleldil (God) comes to him to tell him to battle with the Un-man physically rather than mentally. In the fight with the Un-man that follows, Ransom is able to raise in himself so great a rage at his adversary that he finally overcomes him and puts him to flight.

There follows a pursuit on dolphin-like creatures across the ocean of the planet, a journey through the interior of part of the fixed land of the planet, the final killing of the Un-man, and Ransom's eventual emergence from the darkness onto a hillside that is part of the highest place of Perelandra. Led by an inner prompting, Ransom gradually ascends the heights, until at the far summit he finds the angelic guardians of Mars and Venus and the Lord and the Lady. Ransom is then granted a vision of the cosmic dance of creation before being returned to Earth.

The whole of this story is narrated within a kind of loop. We start with a fictional C.S. Lewis walking on a dark night to meet Ransom at his country cottage, helping to send him off and seeing him return after more than a year; then Ransom comes back into the cottage and tells his story, which is thereafter relayed through this 'Lewis'. In this way the story is not merely Ransom's, but one vouched for by a sober-minded friend who has stayed on Earth. And at the same time, by putting us a little further away from the experience, the author both shows how difficult it is to describe and draws us into it.

In *Out of the Silent Planet* we saw Ransom undergoing, by what seemed accident but was ultimately design - for 'there is no such thing as chance or fortune beyond the Moon' (*Perelandra*, 135) – a training for his role in *Perelandra*. He learned to appreciate and delight in the physical strangeness of 'alien' creatures; he was told of Maleldil or God, and of the past doings of Satan in the cosmic commonwealth; he began to align himself consciously with goodness. On Perelandra he is to meet the alien in a being of human form who is inhuman in soul.

On Malacandra Ransom seemed to wander at will across the face of Mars, but on Perelandra he knows from the beginning that he is part of a plan controlled by the Oyarsa of Perelandra and Maleldil. Where on Mars Ransom's concern was simply to look, meet and learn, on Perelandra something specific is to be done and there is a clear narrative. While a contemplative element is found at the beginning and end of *Perelandra,* when Ransom first experiences the planet and when he is given a vision of the Great Dance, soon the battle over the Lady's soul develops.

Mars is a place of completed actions: the blow of the Bent Eldil that destroyed the planet's surface is æons past, and that world is unchanged and old. The races on it do not develop or 'progress', but are content to be as they are, living their lives in their separate ways but not coming together to create any new dynamic society. The *hrossa* sing and hunt, the *sorns* think, and the *pfifltriggi* carve, and that is all, and enough. With all its beauty the planet is still; and it is composed mainly of solids, and of 'Fixed Land'. Venus however, with its vast, billowing ocean, and its floating, ever-shifting islands, is plastic and in constant movement. Even when one looks at the sky one sees motion, for it is low and golden, and reflects the changing waves beneath it, acting almost as a mirror in which Venus may see herself (30). On Perelandra, Ransom comes to learn, the idiom is one in which '"All is new"' (56).

Perelandra is a young world. Whether that means 'young' in the sense of not having been there for long we do not know. Obviously that is not the case with the planet; and there is no reason why the Lady and her Lord, who do not know the meaning of death or time, and who have never been born, should not have been living there since even our pre-Cambrian period. In such a context, time as we understand it is meaningless: the Lady may have been there for an age, but she and the planet are full of the sense of the new-made. On Malacandra by contrast, life, as in old age, has shrunk back into the valleys of the planet. But Perelandra is bursting with excess life and energy: day is a glory, night sudden and utterly pitch black; the weather is in constant flux like the sea, and every storm seems violent, the expression of prodigal life, 'the laugh, rather than the roar, of heaven' (32).

So far as 'happenings' are concerned, Mars is now out of it – though this does not make it any the less central or important in the great heavenly dance, where all is new, and all supremely necessary and unnecessary. But, in terms of time, Venus is the fulcrum: if Ransom fails there, the Bent Eldil of his world will have established a foothold on another. Great supernatural beings and God himself are much more directly present in *Perelandra* than in *Out of the Silent Planet.* 'Lewis' meets the Oyarsa of Mars himself in Ransom's cottage, and it is this Oyarsa who conveys Ransom to Venus by supernatural means. The antagonist now is not just Weston, but Weston taken over by a devil. And Maleldil is present in the very fabric of Perelandra, speaking sometimes directly to the Lady and to Ransom in their minds.

In *Out of the Silent Planet* Ransom was mainly in flight, or else simply at the mercy of circumstance, driven from one place to another – a prisoner in the space-ship both going and coming, a man having things done to him rather more than doing them. In *Perelandra* he is also to some extent passive, but the passivity is out of trust rather than fear. He gives himself into the management of the great *Eldil*; he goes naked into his coffin-shaped 'space-ship' and is transferred helpless to Venus. He has no knowledge of Maleldil's plan or reason for sending him to Perelandra, and this is only gradually revealed. He lands in a huge sea, an environment over which he has no control, and which is constantly defying his comprehension. And the same is true when he pulls himself on to a floating island, where whatever landscape it resembles is being continually altered. It can seem at one moment as though one is in a wooded valley, but the next moment the bottom of this valley surges far upwards until one is on a hill; and then the top of this hill sinks down and beneath one, back to a valley again (34). Yet all the time Ransom knows he is there for a purpose, and that he will be looked after until it is revealed to him.

Ransom is fed by the rich fruits of the planet, secretly warned against over-indulgence in the fruit, manipulated towards the Lady, pushed by her animal followers to meet her. When he first sees her as night falls, and tries to swim in the dark from his island to hers, he finds himself next morning back on his own – but now the Lady's island has been brought so close to his that he can easily reach it: his will has accomplished nothing. Indeed, whenever he tries to be a separate will, as when after a taxing interview with the Lady he seeks to 'let go', he finds that the oppressive sense of 'Someone's Presence' which had been there during his conversation with the Lady (when Maleldil on several occasions instructs her mind directly) is increased, and only becomes bearable when he accepts it and goes with it. It is intolerable on those occasions when he tries to remain independent of it (64). Going with the grain of reality here means choosing to walk with Maleldil.

But choice here is real too, though hidden. Ransom is to bring the Lady to the realisation that she chooses to accept what every wave sends, that she is not totally passive as she thought. Without being aware of it, she continually wills her own innocence. And Ransom, if under pressure from Maleldil, still makes the (to him) terrifying choice to confront the Un-man. To some extent, as the Lady's awareness of her will grows, so does Ransom's use of his own.

The entire series of the 'space' novels could be seen as a portrayal of Ransom 'growing up'. In *Out of the Silent Planet* he is both weak and wrong-headed; in *Perelandra* he is at first helpless but trusting, then choosing and acting; and in *That Hideous Strength* he has become a soldier of God, a fully choosing agent able to walk in Maleldil's ways while at the same time being in control. Lewis is a master of gradual transitions: what in the first novel is simply a process of finding out something of the makeup of the universe becomes in the next a gradual immersion in its affairs before one knows what has happened, and in the third a clear choice to intervene in a particular and foreknown event.

The story of *Perelandra* is about the discovery of, and then the struggle to maintain, a place of 'otherness', or innocence. The object of the devil in the Un-man is to destroy the beauty of the planet and the innocence of the Lady; Ransom's aim is to stop him and keep things as they are. Ransom is like a conservationist: he wants to keep a natural system from the property developers; he is protecting an endangered species. To an extent Lewis's image of a pastoral planet is of a place that, after Ransom's efforts, will be able forever to escape becoming a built-up area. In *That Hideous Strength*, by contrast, the country and nature come to 'town', which is destroyed.

All Lewis's work is most truly 'a quest for the other', as one writer recently called it.[4] For Lewis, the central purpose of stories was to try to capture that which was wholly beyond, 'that idea of otherness which is what we are always trying to grasp in a story about voyaging through space'.[5] Hence his stories are about 'other worlds' in the first place, and not just 'other' in the sense of being distant from us, but other by being 'supernatural' – 'you must go into another dimension'. Thus we have Narnia, Malacandra, Heaven, Perelandra. It is partly a desire to get away from the self, concentration on which Lewis regards as the signature of Hell. For him Pope's dictate that 'the proper study of mankind is man' is nonsense, for 'the proper study of man is everything,'[6] meaning the objective world outside man, the world of real, concrete, existent, individual things.

In a sense for Lewis 'the other' was no further away than the ladybird crawling over the back of one's hand or the leaf flashing in and out of sunlight in the breeze.[7] For him it is a matter of the sharpness or 'holiness' of one's perception to recover (in Tolkien's sense of the word) a fresh view of the sheer 'this-ness' and separateness of phenomena from all our categorisations of them. But he also had a more distant vision of the other, for in the 'joy' or *Sehnsucht* that the experience of ordinary things could sometimes give him he felt the presence of a different Other who came from far beyond the walls of the world. Moreover, his impulse in story writing was always to get out of the narrowness of this world into awareness of the universe beyond it.

To get out of our world has implications at a psychological level also. It means taking away security and upsetting certainties. Ransom's first experience of Venus is one of complete confusion. After a period of sensing the casket in which he is enclosed to be falling, there suddenly comes 'a great green darkness, [and] an unidentifiable noise', together with a marked drop in temperature. He seems now to be going up, now down, to be horizontal, and then to be descending. Meanwhile he feels the sides of his solid casket yielding and bending under his pressure; then he finds himself surrounded by a viscous white substance which he eventually sees is actually the casket melting; finally, amid a riot of strange colours and indefinite shapes, 'He was turned out – deposited – solitary. He was in Perelandra.'

But if we think we have arrived, and are about to be told of a definite place, we are in for a surprise. For Ransom's first impression is of a slanted line. Then another slant comes before him in place of the first one; then the slants join to become a peak, the peak flattens to a line and the line tilts to a shining slope that rushes towards him. He then finds himself thrust upwards to a great height, and then just as abruptly is sunk downwards into a gulf (29). The perspective creates itself as Ransom perceives it, for we start with two dimensions, first static, then moving, shifting constantly until they 'beget' a third, a solid.[8]

By this point, the scene is no longer something being looked at, it is breaking out of its frame, rushing towards the perceiver, who is not, as he and we thought, detached from it but involved in it – indeed as we are to find, immersed in it. It is doing things to Ransom, lifting him up, high, to a summit, till he sees a huge valley beneath him. Still we are thinking in terms if solids – the valley is land, surely. Then abruptly we realise that it is a sea in which he is floating amid the waves. But it is not just any sea, for it is warm, the waves are far bigger than anything on earth, the almost saltless water tastes like 'Pleasure itself' and above it the sky is a golden mirror that reflects its movements. The whole picture has 'pulled the rug from under us', as surely as Ransom himself has no footing. It is not just a case of Ransom's consciousness gradually building up a clearer picture of the scene, but almost of the scene building itself. This expresses the delight in creativity that is the nature of Perelandra and of Maleldil Himself – all things are both made and make themselves.

But there is another feature of the creation here too. We move up the scale of being (almost à la E. A. Abbott's *Flatland*, a book of which Lewis was very fond). From lines we move to shapes and from shapes to solids, and then geometry turns into life itself. And this is a process that, rather as in *Out of the Silent Planet*, continues throughout Ransom's introduction to Perelandra. After this progression he stays with the elemental sea for a time; then when he sees and finally reaches one of the floating islands of Venus he is with the vegetable – the matted fibres, the trees, the feathery vegetation, the globes of delicious yellow fruit he finds there. Then he meets an animal, a dragon, sees more creatures approaching another island nearby, and a fish with what looks like a malformation on its back, but which turns out to be a human figure that leaves the fish's back and walks on to the island. Thus by gradual transitions we traverse the entire hierarchy of being from abstract shapes to the inanimate and thence to the animate, and so up to the human who is monarch of them all of them all. It is like approaching a throne.

But there is no throne, and the monarch is naked. What is more, it is not a man, but a woman, and not white but green. Ransom has rushed to the side of his island to attract this person's notice, and then when after some time chance has brought the other's island close enough for each to see one the other, each person is shocked – Ransom that she is not the male he assumed, but female, and green in colour; she (as we are later to find out) that Ransom is not her Lord, who has been elsewhere on the planet. And that is the nature of reality in this book. No sooner does it seem to have been grasped than it slips away. In *Out of the Silent Planet* we dealt with a condition in which Ransom's fears of the alien were constantly being brought down to more precise knowledge: but here we are more often involved with a situation where an attempt at exact assessment of reality is continually being undermined by its 'otherness'. Perhaps that is also why the medium in *Perelandra* is the plastic one of an ocean, and why we deal much more with a changing narrative. Reality dips and reshapes itself beneath us as we read, like the floating islands on the ocean (44).

Things are subtly both similar and dissimilar in this book. The ocean of Perelandra is like and unlike oceans we ourselves know, in its immense waves, its warmth, colour and taste, in the many floating islands that ride its waters and the mer-people who live beneath it. More, this ocean is not merely physical, that it is in a sense a person, instinct with the character of the guardian angel or Oyarsa of the whole planet. It is feminine: quixotic, mobile, tempestuous, maternal, softly rounded, beautiful, innocently vain – 'The queen of those seas views herself continually in a celestial mirror' (30). We are drawn in by the seeming likeness of things to our world, but this only makes us feel more forcibly the differences.

So too in the description of the Lady herself, who, aside from her colour, is of exactly the same form as a terrestrial woman: and yet this very likeness heightens the difference of her inner nature and behaviour. Ransom finds that opposites are mixed in her in a way that there are no words to describe. One moment she looks like a goddess, or else like a calm Madonna; the next, she seems ready to 'laugh like a child, or run like Artemis or dance like a Maenad' (57). When the beasts of the island rush forth to greet her Ransom feels that her reception of them was both like and unlike a scene of welcome of an animal on earth: there is a mixture of authority and condescension in her behaviour which has the effect of raising the creatures somehow from 'the status of pets to that of slaves' (57).

No sooner is one classification made than it shifts to another, and then both must be held in moving opposition. No sooner does Ransom perceive her stillness than he is aware of how it could change suddenly into instant movement. No sooner does he see a likeness to the terrestrial than it shimmers into the 'other'. In *Out of the Silent Planet* analogies tended to work: the tall spiky mountains were like pylons, and the red trees were shaped like cauliflowers: and so they remained, even though we knew the differences. But here the no less frequent analogies that are made seem much more like struggles to capture the uncapturable. Of the juice of one of the yellow globe fruits he drinks Ransom could never say 'whether it was sharp or sweet, savoury or voluptuous, creamy or piercing. "Not like that" was all he could ever say' (36). The attempts to make links with Earth continually fail: it is all '"too *definite* for language"' (28). What was more simply the alien in *Out of the Silent Planet* is here the 'other'. It is both like and sheerly unlike what we know.

The most unlike thing of all is the Lady's innocence: and yet it is somehow made real to us through her direct converse with Ransom. Lewis does their meeting very well by having them on separate floating islands. For at his first, distant sight of her, Ransom waves and shouts frantically to her, and eventually the islands are close enough for her to hear him; and she waves back. In this way they start interacting before they actually meet. And when their islands float till they are within sight of one another, their first reaction is shock, as the Lady sees Ransom is not her husband but a stranger, and he realises she is not a white man but a green woman. Familiarity at a distance is ironically followed by alienation when they are closer. Then suddenly the Lady, who is surrounded by animals, points Ransom out to them, and bursts into laughter, to wild animal accompaniment. For she finds his blotched skin, patchily reddened by the sun, quite ludicrous. And Ransom, later realising this, feels as much of a fool as any man laughed at by a woman.

A giant wave has temporarily divided them, and when next they come closer the Lady has forgotten her laughter as though it had never been. Ransom is unnerved by this inhuman-seeming calmness, which he feels might arise from idiocy or immortality or some mental state that has nothing earthly about it. He reflects that on Malacandra he had met creatures that under a non-human appearance were rational and friendly, and wonders if he is now to have the opposite experience (49). But there is time only for a brief, mutually baffling exchange with 'the green Creature' before they are driven apart again and night falls. To Ransom's formal opening words, "'I come in peace,'" the Lady replies "'What is peace?'" For, unknown to him, she has no category to express peace, since she has never known its opposite: she lives inside it.

Next morning Ransom finds their islands almost touching, and they can at last have a longer conversation; and eventually he feels able to ask the Lady if he may cross over to her island. She, having no sense of 'me-ness' or ownership, does not know what he means by 'her island', but bids him come. In these two floating islands, now coming near, now driving apart, but always meeting more closely till they almost but not quite touch, we have been given both an image of the coming of Ransom and the Lady into conversation, and of the limited nature of their meeting. For, after all the incomprehension of one another that accident and ignorance have caused, there is still to remain a vast gulf between his fallen and her unfallen mind.

Ransom is first faced with trying to determine from what mental condition her strange replies to him come. When he asks the Lady where her home is, she cannot understand him, for she sees her home as the whole planet, wherever she is on it. And when she tells Ransom that she has a husband elsewhere on Perelandra, and Ransom then asks if she lives alone, she can only answer '"What is *alone*?"' (58). Later he asks if she does not want her husband the King, and she replies, '"Want him?...How could there be anything I did not want?"' (62). Through this and many other misunderstandings by her of terms that Ransom uses such as 'evil' and 'death', he is brought gradually to the realisation that she is neither stupid nor merely strange but something wholly different from both. She moves in another idiom from anything that we know in our world, and the fact is heightened for us by the conversational proximity of Ransom to her.

But soon Ransom begins to find that somehow he is not always talking to the Lady alone. Sometimes she displays knowledge she could not herself possess; and then she tells him that Maleldil, God himself, is giving it to her, at that moment. When he asks her how she knows about Malacandra's ancient peoples, and she says, '"Maleldil is telling me,"' Ransom suddenly feels that 'the garden world where he stood seemed to be packed quite full, and as if an unendurable pressure had been laid upon his shoulders, his legs failed him and he half sank, half fell, into a sitting position' (54). He is totally unnerved by the realisation that his conversation has a third and awful participant, and that he is sometimes not speaking to the Lady alone, but to Maleldil through her. He says she must have a mother and asks her when she saw her last; and she replies, '"What do you mean? I *am* the Mother"': he feels that not she only but a power beyond her has spoken to him (58-9). Ransom himself becomes increasingly aware of Maleldil's immediate presence, and this in turn increases his sense of the Lady as living innocence. And he comes to see too that the Lady's actions are not as he supposes simply self-directed, but involve the giving of her self into the hand of Maleldil in every instant.

The Lady in contrast is led as we saw by Ransom to realise that her life is not a condition in which she is carried, passive, in Maleldil's good will, but one in which she continually chooses to accept whatever Maleldil sends, whether a big wave or a visitor from another world. She thought that she was carried by the will of her creator, but now she sees that she herself chooses to go with that will. And now she wonders how Maleldil could be so generous as to make her thus able to be separate from Him, realises that the world is far more complex than she thought (62).

This new awareness is one of increasing wonder, but at the same time of increased insecurity. If it is not Maleldil who manages her life, but she who chooses to let him do so, then she could choose not to do so. For Ransom is led by their conversation to reveal to her, without any bad intent, that a creature exists which chose to cling to one good and reject all others Maleldil presented to it – the devil. He also tells her how the prohibition in Perelandra against sleeping on the Fixed Land is not forbidden to other worlds, and that on Earth a different command was laid on Adam and Eve.

There is no harm done, but rather good, in thus increasing the Lady's knowledge of herself, her world and Maleldil – so long as no-one comes to invite her to exercise her choice against Maleldil's wish. By herself she accepts this new reality Ransom has brought, as she has accepted every other wave. What Ransom has done for her is allow her to realise the fullness of her being and separateness from Maleldil: he has as it were helped her into a fuller and more conscious existence, an awareness that is quite 'other' from her present one. In this Ransom is making the Lady change as Maleldil wishes her to do. Her original unthinking innocence is not simply to be rejected as a sleep, any more than the old races of Malacandra are to be rejected, even though in another way they are 'superseded'. It is a condition that we might, so far as its passive acceptance is concerned, liken to the behaviour of a child: and yet it is surely different, for what in the child is a need for the self, is for the Lady a giving away of the self.

Ransom is present on Perelandra not only to witness the 'otherness' of the Lady's innocence, but as we have seen to preserve it; and preserve it not as it was but in a 'developed' form. The Lady at the end continues to act as she did, and yet now has awareness of self and of self making choices which could have been used to bring about her fall, but which, with her still innocent, increase the radiance of that innocence a hundredfold. The whole book is thus about the experience, growth, salvation and elevation of 'otherness' to its rightful throne (literally accomplished at the end).

The motif of otherness appears in other forms in *Perelandra*. When Ransom first reaches an island and finds the yellow globe fruit, the pleasure its juices give him makes him want to repeat the experience. Yet he resists the urge, and the reasons for eating that he surrounds it with, but without quite knowing why (37). Later he finds strange silvery globes or bubbles that expand from the tips of the branches of certain trees, and on touching one he is drenched with a cold shower with an exquisite scent, the experience of which throws new enchantment over all that he sees. Again he wants to repeat the experience, but desists in the same way, wondering whether the urge to repeat pleasures is not the root of all evil (41-2). He goes through a similar physical and psychological experience with some red-centred green berries a little while after (43).

All these experiences reflect the truth caught in Blake's lyric 'Eternity' – only when something is accepted, not appropriated, only when it is allowed to retain its otherness and not become a possession, can pleasure truly exist. That is why on this planet the Fixed Land can operate as a symbol of evil, as the thing prohibited: it is a place of stasis and possession against the free mobility of the island.[9] Evil essentially stops motion. (Yet the fact that it can be symbolic in this way does not mean that the Fixed Land is inherently evil: it depends on why it is chosen, and the novel ends on fixed land with the great celebration.) And evil is sameness and repetition, supremely caught in the hideous picture of the Un-man saying 'Ransom' over and over again, and every time Ransom replies, saying 'Nothing' (111-13). To it there is nothing to communicate, and nothing is all it ever can communicate.

What role does the strange landscape play in all this? In *Out of the Silent Planet* we dealt with landscapes and creatures which were bizarre and alien – the pylon-shaped mountains, the huge, soft, blue trees, the furry, thin, rational creatures the *hrossa* – but on Perelandra we have the much more nearly familiar – an ocean landscape, a human being – and this simultaneous proximity to, yet immense separation from our world strongly evokes the 'other'. For instance, the ocean is a kind of archetypal ocean: it is the reality of which in a sense our seas are shadows.

In the same way, what is myth on our world becomes fact in Perelandra. There Ransom finds the Garden of the Hesperides and its dragon (39). There he feels that he himself is not so much taking part in an adventure as enacting a myth (41, 131). Fiction becomes fact; and seeming accident is shown to be design. Ransom himself becomes 'other': Maleldil tells him, "'It is not for nothing that you are named Ransom,'" and, "'My name also is Ransom'" (134,135). He comes to realise that

> Before his Mother had borne him, before his ancestors had been called Ransoms, before *ransom* had been the name for a payment that delivers, before the world was made, all these things had so stood together in eternity that the very significance of the pattern at this point lay in their coming together in just this fashion. (135)

The otherness of Perelandra also exists in its inversion of some of our presuppositions. To us a paradise that has no location, no single place, comes as a surprise, more so in that it is so elemental. Instead of a constructed place, a garden, we are faced by wild nature in the form of a huge ocean. Lewis shows us that there can be more than one kind of happy place, indeed that paradise can be totally different from our notions of it. Still more, there can be good reason for its being so. There is no fixed living place on Perelandra because fixity is here the enemy, no home because to choose one location is to reject all others. Yet these symbols and rationalisations apply only to this planet. (Perhaps though, Lewis was reacting to the rather more sedentary paradise Milton gives us by making a place where the Lady and Lord have to be actively involved with their environment of waves and islands.)

The title of the book, *Perelandra*, means just what it says, that the planet and the humans together make up a sort of spiritual union; and it is the whole of that, the entire planet and its inhabitants, that is involved in the action and the temptation, and will be in any fall. Such an exposed place on the open sea again may seem to go against our notions of paradise as a protected place (even if the protection did not work in Eden). But here again Lewis is portraying to the full a new yet thoroughly-imagined innocence: the Lady is open to whatever the universe may send, whether a great wave or even a space-ship from Hell; but that does not mean that she will be without the ability to refuse them. It is the mixture of risk and protection, of open-ness and the sense of being fenced in by innocence, that is one of the beauties of Lewis's portrayal. He confounds too any notion we might have of oceans being places of instability and loss of control (a frequent image in our literature); or, similarly, of floating islands being places of delusion: on this planet instability and delusion find their place, so far as the prohibition is concerned, on solid ground.[10]

Further, through Lewis's image of this other world also comes, if his idea of *Sehnsucht* is to be believed, an element of the truly Other, of a kind of final reality. As we have seen, Lewis's conception of *Sehnsucht* was one whereby certain images in his life awoke in him feelings of such a nature and power that only something beyond space and time could satisfy them; and that something was God and Heaven. Lewis felt that the nature of our fallen experience on Earth is such that the images we have give only a broken hint of that holy Reality. But by getting out of this world, our spiritual telescopes might be less distorted by the atmosphere, as it were; and particularly on an unfallen world, even if that is imagined by a mind from this Earth.[11] Whether we feel this or not is for us to determine. Certainly as we have seen Lewis did, when after writing the book he fell in love with the notion of Venus as Perelandra, and the fiction for him almost became fact.

The world that Lewis has created, with its beautiful fullness of being, its great ocean, its living innocence and above all its superb sense of a thoroughly worked-out reality, by which each element seems to be present by inevitability, almost suggests a creating mind beyond that of a man. One moment where *Sehnsucht* seems particularly evoked occurs when Ransom is returning by night on a dolphin-creature's back to find the Lady, and smells through the darkness the warm, pure 'night breath' of a floating island:

> The cord of longing which drew him to the invisible isle seemed to him at that moment to have been fastened long, long before his coming to Perelandra, long before the earliest times that memory could recover in his childhood, before his birth, before the birth of man himself, before the origins of time. It was sharp, sweet, wild, and holy, all in one.... (92)

Whether the longing is for something that lies through and beyond the image and the lyrical style one's own experience will decide.

The otherness that is portrayed in *Perelandra* receives its most complex expression in the later stages of the 'temptation' of the innocent Lady. Professor Weston has arrived on the planet, has been taken over by Satan to become 'the Un-man', and has met the Lady and begun to tempt her to disobey. This Un-man has claimed to be Maleldil's messenger to her, and this makes her heed what it says. Ransom, meanwhile, offers what counter-arguments he can. For two days the Lady has been listening, as she feels it is her duty to, to the arguments of them both. Throughout, her innocence has been realised by the way that both her companions have had to mould their speech to her condition. The Un-man, using her idea of experience as a series of waves to be accepted, has sought to portray staying on the Fixed Land as another wave – which, since Fixed Land is solid, is inherently a contradiction.

The object of the Un-man is in effect to destroy otherness, to make the Lady behave as the fallen women of Earth behave. It wants her being to become less, rather than more herself. Its own being is a nothingness: it is a walking nonentity seeking to propagate itself. It argues that it is Maleldil's secret wish that she should disobey His command, a command which is really there only to test her boldness in breaking it. It tells her that Maleldil speaks through it because were He to tell the Lady directly she would simply once more be obeying Him when she broke the prohibition. Then it proceeds to use earthly history as a pattern for her to follow, as though the Lady's situation could be reduced entirely to the standards of terrestrial behaviour. It says that women on Earth have learnt to take goods for themselves and do not have to wait for Maleldil to tell them what is good (95); it portrays human progress as the result of the exploring and heroic spirit of terrestrial womankind (114,120-2). The Lady should submerge herself in this collective female will, should ensure its propagation on her own world.

Ransom warns the Lady that man's fall was not the origin simply of the heroism and creativity that the Un-man has described, but also of pain and misery and death. But she knows little of these categories, and the Un-man produces what is for Ransom a devastating answer: it says that but for the Fall, there would have been no Incarnation and no Redemption; Earth would never have experienced that enormous glory by which Maleldil gave Himself to man (109-10). The implicit argument is, 'Fall here, and this planet will benefit by an even greater Redemptive act on Maleldil's part.' Ransom cannot see that this too is a perversion of the facts: that man's evil cannot call God down from Heaven, but only the divine mercy, freely given in a universe where 'All is gift.'

The Lady's innocence is such that the evil of the Un-man is invisible to her. She sees it as a wave of experience sent by Maleldil that she must plunge into gladly, and she also views the Un-man's temptations as material sent to her for her consideration. She may be puzzled at times by the Un-man, but it is in a mood of 'cheerful curiosity' that once, while seated, she looks up at 'the standing Death above her'(108). She is both guilelessly trusting and intellectually rigorous during the temptation. She trusts both her interlocutors to be speaking the truth and, knowing nothing of evil (except going against love), cannot perceive the moral difference between the arguers and their arguments. Yet at the same time she demands that a case may be thoroughly watertight, and is continually raising problems that force the others to extend and elaborate their arguments. This mixture of the trusting and the penetrating is another side of the strength of her portrayal, and illustrates how opposites meet in her.

The Lady is immune to temptation of the straightforward sort. Because she will not cease loving Maleldil or her Lord the King, she can only be persuaded to fall through love for them. Indeed she can fall only insofar as she can be brought to believe that Maleldil really wants her to disobey Him, but cannot tell her directly because He wants her to do it on her own. The Un-man has to argue that Maleldil wants the Lady to cease being passive in His hands or waves, and become fully independent of Him. And it backs this up by saying that Ransom himself began the process in teaching her to be more conscious of her free choice and its exercise.[12]

There might seem to be a problem here. For if the Lady chooses to disobey the prohibition out of love for Maleldil, her husband and of her unborn children (121), she will, it will seem to our eyes, be doing it out of innocent motives. But such a view may be the result of our own 'fallen' understanding, and a test on us. What do we, finally, know of the nature of evil with our little quantifications of motive and act? Maleldil told her 'not to': surely the act itself, irrespective of motive, could be all – could in a sense 'contain' an 'evil motive' without there being any evident sign of one. Who knows? Again, it was Maleldil Himself who told her not to sleep on the Fixed Land. He has not told her why she should not do so. It is not He who appears to her to reverse this decree, and the creature that does so gives her reasons, but no living voice. True, it tells her why Maleldil cannot appear to her directly, but these are still only explanations.

If the Lady now chose to fall she would be putting arguments before fact, would in a sense be disputing Maleldil's prohibition, which was accompanied by no arguments and demanded obedience simply, for itself, without question, however induced. Ransom at one stage puts this point to her, and she accepts it delightedly. They are debating whether there is any 'reason' behind Maleldil's command, and Ransom says to her that while all her other 'obediences' of life on the islands are evidently good to her as to Maleldil, the one relating to the Fixed Land has no evident point in it – and that is just its point, for here Maleldil wanted an obedience that was purely for His sake rather than because it seemed good to her too (107).

In another place the present writer once argued that the portrayal of original innocence is inherently problematic. If the innocence is open to blandishments by that which is evidently evil, if evil can find a handhold on it, then it might seem that it could never have been pure innocence in the first place. The example used was Milton's portrayal of Eve, who can seem to fall very quickly into open hostility to God under the arguments of the serpent. But if, on the other hand, one makes the innocence perfect, then it becomes immune to temptation. There seemed no way out of the problem: if innocence was open to temptation it could not be innocence; if not, there could be no true fall.[13] On reflection, however, this may be a limited view. Certainly, in any case, as Lewis points out, we know nothing of what happened in Eden (133). And certainly here he has shown how innocence could be open to temptation without ceasing to be innocence as we fallen mortals understand it.

This issue of the Lady's potential culpability relates more to the intellectual consistency of Lewis's book than to its narrative actualities, for we are told that the Lady is not left to fall in this way. Nevertheless, we have for long felt that she could do so, that great issues hung on every argumentative point scored by Ransom or the Un-man; and for pages we have followed the to and fro sway of the debate. Finally, it seems, the Lady is resistant to the idea of breaking Maleldil's prohibition, so long as it comes to her as mere argument: 'perhaps no rational creature... could really throw away happiness for anything quite so vague as the Tempter's chatter about Deeper Life and the Upward Path' (121). This is not quite what we have felt: but still.

The Un-man, at any rate, is now forced to change the nature of its persuasion. Instead of arguments, it will resort to ceaseless propaganda. It begins to tell the Lady endless stories about heroic females of Earth who disobeyed Maleldil and experienced noble and tragic lives (114). It goes on telling these stories by day and night, and Ransom, who eventually needs sleep, is unable to intervene effectively anymore, while the Lady, needing sleep less, and full of the sense of duty to her world, makes herself listen to it. As she does so, she gradually begins to be taken over by the Un-man's images of the heroic female. To Ransom she seems to be very faintly reminiscent of a tragedy queen (115), and later she has 'the faintest touch of theatricality, the first hint of a self-admiring inclination to seize a grand role in the drama of her world' (121).

She begins to pay less attention to the real issues and to the facts of the situation – Maleldil's prohibition, the unknown results of breaking it, and to the happiness she presently has – because her mind is being swept away in a flood of hypnotic imagery (122). Ransom sees that she is still innocent, but that if her will is uncorrupted her imagination has begun to be taken over. He says, 'this can't go on,' but it does. The Un-man sets about giving the Lady an image of her beautiful soul through realisation of the beauty of herself: it dresses her in feathers (torn, unknown to her, from Perelandrian birds), and then shows her her face in a mirror. At this stage Ransom feels that the 'Third Degree Methods' are being used. It seems to him that these will break the Lady's resistance in the end. He cannot understand why, since Maleldil has permitted a 'miraculous' force of evil to appear on the planet, He has not produced one on the right side (128).

But Maleldil's 'standards', if we can call them that, could be wholly other than ours. He gave no explanation for His prohibition: why should he justify Himself to us? Why should we not obey Him and accept as the Lady does whatever He sends, simply because He is Maleldil and Love, and not when it makes sense to our limited understandings? Ransom is at this stage himself about to undergo an interview with Maleldil that will pose some of those matters until his questioning intellect dies away.

Nevertheless, were things to be left like this, *Perelandra* would be portraying an otherness in Maleldil far beyond the kind so far seen in the world of Perelandra. This would be an otherness that required blind faith in the goodness of God when His acts seem cruel or unjust. It is the kind of otherness to which the only answer is Vertue's final admission in *The Pilgrim's Regress*, "'Thou only art the Lord.'" That would be a pretty Himalayan truth for us to scale, but it is one that is in the Bible in the story of Job and in some degree is the experience of every Christian.

However, Lewis does not leave us with this view of Maleldil's power, for in an 'interview' that shows His mercy, He tells Ransom that there is still a way to overthrow the Un-man. That way lies in Ransom himself: he can fight the Un-man physically, can attempt to destroy it with his bare hands. In this sense Ransom himself is the miracle 'on the right side' that he was looking for. There may be nothing he can do by way of argument to stop the Lady's mind being overwhelmed, but still he can remove the tempter physically.

Ransom's 'voluble self' protests however that a physical battle between himself and the Un-man would be unfair, since it would not answer the enemy's arguments, only stop them. And if the Lady was to be kept innocent only by removing her tempter, her innocence would be made a poor thing that could not stand on is own. What could such a salvation prove? (132). But here again Ransom's argument drives us towards realising how inadequate our standards are to encompass divine reality. Ransom, who previously said it was unfair to the Lady to give the devil the stronger hand, is now almost saying it is unfair to the devil to reverse the situation. The whole concept of 'fairness' takes rather a knock from this.

Moreover the Lady is not being 'fairly' tested: she is being driven into the ground by what Ransom has himself just called 'Third Degree Methods'. These methods are no longer a temptation that involves any real spiritual issue: they are the crushing methods of continuous propaganda. The Un-man is now superhuman in that it needs no sleep, and the Lady, increasingly exhausted, is forcing herself to stay awake because she believes the Un-man's assertion that it is Maleldil's messenger. Her mind is being overwhelmed. And Ransom is likewise too exhausted to offer sufficient counter-propaganda to the Un-man's, even if he had wished to resort to such methods. It is thus 'fair' that he should himself resort to the Third Degree Methods of physical intervention against the Un-man.

As for Ransom's asking what it would 'prove' if he uses physical force to stop the Un-man's temptation, that is a mortal man's question. Maleldil has nothing to prove, for He is Himself Proof, and the 'temptation' need not be any more of a 'significant' event than any other. Why should meaning have to be separable from experience? Where all is equally at the centre or the periphery of 'importance' in the universe, why should any act be more crucial than another? Ransom is to realise that it could have been another as much as he who helped the Lady, that he both is and is not marked out: 'It might as well be any other choice as this. The fierce light which he had seen resting on this moment of decision rested in reality on all' (137). This takes us into a deeper awareness of how limited is the human understanding of divine truth.

All attempts to look away from the actual event ignore Reality for what the book calls an 'alongside world'. Ransom tries to compare what is happening on Perelandra with Eden. It would have been absurd, he says, if the elephant had come along and trodden on the serpent when it was on the point of persuading Eve to fall (132). He wonders whether Eve resisted, and if so, for how long. Still more, if the serpent had returned day after day, would Maleldil not have stopped it (133)? But Ransom's two positions concerning Eve's predicament have cancelled out, just as before: now it would be unfair to save her by miracle, now Someone ought to have intervened to rescue her from an interminable blandishment. To all this he is given no answer, only drawn back to the here and now and what must be done (133). We are to face only the event itself. 'This chapter, this page, this very sentence, in the cosmic story was utterly and eternally itself; no other passage that had occurred or ever would occur could be substituted for it' (133).

Such facts are not to be argued away: the universe in many ways operates on principles beyond our comprehension. God and goodness may be far more terrifying than we know – equally they may be far less remote than we suppose. The pure, intellectual love that shoots from the faces of the Oyéresu at the end is 'like barbed lightning' and 'so unlike the love we experience that its expression could easily be mistaken for ferocity' (185). The vision of the Great Dance given to Ransom at the end serves partly to show him how much wider and more strange is Reality than the human mind could ever grasp.

For instance, if Ransom had been overcome in the physical struggle with the Un-man, would the temptation of the Lady then have resumed where it left off and she been allowed to fall? Or was Ransom's hard-won decision to fight the Un-man rather than the fight itself the Lady's salvation? Or are we wrongly dividing the two? Perhaps the decision and the fight are in a sense, as Charles Williams would have put it, 'categories of one identity' – after all, when Ransom comes to his decision, he says it was as if the act of fighting was already performed (136-7). Then again, if the Lady can see nothing hideous in the Un-man, but accepts it like any other wave, would she not equally have rejoiced in the trail of torn frogs or birds later ripped apart by it? – the question is potentially there, even if Lewis never gives it scope.

At the end we are again shaken out of our ways of thought when we meet the King. Ransom cannot see how the King knows so much about evil when it is the Queen who has been up against it, nor can he quite accept, as the King remarks to the Queen '"that you suffered and strove and I have a world for my reward"': but he is told that Maleldil always goes above justice, and that '"All is gift... The best fruits are plucked for each by some hand that is not his own"' (194). Then the King adds a wider dimension to the earlier issue of the Lady seeming to be able to fall without a sinful motive. He says that *while* she was being tempted, not *after* (which was when her eyes were opened to the truth), he was taken by Maleldil to a place where he was instructed in the nature of evil, and saw the threat to the Queen. There he determined not to fall himself. And he believed that even if the Queen fell, he might be able to 'recover' her (195). The fall of the Lady would not then be so final as we had supposed, and our earlier judgements would have proved again inadequate to the variety of divine fact.

Our compartmentalisations of reality are broken down within the whole structure of the book. We think that Ransom arguing with the Un-man and the Lady is a 'mental' or 'intellectual' action and that the subsequent fight between the two human bodies is 'physical'. But we have seen enough of mental and spiritual life in the joy of the physical ocean or the radiance of the Lady's body to undermine this. And Lewis has deliberately shuttled between what may be called 'physical' and 'mental' sections throughout the narrative, to prepare us for the idea that in Reality a blow with a fist can be as much a thought as an act. He starts us with the 'mental' struggle of the narrator as he tries to reach Ransom's cottage; then when Ransom has arrived on Perelandra we are given his 'physical' experience of the ocean and the islands. Then there is a more or less continuous discussion with the Lady, later joined by the Un-man; after which we move to the physical fight with the Un-man, and the pursuit of it both across and inside Perelandra. And at the end we seem back again with the 'mental' in the long hymnal discourse of the Oyéresu on the nature of Maleldil's universe. Discourse and action are thus interwoven throughout to suggest that they are interchangeable.

At times however this idea of an exchange of categories can be too theoretically put. When Ransom objects to the idea of fighting with the Un-man with his fists on the ground that it 'would degrade the spiritual warfare to the condition of mere mythology', he is checked by the realisation that, through all his experience on Mars and particularly on Perelandra, he 'had been perceiving that the triple distinction of truth from myth and of both from fact was purely terrestrial – was part and parcel of that unhappy division between soul and body which resulted from the Fall'. Ransom then thinks how, on earth, the fact of Christs' life on earth is also a myth, and how the sacraments continually re-enact it. He concludes that whatever takes place on Perelandra will be of such a nature that earthmen (who are fallen) 'would call it mythological' (131). This idea may be correct, but it is one more imposed than worked out through argument with someone else.

And Lewis as an earthman himself does not always keep to these transcendental perceptions. For all his sense that Reality, Love and Justice go far beyond our notions of them, he has to some extent 'descended' to our notions in the narrative. And the very fact that Ransom is there to answer to 'unfair' methods of the Un-man with the 'unfair' interruption of those methods provides a sop to the merely human sense of imbalance.

More questionable is the treatment of the prohibition. During the Lady's temptation it is as we saw one of Ransom's strongest arguments that the prohibition should have no inherent significance at all, save that Maleldil forbids it. If He forbade her to starve herself, there would be no real obedience, since it is what she wants to avoid herself. But her not sleeping on the Fixed Land is a command that seems meaningless, and her obedience to it will not be because she sees why, or wants to obey it: she will avoid doing it simply because Maleldil wishes so. It is an opportunity for her to obey Maleldil directly, to give her love back to Him by continually choosing to follow in His ways (107). The command is there not simply to forbid, but for the creation of more love, for every instant that the Lady continues in obedience is another compact between her and her creator.

Our fallen minds may however still ask why the prohibition is the particular one of not sleeping on the Fixed Land rather than any other 'meaningless' command, as Ransom does once early on, before the Lady changes the subject (67). And the Lady is surprised to find that on Earth Adam and Eve were never forbidden to sleep on any fixed land, but had a quite different demand to follow. But for a long time we have no cause to see what is forbidden on Perelandra as being significant.

What may also occur to us is that the command not to sleep on the Fixed Land is not a hard one for the Lady to obey. She is perfectly happy to move with the floating islands, and has no particular wish to stay on the Fixed Land. She takes Ransom to it once so that she may climb to one of its higher places and see whether her missing husband the Lord is on any of the farther floating islands. But while they are there, she shows not the slightest interest in staying there. If we compare this to the stories of Adam and Eve, the forbidden fruit was at least attractive to them before the arrival of the serpent. Ransom raises the issue of 'this forbidding... [being] no hardship in such a world as yours'. The Lady finds this strange, replying that whatever Maleldil tells her to do is a joy to her, however easy or difficult it may be (67). But Ransom's point was not so much what she felt about it, but whether or not it could be called much of a command at all – for the easier it seems objectively, the more we feel that nothing is at risk. And if nothing is at risk, and innocence is more or less assured, how can love for Maleldil be truly shown?

But we are to find that in fact the command by Maleldil is not finally meaningless at all. For at the end of the adventure, when Ransom meets the Lady again in the high place of Perelandra, she tells him that as soon as he chased the Un-man from her island, her eyes were opened to hidden significance of the forbidding of sleep on the Fixed Land:

> 'The reason for not yet living on the Fixed Land is now so plain. How could I wish to live there except because it was Fixed? And why should I desire the Fixed except to make sure – to be able on one day to command where I should be the next and what should happen to me? It was to reject the wave – to draw my hands out of Maleldil's, to say to Him, 'Not thus, but thus' – to put into our own power what times should roll towards us.' (193)

The prohibition thus becomes self-explanatory. It would have been quite possible, knowing Maleldil's and the Lady's natures, to have worked it out – to realise that the Fixed Land, which does not move, can be seen as a symbol of the rigid and unyielding self, the self that will not give itself like the islands to the changing shapes of the waves. And while the Lady would not have wanted to do this in innocence, it was the Un-man's object to turn her into just the kind of person who would.

And *sleeping* on the Fixed Land – well, that is an image of death; but as a state of unconsciousness, it is also, on the Fixed Land, an emblem of the no longer clear-seeing or free self – for to choose Maleldil is to be fully conscious and free, while to assert the self and (paradoxically it might seem) to sleep, is to diminish it. Thus the entire landscape of Perelandra, Fixed Land and prohibition included, becomes significant, available to explanation. The Lady says to Ransom that it was a wonder that she and he failed to see 'the point' of the prohibition: and indeed in a sense it is. Had they seen it, had the Lady understood exactly what was wrong with the Fixed Land, the Un-man might not have succeeded in its temptation.

But only *might* not – for we know that the Lady feels she must listen to it, and that it resorted in the end to the Third Degree Methods which might have worn her down whatever larger perception of the issue she had hit on. It may be that Maleldil inhibited her and Ransom from making the connection before (after all, He opens her eyes to it after the Un-man has been removed), so that the temptation has to proceed as though the command were meaningless. This was the only way to make the temptation of the Lady a real one, with no holds barred.

But in the end Lewis will not leave the command 'meaningless' and 'other' because it is part of a gradually revealed cosmic pattern behind the story. The revelation of pattern is central to the book: even the story of the averted fall is subsumed in it. The Lady seems at first only a green woman, but then turns into the Mother and her predicament into that of a crucial moment in universal history. Weston comes as the human scientist we know to the planet but then becomes caught up by a Spirit far larger than he. Ransom is a 'mere' Cambridge philologist who finds himself called on to act something of the role of a Christ – he is 'forced out of the frame, caught up into the larger pattern' (135). Making the landscape of Perelandra significant fits with this kind of concentric patterning and also gives the book more organic unity. However one also feels that Lewis has given way to a wish to avoid mystery and to make the universe intelligible to us. The intellectual and argumentative core of the book here wins over that other side of Christianity which Lewis once called 'big medicine and strong magic'.[14]

To return now to the story: after Ransom's interview with Maleldil, his fight with the Un-man is a mixture of the everyday and the terrifying. At the level of physique it is 'one middle-edged, sedentary body against another' (134). The Un-man, devil though it is, can operate only through the flabby body of Weston – though it has hideously long fingernails for rending. Ransom is the better boxer, but the Un-man's slashing slowly saps his strength through loss of blood. However at one point in the struggle Ransom comes to a point of so great a hatred for the devil in the Un-man, 'the living Death, the eternal Surd in the universal mathematic', that he becomes able to smash it into defeat and force it to flee (143). It seizes one of the dolphin-like creatures by the shore of the island and forces it to bear it away; and Ransom, following close behind, takes after it on another dolphin.

Eventually, out on the wide ocean of Perelandra, with his enemy lost to sight, Ransom feels another kind of otherness from that in Maleldil's words to him. Maleldil told him that on him depended the fate of a world; revealed to him the awful significance of his name Ransom. But now, instead of being brought from a sense of his unimportance to knowledge of his absolute 'importance', Ransom experiences the reverse emotion – and not only about himself, but about the Lady and her concerns too. Now everything he has experienced seems little, insignificant, peripheral. The world of Perelandra becomes suddenly quite 'other' from these human concerns:

> As for the great prohibition, on which so much had seemed to hang – was it really so important? What did these roarers with the yellow foam, and these strange creatures who lived in them, care whether two little creatures, now far away, lived or did not live on one particular rock? (150-1)

This perception is ultimately inaccurate: Ransom's imagination is being overwhelmed by terror at mere size and vacancy; and the littleness of a thing does not make it unimportant. Yet part of this feeling is, in its cloudy way, right. All that he does, all that the Lady does, all Perelandra, all creation, are sublimely unnecessary, 'unimportant' to Maleldil; even while at the same time they all matter supremely to Him. Both views are needed, and both views are to be given in the hymn of the Oyéresu at the end. No one view is sufficient, yet each is opposite or wholly 'other' to its partner, so that it is hard to hold both together in one act of mind. Experience therefore is mobile and dialectical, moving back and forth from one side to another, just as in his own way Ransom has moved from a view of himself as a mere mortal helper of the Lady, to the realisation that he is Maleldil's agent and thence back to a notion of himself as supremely insignificant. Only the innocent perhaps, and those who live in Heaven, can turn the shuttlings of mortal dialectic to lived paradox.

As a book by a 'fallen man', *Perelandra* has to enact the dialectic of meaning and apparent meaninglessness sequentially. We start with the narrator 'Lewis' walking alone to Ransom's country cottage in the dark and becoming increasingly terrified, especially when he finds the cottage empty. Then Ransom comes to give purpose and order to events, and they are together as old friends for a time in the cottage until Ransom leaves. On his first arrival in Perelandra, Ransom floats in the ocean on his own, ignorant of what he has to do; then he meets the Lady and stays on her island for a time, learning her nature and the significance of his having been taken to meet her. Then again he is on his own again, journeying over the now seemingly waste and dark places of Perelandra; and finally he is with men and with angels who reveal to him how the universe is a dance of opposites in which the duality of his experience is made one.

Another double view of the world is that between random and the planned. The dolphin-creatures that carry the Un-man and Ransom are going no-one knows where across the face of the planet. Eventually they come to a coast and great breakers. The Un-man seizes Ransom in a frenzied grip and drags him down with it as the seeming end approaches: but after a long descent into the ocean depths Ransom feels himself come up into air in a place of darkness. At length he realises that he is in a cave with a submerged entrance, and finds a possible way out which involves climbing upwards into the darkness. And so Ransom begins a long journey through the deep places of Perelandra, during which he encounters a huge insect-like monster that proves quite harmless, sees at one point far below him some human-like figures drawing a strange cart, and re-encounters and finally destroys the Un-man. Nearly all this journey seems haphazard, without direction.

Yet it is also part of a plan. For one thing, in a sense Ransom is, as he knew before, enacting a myth. In his loneliness and terror on the ocean, in his 'death' in the waves, in his gradual climb through the dark to the light, in his final wrestle with and victory over this devil, he relives in his way the story of Christ from His loneliness in Gethsemane, to His death, His overthrow of the Devil and His Resurrection. If we like, the whole book has enacted the story in the Bible, from the creativity that is in Perelandra to the story of the averted fall to the new 'Christ'

– and thence to the vision of the 'Last', but here eternal Things, given to Ransom at the close.

And there is another 'planned' aspect which is present, though hidden. By being taken out from the fairly narrow personal context of the first half of the book to the wide wilderness of the whole planet, Ransom's consciousness is being opened out from its previous confines; and at the same time he is being made ultimately more aware of the fact that it was not 'just' the Lady he saves but the whole world of which she is an organic part. In being Queen of Perelandra she is the planet in microcosm, and after Ransom has met her as a single human, he is as it were being introduced to her in macrocosm.[15] The merging of the apparently random into the patterned, of the unplanned into the planned, is caught by the Oyéresu at the end: "'There seems no plan because it is all plan'" (202).

The Un-man by contrast has no interest in dialectic or dancing opposites; it is on the planet to destroy the 'other', to make the innocent lady fall into the common ways of man. It seeks to reduce all things to one, and beyond that, to turn them to nothing. Weston feels himself driven by a 'Force' that finally takes him over and makes him the Un-man. He has denied the existence even of final opposites such as good and bad, God and devil, saying they are portraits of different actions of one cosmic Spirit (84). He has asserted that there is no gulf between self and world, perceiver and perceived: "'In so far as I am the conductor of the central forward pressure of the universe, I am it... I *am* the Universe. I, Weston, am your God and your Devil'" (86). For him nothing is 'other' because all is reduced to him. And at that very point, as he is taken over by Hell, he becomes 'other' in a way he could not have guessed and will forever suffer.

The book has moved towards the view of reality that the Un-man rejects, and it is with this that it ends. In Maleldil the opposites of the Great Dance of existence find their true nature, and all things finally merge into one great light (203). There lies that resolution of all paradox which we call heaven. But the insistence of *Perelandra* is also on the evasiveness, the simultaneous familiarity and 'otherness' of reality to us as fallen creatures, like the strange shy singing beast that Ransom finds on the great mountain (176-7). Between the vision of opposites and the great light of their resolution, Ransom alone of fallen men has been permitted to move.

Certainly Ransom's experience of the 'other' throughout the story, and his questioning of the often incomprehensible ways of the Lady and

Maleldil, have been the measure of his and our mortality. Yet that very fallen mortality has with Maleldil's encouragement been able to save a whole innocent world from a disaster of the kind man brought upon himself in Eden. At the end, Ransom, so long the recipient of longings that come from far beyond himself, is drawn through the whirling vortex of creation to be one with that far and yet near source from which he has been so mortally divided:

> a simplicity beyond all comprehension, ancient and young as spring, illimitable, pellucid, drew him with cords of infinite desire into its own stillness. He went up into such a quietness, a privacy, and a freshness that at the very moment when he stood farthest from our ordinary mode of being he had the sense of stripping off encumbrances and awaking from trance, and coming to himself. (203)

There, taken furthest from himself, he is most truly what he is; taken to the wholly and finally 'other' he will never quite see things as 'other' again. His free choice has made him one with the purposes of Heaven; and from now on his will is with Maleldil. In the next book, *That Hideous Strength*, we will find a Ransom who has ceased to ask querulous questions, a wholly confirmed person living freely in the idiom of the celestial commonwealth, as free from sin almost as one of his beloved *hrossa*, yet still with the mark upon him of his mortality in the form of his continually bleeding heel.

Endnotes

1. Roger Lancelyn Green and Walter Hooper, *C. S. Lewis: a Biography*, 170-1.
2. Ibid. 171.
3. Lewis, 'On Stories' (1947), repr. in *Of Other Worlds: Essays and Stories*, ed. Walter Hooper, 20-1. On *Perelandra* as the most 'other' of Lewis's fictional other worlds, see Manlove, *Modern Fantasy*, 102-6.
4. Meilaender, op.cit.
5. Lewis, 'On Stories', *Of Other Worlds*, 12.
6. Lewis, 'On Science Fiction' (1955), repr. in *Of Other Worlds*, 65.
7. See e.g. *Surprised by Joy: the Shape of My Early Life*, 14, 22. Glover, *C. S. Lewis*, 94, cites a letter by Lewis to Ruth Pitter, of 4 Jan. 1947, 'And oh how much sweeter is this *longing* than any other *having*.... What you are really wanting will never be any finite *here* and *now* (God bless us. You know that as well as I do) and the rabbit in Magdalen grove may mediate it as well as a hross.'
8. In Manlove, *Modern Fantasy*, 117-18, this passage is also seen as serving to put us close to Ransom as he tries to decipher his experience, and as portraying the precision and clarity typical of the picture of innocence on Perelandra. Almost the same image is used at the end, of the Cosmic Dance (199).
9. See also Meilaender, op.cit. 15-19.
10. For more extensive treatment of some of these points, see Manlove, *Modern Fantasy*, 119-21.
11. For Lewis's views on *Sehnsucht* and 'joy' see the references cited in Chapter 1, note 14; see also Corbin Scott Carnell, *Bright Shadow of Reality: C. S. Lewis and the Feeling Intellect*, and, on the particular intensity of *Sehnsucht* in the unfallen world of Perelandra, *Modern Fantasy*, 109-13.
12. For a fuller analysis of the temptation, see *Modern Fantasy*, 129-34.
13. Ibid. 136-8.
14. Lewis, *Letters to Malcolm: Chiefly on Prayer* (London: Collins, Fontana, 1966), 105. Lewis is discussing his difficulty with the Sacraments.
15. On this idea see also Lewis's poem 'The Adam at Night' (1949), repr. in Walter Hooper (ed.), Lewis, *Poems*, 45-6.

CHAPTER 5

That Hideous Strength (1945)

That Hideous Strength was not needed to complete the story of the first two books of the space trilogy. In *Perelandra* Ransom had successfully carried out the task he was partly prepared for in *Out of the Silent Planet*. The Lady and Lord had been saved, Satan defeated, Weston killed, and Ransom returned to Earth to tell the tale. *That Hideous Strength* gives us entirely new protagonists, in the sociology lecturer Mark Studdock and his wife Jane; and new antagonists, in the scientists of the N.I.C.E., or National Institute of Coordinated Experiments. And where the earlier two books involved space travel, this one is set throughout in one place on Earth, the provincial university town of Edgestow in mid-twentieth-century England. Ransom is still present, but he is now more distant, as director of the Company of St Anne's, a religious foundation with its centre in a hilltop village just outside Edgestow. In addition, the mythology of Arthur and Merlin now makes an important appearance.

There could be a certain connection with the earlier books if we considered the action of the 'Bent One' or Satan as a sort of solar flare of evil: for, once thrust back to Earth again from his sortie to Perelandra, Satan might well wish to expend his energies on destroying Maleldil's creations on Earth. This connection is however only implicit. And when Lewis tries to make a link with the earlier books he does not use it. Late in the book Ransom learns that it is because the forces of Hell have broken out of the Earth to which they were bound, that the powers of Heaven have come down: '"They have gone to the gods who would not have come to them, and pulled down deep heaven on their heads"' (294). This is fine as an explanation, but it is offered too late to do much to pull the books together.

It is not surprising therefore that readers often feel puzzled by this novel. And it not only lacks clear narrative links with the rest of the trilogy: it feels quite different, and even unpleasant, by comparison. It deals with the near and everyday rather than the remote and romantic; for much of the time it concentrates on the psychology of a married couple in England, almost like a 'realistic' novel; it offers nothing of the great adventures and wide-open spaces of the first two books; it deals with what is evil and sordid much more than what is innocent, beautiful or desirable. Beyond this it is a complex and sometimes cumbersome mixture of scientific theory, Christian supernaturalism and Arthurian mythology that can crush the believability of the characters.

Many, though not all, of these criticisms can be answered. In the first place, the setting of the book on Earth makes a complement to the earlier two. In *Out of the Silent Planet* and *Perelandra* Ransom was engaged in finding out the real and objective nature of the universe beyond the Earth – which turned out to be supernatural. He was continually going outwards, not only physically by spaceship, but also spiritually, in having to encounter first the alien, and then the 'other', at increasingly trans-mortal levels. But we find no such physical journey in *That Hideous Strength*; and the spiritual journey we are given is not outwards to increasing levels of truth, but ever inwards through deepening circles of subjectivity towards falsehood. A kind of vortex is at work throughout on the confused mind and feeble will of Mark Studdock, drawing him in to creatures that are not the absolute being embodied on Maleldil, but the utter nonentity that is Hell.

It has often been said that in this book Lewis comes nearest the novels of his close friend Charles Williams. In a sense this novel can be seen as Lewis's recreation of Williams's *Descent into Hell* (1937), in which we watch the cold historian Wentworth fall steadily towards the pit. As in that novel, the emphasis is psychological, and the focus is on the workings of the mind and moral nature of a character faced by temptation. The theatre of *That Hideous Strength* is the inner rather than the outer self. At the centre of the N.I.C.E.'s purposes is a human head, a brain, severed from the body and kept alive by machines. Throughout the idea of an 'Inner Ring' obsesses Mark Studdock: he longs to be 'in the know' with those who 'matter', he wants to penetrate to a secret inner centre from which he feels excluded. His lust is for the esoteric, powerful knowledge of the magician, rather than the exoteric, true knowledge available to all men.

In keeping with this, the novel is most commonly set in houses and rooms. We start in the Studdocks' home, move to the committee room at Bracton College, and from there Mark goes to Belbury and the complex of buildings that makes up the N.I.C.E. Soon Mark finds himself forbidden to leave. He is taken to see the Head in the secret room at the centre of Belbury, and his horror leads him to break out of the complex and escape to Edgestow. But he is quickly recaptured, and is now falsely accused of murder, so that he may be confined to a cell by the N.I.C.E. and moulded more easily to their purposes. Meanwhile Jane has gone in the opposite direction. She is drawn towards the community at St Anne's, is eventually admitted to their house, and gradually becomes a believer. People are enclosed: even Satan is shut in the confines of this world, and at the end beneath it.

There is also a sense of increasing focus on one spot throughout the novel. There is little travel aside from going from one side of Edgestow to another, and the town is seen as isolated from the rest of the country. This particular spot matters to both camps because they have found that Merlin is buried somewhere there, and is about to rise again with all his great magical powers. The 'Macrobes', or devils, have bent their energies on Belbury and the N.I.C.E., seeing them and their beliefs as a means of extending their own power over humankind. And at the end the powers of the five planets Mercury, Mars, Venus, Saturn and Jupiter, embodied in their guardian intelligences, and represented on Earth in the five wits of man, are focused on St Anne's to transform its people for action. The devils are thrown back to Hell in a vortex that takes in Belbury and ruins Edgestow.

It can be said that where in the earlier books of the trilogy a man went outwards to find God in what we call the solar system, in *That Hideous Strength* another man is forced to make a journey inwards to find whether God or Satan lies at the bottom of his soul. What Mark finds in himself however is not so much any immediate sense of God, as a final preference for 'the Straight' rather than 'the Crooked'. Nevertheless we are to suppose that this feeling also comes from the working of divine grace in him. When Mark refuses the demand by the scientist Frost that he stamp on a figure of the Cross, the door to his cell suddenly opens to admit Ransom's agent Merlin, and Mark can at last escape from the narrowing vortex in his mind.

In these ways, *That Hideous Strength* is not meant to be a continuation of the two preceding books so much as the third panel of a triptych, completing a picture of God's workings in the universe. And this will explain why the book is as it is. It may even be argued that the book is without obvious links in order to make us look for these deeper connections. And certainly this is of a piece with the wider character of *That Hideous Strength*, which is finally analytic, taking us down through layer after layer of knowledge. Only gradually do we find out the true nature and connections of the N.I.C.E.; for long the Company at St. Anne's seems a frail thing against the powers of evil; and for long Mark Studdock journeys downwards through the layers of his soul to find out who he really is.

This is Lewis's most negative book on the subject of the potential uses of science. To science as 'scientia' or knowledge he had no objection – indeed Ransom's use of it in *Out of the Silent Planet* was an almost heroic activity - but when in that book the exploration of phenomena turned men into materialists who denied God and the spirit, then Lewis objected to it. Here he is exploring another of the dangers of science, namely, the crushing of human values in its cause. The experiments of the N.I.C.E. are designed ultimately to 'improve' humanity to the point where it will be human no more, and to exterminate all the unfit and unintelligent: Lewis portrays this as furthering the cause of the Macrobes.

Opposed to the N.I.C.E. is a Company, led by a Director, who is in fact Ransom, and made up of a variety of humans and of animals, including even a bear, Mr Bultitude. The Company lives outside Edgestow, in a large house in the hilltop village of St. Anne's. The N.I.C.E. never finds the location of the Company nor its membership. Merlin goes to Ransom, led there by a heavenly prompting. The planetary intelligences, or Oyéresu, descend on St. Anne's and their influence enters into Merlin, who is then sent to Belbury with others of the Company to destroy the N.I.C.E. All at Belbury are killed, and the black powers return beneath the earth. After that Merlin, and a little later Ransom, are taken into Deep Heaven.

But the forces of evil have not finally been destroyed: rather, a balance has been restored. There are, Ransom says, two Englands, as there are two aspects of any land: the one is Logres, the Britain that belongs to old and traditional values, and is in Maleldil's hand; and the other is plain 'Britain', the secular humanist state of scientific progress, always in danger of slipping into contact with the forces of darkness. (This Britain is presumably to be identified with that celebrated by the Labour Prime Minister Harold Wilson in his speech to the party conference in 1963, when he looked forward to the Britain being 'forged in the white heat of [scientific and technological] revolution'.)

Logres is very 'small': in this book it is confined to the Company in St. Anne's; and it certainly would have been overwhelmed had it not been for divine intervention. Nevertheless there is a sense in which the small can defeat the large merely by being small: for one thing, its whereabouts and members are unknown;[1] and Lewis never believed in the final power of mere size (see also 292). There are of course analogies too with wartime Britain surrounded by the forces of Nazi darkness: and the Nazis too put into practice many of the sorts of ideas that are portrayed in the N.I.C.E. Ransom is the Pendragon, protector of Logres: he has been made the successor in the whole line since Arthur, and he goes to join Arthur in the island of Aphallin (compare 'Avalon') in Perelandra at the end.

This is the larger area of the narrative, concerning the battle of two kinds of society: and in fact it only becomes prominent as the book proceeds. What we are first faced with are the doings of a married couple who are becoming separated. Apart, each of them drifts towards different people to whom they feel akin. Throughout, wider contexts of opposition are opened up, until we are dealing with planetary powers, and beyond them God and Satan. In a sense this book deserves the title *The Great Divorce* as much as the book that has it (and was written and published at almost the same time).

The Studdocks' marriage has got to the point where Mark scarcely attends to Jane, and she is embittered. Mark becomes mixed up with the N.I.C.E. because he has very little moral sense and is concerned only with personal advancement. But as he dabbles further with the N.I.C.E., he finds himself increasingly forced to compromise with even his limited standards. Always before him is the threat of exclusion from their society, or else, as he begins to find that society less than pleasant, the threat of punishment should he attempt to leave it. He sponsors evictions in and around Edgestow; he writes false newspaper articles defending the actions of the N.I.C.E.; he almost brings his wife to the N.I.C.E. as his masters wish. But in the end, as the central figures in the N.I.C.E. begin to initiate Mark into the innermost 'mysteries' of their supposedly scientific fraternity, and he is asked, among other obscenities, to trample on a crucifix, he suffers a revulsion of his soul, and begins a slow journey towards Christ – or rather, towards Christ in his marriage, a marriage which has never yet been truly Christian. For his escape from the wreck of Belbury takes him to St. Anne's and to Jane awaiting him, under the presiding influence of Venus, agent of Maleldil.

As for Jane, she has spent much of the narrative resisting her desire to go to the Company, and then when she goes there, in refusing the truth of Maleldil. She has a peculiar ability to dream true dreams, and to see into what is at the heart of the N.I.C.E. without knowing anything about that organisation herself. She is given a vision of a man whose head the N.I.C.E. will use in an experiment: he is a French murderer, Alcasan, who is to be guillotined. Then she has a vision of the head itself, fixed on a bracket in a sterile room, with a mass of tubes running from the neck through the wall. At another time she has a picture of Merlin and his awakening, though she does not know who he is. The N.I.C.E. come to know of her powers, and try to get hold of her through Mark.

But eventually, through all her primnesses, evasions and insistences on her self, Jane lets herself gradually become more a part of the Company. She is, simply, frightened of her dreams, and the Company offer help (though there is more at work in her than this). Her dreams are of direct use to the Company, particularly in determining the ultimate objectives of the N.I.C.E., and in being able to pinpoint where Merlin is in Bragdon Wood and when he will arise. (Actually, nothing the Company do as a result secures Merlin. A group of them go to the wood but they are too late to catch him, and he makes, or is made to go, his own way to St. Anne's.)

With Jane we follow a process of growth towards belief, while with Mark the movement is rather away from disbelief, but such inequalities on the road are to be seen as part of the delight in reciprocity that is Heaven. After the first chapter, they are apart until the end when Mark escapes the N.I.C.E. and returns to her and their house. The story ends with a wider coming together in love – both human and animal – within the Company, and then the Company's dissolution, as Ransom goes to Venus for the last time, to be healed of the wound in his heel.

An extraordinary amount of material and implication has been packed into the novel – and one says 'novel' as it is focussed on English society - but the technique of progressive revelation via the widening awareness of Mark and Jane makes it easier to assimilate. The point of the book is indeed that our lives are always potentially brim-full of significance. The most ordinary events, such as a discussion of the sale of college land or a seemingly harmless after-dinner conversation, may contain the deepest of implications. Like Charles Williams, Lewis has set his novel in the apparently everyday world of modern Britain to show how it is much other than everyday, how permeated by the numinous, as well as being itself.

This novel has always caused difficulties with critics, because of the mixing of reality with fantasy.[2] Lewis's object was of course to show that 'reality' was merely a crust over 'fantasy': but the objection is also to the mixing of science and devilry, and the planetary intervention, a once-for-all and fictional occurrence rather than a continuous and 'believed' situation. But it can be argued that Lewis intended the intervention of the Oyéresu to be a measure of the threat that is posed to humanity by the pursuit of technical advance in a moral vacuum. (Lewis did not object to science or interplanetary travel *per se*, or he would not have had Ransom explore the delights of Malacandra or Perelandra: what he saw as evil was science used as a means of increasing man's dominance, or sense of it, in the universe.[3]) Thus seen, the action of the great *eldils* is a means, in its way, of further characterising the nature of the evil that we are up against.

A more telling difficulty is caused by the clash between assumed realism and apparent extremism of stance. When one finds a university teacher, even after a tiresome committee meeting, being prepared to swallow without demur statements of N.I.C.E. policy on which even the present-day British National Front would be evasive, we begin to wonder just how we can take him. Mark Studdock is listening, it must be admitted, to his admired Lord Feverstone and enjoying a sense of 'being in the know' with him, but the statement of the sort of thing the N.I.C.E. have in mind is brutally stark:

> 'Quite simply and obvious things, at first – sterilization of the unfit, liquidation of backward races (we don't want any dead weights), selective breeding. Then real education, including pre-natal education. By real education I mean one that has no "take-it-or-leave-it" nonsense. A real education makes the patient what it wants infallibly: whatever he or his parents try to do about it. Of course, it'll have to be mainly psychological at first. But we'll get on to biochemical conditioning in the end and direct manipulation of the brain...' (42)

These totalitarian sentiments, with which Mark excitedly concurs, would not find such an eager response in our more careful age. We are reduced to seeing Mark as singularly naïve for a university teacher – even of sociology, which Lewis doubtless detested as a new pseudo-science. But we have to remember Lewis was writing at a time when such attitudes to treating people en masse were common currency, even among those cultures opposing Hitler; and it was not unknown for 'perfectly intelligent people' to assent to them.[4] When Mark cooperates in a plan to destroy the rural beauty of the village of Cure Hardy and construct a 'model village' instead (85), he does not have the post-war decades of rural despoliation with which we are now familiar to condition his choices. Now it would be simple anathema, while then the idea of improving the collections of insanitary hovels that often made up the English village might not have seemed so bad an idea. As twenty-first century readers we have therefore a problem in understanding some of the motivations and the behaviour in this novel. Lewis argued that we cannot see the literature of the past in the same terms as ours, and that to read, say, Chaucer, it is necessary to become familiar with the medieval culture and society in which he wrote. Doubtless he would wryly accept that the same might eventually be necessary to appreciate some of his own books.

But irrespective of when Lewis wrote the book, or of whether we have in our wisdom more complex moral scruples and reticences than he lets into it, the issue is also the particular conditions he has set up in the book that determine this sort of behaviour. Existence has come to a point in this sudden focus of evil: evil has as it were lurched out of the solution of ambiguities and mixed responses with which it is usually merged. As such, it makes for a polarising medium in the novel. Dr Dimble of the Company sees the process as one of a continuous sharpening: "'there's going to be a time... when there is even less room for indecision and choices are even more momentous. Good is always getting better and bad is always getting worse: the possibilities of even apparent neutrality are always diminishing'"; "'Everything is getting more itself and more different from everything else all the time'" (283, 284). The extreme behaviour of the characters, which we might not accept as 'true to life', is true to the kind of life reflected by this novel.

And there is one more point. We are to learn later in the novel that the true dealings of the N.I.C.E. are with the 'Macrobes', and the final ones of the Company are with Maleldil and the Oyéresu. Jane's visions are throughout 'supernaturally' given. What we have is a context in which *eldils* are already at work on the mind of man. In Wither, Deputy Director of the N.I.C.E. (which in a way poses the question of who, more than the figurehead Director Jules, is really in charge), we have a person 'withered' by his contact with the Macrobes into a front of eloquent evasions, behind which is a ghost. We can feel, with Straik, that he is perhaps so extreme as almost no longer to be in control of himself. Most particularly, we can feel, in that early College committee meeting in which all goes so disastrously wrong for the good characters and for Bracton, that the inability of the good to resist is not just a result of Feverstone's manipulative skills, but of a curious paralysis on their part. In short, the N.I.C.E., and through it the Macrobes, radiate evil: and, until the Oyerésu arrive, whatever in Edgestow does good, does it with difficulty.

Seen in this light, the complete absence of human feeling or scruple in some of Mark's responses becomes the sign of the dark powers already working unseen on his will and sensibility. So too, the extremity of the evil of Frost, or of Wither or Filostrato or Straik, is not an expression of them alone, but the result of their near-complete absorption by the black forces. To live in Edgestow, as the N.I.C.E. come nearer and then take it over, is then like living near the unseen but sapping influence of an electric pylon. That may in one way be why the Company has its place outside Edgestow. But in the same way as the Macrobes are working on Mark to erode his moral nature, and drive him towards the N.I.C.E., so other powers are acting on Jane through her dreams to drive her increasingly towards the Company.

In the light of this secret working it becomes possible to explain the otherwise questionable assent of the government of the doings of the N.I.C.E. at Edgestow, not to mention the gullibility of the Edgestow police and press, and the curious apathy of the people generally. And perhaps finally it becomes easier to understand why all of Edgestow, apart from those of its people given secret monition to flee, must perish in the earthquake, the seemingly innocuous with the evidently guilty. It is true that we are not made directly aware of this involvement of Macrobes and *eldils* till later in the novel, and before then we will have felt our incredulities and outraged reasonabilities: but it seems on the evidence to have been Lewis's aim to shake us out of our easy self-protective shock. Of course, people don't behave like that! But under certain circumstances, circumstances made all the more real and terrible when they are suddenly perceived, perhaps they do. It is a measure of the success of the structure of this novel that it becomes something of a journey towards Reality for the reader as well as for the characters.

The book is also an analysis of what Lewis saw in certain social tendencies of his own day, and to that extent it is directed much more at contemporary society than either of *Out of the Silent Planet* or *Perelandra*. Those books were about the alien, which had little evident connection to us: their aim was to draw us out of our human view of things to an 'other' one. Because *That Hideous Strength* is concerned with human beings on earth, and with issues that Lewis felt were real and immediate, it has a more moral and hortatory tone. Though in the story evil is overcome, in reality Lewis is pointing out what he feels is the spiritual knife-edge on which we all live.

The narrative itself is not so much causal or linear as things (literally) 'coming to a head'. As far as any pattern of development is concerned, it relates only to the growth of the souls of Mark and Jane and the decline of the souls of others. There is not much of a sequence of action. Jane's dreams give disconnected, portholed views on what is going on at Belbury. Merlin suddenly appears; as he does the Oyéresu descend: and that is the finish of the N.I.C.E. The suspense in the narrative is to find out what the N.I.C.E. and the Company are and intend, rather than what they do. Actually, neither *does* anything. The N.I.C.E. get hold of a tramp in the wood and think he is Merlin; during the narrative they do no more than consolidate their hold on Edgestow, and none of their larger plans is yet carried forward. In fact, when it comes down to it, they have no plans at all. Merlin comes to the Company of his own accord, not through any human agency; and he is transformed by powers from beyond Earth. Not that humans are irrelevant: far from it, they are essential channels for the operation of these 'supernatural' beings. But action when it comes is abrupt and unpremeditated.

Indeed the novel is rather like a seventeenth-century courtly masque, in which ideas are pictured in a progressive way until in a sudden intervention all is resolved. For a further difference of *That Hideous Strength* from the earlier books of the trilogy is that here we deal with absolutes directly. In *Out of the Silent Planet* and *Perelandra* we had in Ransom and Weston carriers or agents of Maleldil or of the Bent Eldil; but here Ransom, even while he is far more in control than in the earlier books, 'does' nothing and it is the Oyéresu who intervene directly to transform Merlin.

Lewis has given his characters and their behaviour a great deal of intellectual and moral analysis to explain the roots of their behaviour. There are those who may baulk at this constant 'intellectualising' but, not to imply any comparisons of merit, it is really no more than George Eliot does with her characters in *Middlemarch*, or D.H. Lawrence with his in *Women in Love*. What Lewis is trying to do is to show what lies beneath the deceptive surface – indeed the motif of concealment and of penetration beneath surfaces is central to this novel – and thus to make us learn something about ourselves. And, as with Charles Williams, whose novels are also shot through with thought, the thoughts are no dead things, but parts of an active process of progressive realisation of truth going on throughout the story.

The central line of development in the novel is that of Mark, as he has 'further to go' than his wife. At first he is shown as almost devoid of any moral sense.[5] He has put aside his pleasant childhood and his friendship with his sister Myrtle for a false 'adulthood' to which she can look up with foolish admiration. We are told that he has abandoned all that is natural and spiritually healthy - his roots, the countryside, old values, loyalty to his college, his wife. Later he is shown losing touch with the truth, when he writes lying articles on behalf of the N.I.C.E. for the press, turning evil into apparent good, acceding to riot, laying the ground for the takeover of Edgestow by the brutish Institutional police. Morally 'neutral' at first because as yet untested, he is revealed to have not the least shred of morality to oppose to the blandishments of the N.I.C.E., apart from an occasional personal dislike of some of its adherents. And so begins his journey into the dark.

The stages of his decline are well portrayed. At first he is one of the college 'progressives', actively supporting the sale of college land to the N.I.C.E.; then he is delighting in the superior company of Lord Feverstone, realising how foolish and laughable even those colleagues he supported or liked are, and being invited into the N.I.C.E. Lewis finely captures – how poignantly he himself hated[6] – the insidious intimacies of the 'inner ring', the group of people 'in the know' that can draw a man to give up even his soul to join them. Mark is delighted at being 'accepted' by the College Bursar Curry, by Lord Feverstone, by the head of the Institutional police, 'Fairy' Hardcastle, and eventually by the inner members of the N.I.C.E. itself. Lewis shows how the desire for acceptance by an inner ring expresses a need for security that emerges from refusal to accept the self: Mark wants someone else to approve of him as he himself cannot. In a sense therefore the quest for a place in the inner ring is at once a journey away from moral values and also, just possibly, a journey towards them: for Mark is also looking for some kind of absolute beneath his shifting life.

However the absolute he is most likely to find during much of his story is one of the Macrobes, and it seems for long that it is that or some other utter corruption which he will reach, as he accedes gradually to first one and then another demand of the N.I.C.E. Eventually he is far enough 'in' to be taken to visit the ghastly Head; and then Frost, one of those at the centre of the N.I.C.E., begins to initiate him through some of the further, and more obscene, mysteries.

But by now Mark has begun to have scruples and to make protests. He has annoyed Wither by demanding a fixed contract and a clearly-defined job at the N.I.C.E.; he has had early doubts about the N.I.C.E. and its purposes, but only because they do not seem to include him; he has intermittently resisted Wither's request that he bring Jane to Belbury; he is sick at the sight of the Head; and when he hears that Jane has been hurt, he manages to escape Belbury for their home. But she is not there, and when one of her friends offers Mark the chance to join the Company at St. Anne's of which she is now a part, he puts off a decision. When he leaves this friend's house he finds himself arrested for the supposed murder of a former academic colleague, and placed in prison to await trial for his life. His indecision has thrown him back into the clutches of the N.I.C.E., who have arranged this scheme to recapture him.

Now that his death seems closer than he has ever known it, Mark is shown gradually coming to himself. He sees that the N.I.C.E. has been one tissue of deceit from the first. They have gradually charmed him into complicity with what he now sees is evil. And he realises how easy a prey he has been for them. He sees that all his life, in the name of being 'adult' or 'in the know', for the sake of cheap flattery and false security, he has given away all that he truly loved and enjoyed: his open friendship with Myrtle; his school friendship with a man called Pearson (Pierce-one) for a wretched society called 'Grip'; his sense of all that was good and true in Jane; everything that might have been good in himself. Faced by death, Mark finds all this thrown into relief, until he is amazed that he did not see it before.

At first this perception is not a moral one: it is rather more a sense of his life as an enormous waste of time (246). But then, thinking less of the folly that he has done and more of the joys that he has not had, Mark begins his first halting step on his long journey upward. He is glad that his death will release Jane from him: he realises that he had planned to draw her into the Belbury orbit and turn her into a great hostess, as a sort of magnificent front for himself. And as he mentally releases her, he sees and appreciates from afar as never before the spiritual beauty in her: 'She seemed to him, as he now thought of her, to have in herself deep wells and knee-deep meadows of happiness, rivers of freshness, enchanted gardens of leisure, which he could not enter but could have spoiled' (247). At this point there comes 'the sound of a key turning in the lock of the cell-door' (248).

But the person who enters is not however some good soul, but the horror of evil that is Frost. Mark's good thoughts are as yet temporary, and he is doomed to learn more about good through deeper knowledge of, and temptation by, evil. Frost tells him that his execution for murder is not as certain as he thinks: and that he comes with an offer to make Mark part of the Inner Circle of the N.I.C.E. The whole business of Mark's arrest and the threat of death have been arranged by the N.I.C.E. to make him more agreeable to their wishes when they 'save' him. Frost now tells Mark about the deepest secrets of the N.I.C.E., and about the Macrobes. Mark is fascinated, full of 'ravenous curiosity' (256); he has as yet no real sense of evil. Frost tells him how the wars of the twentieth-century, of which there will be many more, are designed in concert with the Macrobes to destroy all people save the intelligent. Mark is not interested in these matters, as he realises that the broad aims of the N.I.C.E. have never really concerned him closely. Despite his distrust of all the people of the N.I.C.E. he is drawn to it by a deep fascination:

> For here, here surely at last (so his desire whispered to him) was the true inner circle of all, the circle whose centre was outside the human race – the ultimate secret, the supreme power, the last initiation. The fact that it was almost completely horrible did not in the least diminish its attraction. Nothing that lacked the tang of horror would have been quite strong enough to satisfy the delirious excitement which now set his temples hammering. (259-60)

It reads something like *Nineteen Eighty-Four* and loving Big Brother, though that stops short at politics.[7] This is the true direction, Mark realises, in which his life has been going. He joined the N.I.C.E., finally, because the search for an inner ring was ultimately a search for Hell. Yet, seeing this more plainly, he is still the more tempted by it.

At this point Frost has to leave temporarily, and several scenes with other characters take place before we return to Mark. When we do so it is to see him just after Frost has left, resolving now to oppose the N.I.C.E. This seems quite inconsistent with his readiness a moment before to enter to the centre of their circle. He says that he feels a strange sense of liberation: now that he is no longer afraid for his life, now that he no longer feels drawn to toady his way into an inner circle (and that is a change), he is ready for 'a straight fight'.

The hidden explanation for this change of heart is that Frost, and what came with him, is no longer active in Mark's mind. For we are soon to understand that Mark is being influenced by the Macrobes, or devils filling his mind with desire for the evil that most draws him. Temporarily they have withdrawn, and he can revert to his shaky resistance to the N.I.C.E.: but they will be back.

Meanwhile Mark excitedly fills this interlude with avowals. He tells himself that he may lose the fight against the N.I.C.E., but 'at least it was now his side against theirs. And he could talk of "his side" now. Already he was with Jane and all she symbolised. Indeed, it was he who was in the front line: Jane was almost a non-combatant...' (268). This is a typical example of Lewis's skill in moral analysis. Mark is in fact enjoying once more the idea of being an insider: he needs to talk about 'sides' because he needs to feel a member of a wider club (in doing right he is one, far more than he knows). He is taking pleasure in having an emotion and even indulges the feeling that he is more of the inner ring on the 'right' side than Jane: he 'divorces' her again even as he thinks to go towards her.

Mark pursues his vision of himself as a hero, but as he does so, he begins to fall back into precisely the pit from which he prides himself on escaping: 'it wasn't everyone, after all, who could have resisted an invitation like Frost's. An invitation that beckoned you right across the frontiers of human life… into something that people had been trying to find since the beginning of the world… a touch on that infinitely secret cord which was the real nerve of all history. How it would have attracted him once!' (268). But it is attracting him now; and now he finds himself subjected to the most awful pull of black hunger from a force outside him that he has yet experienced. He is utterly helpless before it, without a moral rag to put in its way (268-9). He knows now that the Macrobes are with him in his cell.

What saves him is a plain fact, the return of the realisation 'that he would probably be killed'. This brings him back to earth, to his bare cell and its glaring light. The light is almost a symbol of his returning reason: 'He could not remember that it had been visible for the last few minutes' (269). He thinks starkly, 'Of course they meant to kill him in the end unless he could rescue himself by his own wits.' But this is not enough. He thinks that, having made his good resolutions, it was then for the universe to help him, not turn against him; he moves towards cynicism and receives another attack.

This time, however, instead of assenting to it, he loathes and is terrified by it. For the first time he calls for help:

> 'He wanted Jane; he wanted Mrs Dimble, he wanted Denniston [a member of the Company]. He wanted somebody or something.

"Oh don't, don't let me go back into it," he said; and then louder, "don't, don't." All that could in any sense be called himself went into that cry and the dreadful consciousness of having played his last card began to turn slowly into a sort of peace. There was nothing more to be done.' (270)

He lets his body relax; he sleeps. Grace has come to him through nature. He has been led to a point where all attempts to help himself have proved futile, and only another can do it. In a sense, he has unknowingly received Christ into him; has let the little cell of his self be invaded. He has much more to suffer, and eventually to resist, but he is genuinely, if unwittingly, on the 'right' side now.

Frost now returns and takes Mark out of the cell to begin a conditioning of his spirit which will fit him for entry to the Inner Circle of the N.I.C.E. Throughout this conditioning, which involves Mark in all sorts of trivial, absurd or obscene acts designed to burn out his feelings and his self, he keeps himself as far as he can detached. He begins to realise the good more fully by immersion in the bad. He is put in a strange lop-sided room with odd patterns of black spots on the ceiling and of white spots on a table in it, and with surreal or twisted religious pictures on the walls: and he sees that the aim is to disorientate and dislocate his being.

However – and it is curiously typical of Lewis throughout the book to put it as a series of alternatives – whether because Mark has survived the last night's attack, or because his fear has forever destroyed his desire to belong to an inner ring, or because he has called for help, he now finds that 'the built and painted perversity of this room had the effect of making him aware, as he had never been aware before, of this room's opposite.' This crooked room does not make him crooked too: rather it makes him long all the more for the straight. As his initiation in evil proceeds, so in parallel is Mark being initiated further into the objectivity of good: good is here literally made out of evil. He finds himself 'choosing a side: the Normal' (299). He has been chosen by good: now he chooses; he understands at the root of his being what morality is. And as day follows day in his cell the idea of 'the Straight and the Normal' grows until it is as strong and solid to him as a mountain (310). He has arrived at what Lewis called the *Tao* – the conviction that certain values are absolute.[8] But he has not yet moved in this beyond nature towards supernature.

The focal stage of Mark's initiation into the ways of Christ occurs when he is ordered to trample on a crucifix in the 'Objective Room'.

Here he has to bring what have so far been his inner refusals of evil out into the open, in an act of choice made in front of Frost, one for which he will undoubtedly have to pay a deadly price. He has not until now admitted any belief in Christ: he has only got to the point of acknowledging the truth of right and wrong behaviour. The quiet way Lewis has managed this process of development is detailed, subtle and convincing. Mark, who has never believed in the 'supernatural' (the Macrobes are described to him in scientific terms and are therefore assimilable), is suddenly faced by it: it seems so simple and pointless to trample on the cross – of course there never was a real Christ, who can it hurt, it is only a symbol – and yet somehow the thing cannot be done. He begins to see that 'his simple antithesis of the Normal and the Diseased had obviously failed to take something into account. Why was the crucifix there?' (335). He feels sentimental emotion over the mere helpless wood of the cross and the figure, lying so passive, on it. He realises that the Cross represents what the Crooked does to the Straight. Without yet acknowledging Christ, he still feels it is better to align oneself with the Straight rather than with the Crooked and its picture of the universe. He tells Frost, in words truer than he yet knows, "'It's all bloody nonsense, and I'm damned if I do any such thing'" (337). He has made his choice, and accepts its consequences. Now he has made his first step as a Christian.

At this point Mark is saved from Frost's rage, and saved more finally too, by the opening of the door to the room, this time to admit the Straight in the form of Merlin and a tramp – though both disguised. It is Merlin who will save Mark from the approaching wreck of Edgestow, thrusting him out on the long walk to St. Anne's and Jane. Mark is ashamed of himself, he does not believe that Jane should have him back again, but still he goes, like a sinner to Christ, and the Company and its charity under Venus receive him.

Compared to Mark, Jane is far less difficult to convert. True, she is, like Damaris Tighe in Charles Williams's *The Place of the Lion*, cut off from the realities behind her literary researches; and she herself has also kept herself aloof and untouchable in relation to others – other people, the lower classes, her own husband. Yet from the start her little 'enclosure' is being invaded by her dreams, which eventually force her towards St. Anne's. She resists – what claim have these people on her? – but eventually agrees to co-operate with St. Anne's so far as keeping them informed of her dreams. She comes to view them as 'nice' rather than 'nasty' people (137). Eventually she is introduced to the Director,

Ransom, and becomes partly infatuated by him (144). But he tells her that she cannot yet come into St. Anne's but must try to remove Mark from the N.I.C.E.

Half in love with him and with herself, she is taken by the N.I.C.E. police under their chief Fairy Hardcastle and tortured by the application of a burning cigar to her skin; the flesh is being punished for its rebellion. After that she is received into St. Anne's. From this point on, as part of an organic community, her individual failings are no longer so much attended to. She is part of the body of Christ, even if it takes her some time fully to accept the fact (229-30, 233-4, 303-6, 314-19).[9] What we have at St. Anne's is a company of many and varied members, but the variety is not really a moral one, rather one of personality and species, a mixture of different human temperaments with different animals in one whole.

Unlike Mark, Jane knows and accepts the supernatural almost from the start, for it comes to her in dreams: she sees into the future; she dreams of people whom she later meets as realities; she penetrates in her mind to the innermost recesses of the N.I.C.E. In a sense she starts from where Mark leaves off: most of her journey is in Christ, or 'under the protection', while Mark's is towards Him. Such distinctions are not of course finally real in Maleldil's hand: perhaps it is truer to say that through both of these characters we see the workings of Christ under different aspects. Mark may have to suffer for his moral inaccuracies in the fog of Edgestow, while Jane can ascend to the clearer air of St. Anne's (137-8): yet finally their separation is not a hierarchic difference, but a divorce of equals before God, who at the end base their new and truer marriage on humility (382). What the contrast in their journeys does is remove Mark's imagined superiority to his wife.

Manifestly though, Lewis has intended the two to be a contrast for much of the novel, the one entering on to a journey into evil, the other on one towards goodness; Mark is eventually to resist the Devil, Jane holds out against Christ. Mark travels inwards towards the esoteric and the inner circle, Jane outwards to the fog-free sky of St. Anne's and openness to Christian and heavenly influences. St. Anne's is up a hill after a long rail ascent from Edgestow: the one high, the other low.[10] The contrast between Mark's journey and that of Jane (though it is still not *her* journey) is caught early on in a description of Mark's being driven to Belbury in Feverstone's big car while Jane travels to St. Anne's in a rattly country train. Feverstone's car rushes along, full of power, 'devouring' the country and even killing a hen. But Jane's train is less a machine than an amiable creature, wandering along no direct course, and stopping at numerous little stations with rustic names (almost like the errant train from Leatherhead to Bookham Lewis describes in *Surprised by Joy*, on which he first read George MacDonald's *Phantastes* [11]). When Jane's train stops at a station it settles back with 'something like a sigh'; and in the pause after the activity on its arrival, 'the autumn sunlight grew warm on the window pane and smells of wood and field from beyond the tiny station floated in and seemed to claim the railway as part of the land' (50). It is an arranged contrast, perhaps: but through it we learn more of the different idioms in which good and evil move.

Just such a contrastive technique is at work throughout the novel. The Institute that is the N.I.C.E., suggesting the reduction of humanity, is set beside the Company of St. Anne's, which rejoices in a free society which is as wide and varied as possible, taking in animals as well as humans. The N.I.C.E. separates itself from nature and even from self. All the lower orders are to be wiped out. Organic life is to be obliterated: there are to be no plants, only artificial ones, no animals, except for experiments; and in the end no bodies, feelings, motives, simply heads. And those heads will not actually be in control of themselves, they will simply be empty receptacles for the instructions of the Macrobes. Wither is already a not-self; Frost halfway to the vacuity of a demon. In the end there will be nothing at all.

Mark asks Frost what the N.I.C.E. really exists for – along the way there has been vague talk of organising humanity to more directed purpose, or even travel to other planets – and is told that ultimately it has no purpose at all; it is in effect like the Un-man in *Perelandra*, mere motiveless malignity: '"The present establishment of contact between the highest biological entities and the Macrobes is justified by the fact that it is occurring, and ought to be increased because an increase is taking place"'; '"When you have attained real objectivity you will recognise, not *some* motives, but *all* motives as merely animal, subjective epiphenomena. You will then have no motives and you will find that you do not need them"' (295, 296). In a sense, in Heaven love needs no motive either: but that is because the 'feeling' is simply there; here there is neither feeling nor cause.

One has the impression, in penetrating to the inner rooms and secrets of the N.I.C.E. with Mark, that one is discovering not more, but less: the Head itself proves unimportant, the biggest mystery of all is a mere perverted room (297-8). This is in contrast to the early account of

Bragdon Wood, inner sanctum of the college (20-2), or of the Director's room into which the Celestials descend (320-7). But everything about the Company is different. The organic, even the flea-bitten, is present in the form of Mr Bultitude the Bear (261,206). People are made not less but more themselves, as imaged in the scene where the women dress in clothes instinct with the characters of the Celestials (360-4).

And people speak to one another, and across class and even 'species' boundaries in the Company: whereas in Belbury they are at best spoken at. In this book Ransom's interest in language and communication becomes even more morally significant than it was in *Out of the Silent Planet*. He can speak to Merlin in the hidden tongue or 'Old Solar', and because of his meetings with the Oyéresu of Malacandra and Perelandra, he can answer three questions that Merlin asks to find out whether he is addressing a true master. One of the chapters in the book is called '"Real Life is Meeting"'.

At Belbury by contrast all meetings are fraudulent or manipulative: people are pleasant to others only to weaken their resistance, and angry when they resist. All emotions are finally means, merely used and discarded as the Un-man used and discarded reason in *Perelandra*. So too with language. The aim is the ultimate absorption of all separate egos, when there will be no need for language at all. This does not go unpunished. Because the evil have thus abused the means of communication, these are taken away from them: in a fantastic scene at a dinner at the N.I.C.E., all the speeches turn to gibberish, and people find they can no longer speak or write in any sensible language. At the same time, the animal natures that they have rejected return in the form of the beasts from St. Anne's to devour them.

Such contrasts can also be seen between leading figures from St Anne's and Belbury. There are the rich fullness of Ransom on the one hand, the ghostly vagueness, both physical and linguistic, of Wither on the other; the love of nature and all organic things in Mother Dimble, the detestation of them in Filostrato; the austere charity of Grace Ironwood compared to the cold misanthropy of the cleric Straik; the healthy scepticism of MacPhee beside the nihilism of Frost. There are far fewer women at Belbury than at St. Anne's, apart from the denatured lesbian thug Fairy Hardcastle – symbolising not only the rejection of sex but of true marriage between people.

Throughout the book Lewis underlines all these contrasts by alternating scenes at Belbury with scenes at St. Anne's. There are also sharp local contrasts and ironies between one section and another. At the end of chapter 11, when Mark at Belbury suddenly realises the full horror that is Professor Frost, chapter 12 begins, '"Well," said Dimble. "There's no one here"' (249). Dimble is speaking of Merlin, for whom he and some of the Company are searching in Bragdon Wood, but the juxtaposition with the end of the previous chapter makes us also consider the remark in relation to the nonentity that is Frost. A little later, a terrifying scene in which Frost tries to break Mark down, is abruptly succeeded by a new section beginning '"What friends those two are!" said Ivy Maggs. She was referring to Pinch the cat and Mr Bultitude the bear' (260).

There is a sense, perhaps, in which these are not simply contrasts. Throughout the novel, the evil do not know who the good are, or where they have their centre. But the good know these things of the evil, and through Jane they know much of what their opponents intend. These factors can be taken as images of superior insight. Equally they symbolise the sensitivity, the receptiveness of the Company to all forms of communication. It may be that in these examples Dimble and Ivy Maggs are responding at an instinctive and unconscious level to promptings set up in them by the contemporary events at Belbury; and that, just as Jane's unconscious mind is open to forces outside its knowledge so, to a lesser extent, are theirs.

Perhaps the central contrast in the book is between what one might call the reductive and the expansive. This is most fully seen in the stories of Mark and Jane. At first Jane keeps 'herself to herself', while Mark continuously gives himself away in a kind of spiritual prostitution. Mark starts inside a society and has to reject it: Jane holds to herself and has to give herself up to other people. The society of the N.I.C.E. is actually an assembly of isolated egos, and its object is the reduction of all things to nothing. Mark's journey goes ever inwards, to further and further rooms: the process is like an inverted funnel, as in Dante's Hell. But with Jane the funnel opens out. The society of St. Anne's, and her knowledge of the Oyéresu and of Maleldil gives her her true self. Mark's experience of the pull of the Macrobes 'disenchants the entire universe'; this is the Hideous, the Annihilating Strength (268-9).

The Macrobes draw all things inward and downward to one undifferentiated lump or even a point – Hell as a black hole. The Oyéresu, by contrast, are many, rather than one devouring centre. They focus themselves on to one spot on Earth from their different regions of the Heavens. They give all of themselves, rather than seek to draw to themselves (each is shown diffusing its influence over the company at St. Anne's); they come down to men, where Hell draws men down to it. Hence the sense of expansion in Jane's journey – contrasting to Mark's – is additionally appropriate: she is journeying to that wider realisation of the self that can only fully be accomplished amongst the airs of Heaven and of Maleldil. The two movements, of deadly shrinkage and widening joy, play against one another throughout.

The dominant motif of the book is exposure. Mark's ever-inward journey in the N.I.C.E. has the effect of exposing its people to him, for his experience ultimately converts him. Progressively during the story, not just the inner nature of the N.I.C.E. but the full horror of the characters running it becomes revealed – the courtly Wither gibbering in vacuous ape-like embrace with the ascetic Frost, ruthless blood-sacrifices to the Head, the nudity of the figures as they meet the Head, the awful aridities of Frost. As we have seen, those at the periphery of the N.I.C.E. seem full of purposeful activity, taking over Edgestow, bulldozing houses and erecting new structures, organising the policing of the district, all with some secret and very important plan in view, not excluding "'the interplanetary problem'" (41-2): but when the truth is revealed, nothing is really planned or 'happening' at all. (The opposite is the case with the Company: they appear to do nothing, but in fact have an increasingly, not diminishingly, clear plan.) The enclosure of Bragdon Wood is broken into. Merlin emerges from his burial place. Merlin is exposed to the terrible truth in Ransom and then to the influence of the Oyéresu: his old self is burnt away. Jane's refusals of the 'other' are broken down, first by her frightening dreams, and then through her gradual surrender to the Company. Most of all, the Earth itself, at least this area on it, hitherto fenced off from Deep Heaven, is invaded by the guardian intelligences of five planets. The imagery becomes almost that of the Last Judgment as the good remaining in Edgestow are secretly admonished to leave while the hidden evils of the place are thrown open and destroyed.

In a sense the whole space trilogy from *Out of the Silent Planet* through *Perelandra* to *That Hideous Strength* has followed the sequence of Christian history from (blighted) creation on Malacandra, with its accent on making and creating identity, through averted fall and Christ-like acts on Perelandra, to a vision of the Last Things, where all existence comes to a final point and exposure on Earth (see also 290). Seen in this light *That Hideous Strength* is a more fitting conclusion than it seemed to be.

Looking back, what is our general impression of this book? One is that it is a remarkably conscious piece of work. One feels the effects are arranged, not happened on; thought out, not instinctual. For instance, the evil characters are all known only by surnames, where the people of St. Anne's have Christian names. The whole of Mark's conversion may be psychologically convincing, but it also feels carefully staged. And this is of a piece with the book's being much closer to direct spiritual instruction than the earlier ones. Throughout, Mark and Jane are being shown what is wrong with them, and directed along the path to the Cross. Both the preceding books were explorations of territory for which this one is drawing a map. The Macrobes who exert a tremendous pulling power on Mark's spirit are inverted images of the pressure of the book on us. Unlike the earlier books, this one has a programme. And because it has a programme there is sometimes a sense of strain: Mark's fascination for inner rings is made fatuous when he sees Feverstone driving his car as 'a big man driving a big car to somewhere where they would find big stuff going on' (32).

Endnotes

1. Further, as Richard Purtill points out in his *Lord of the Elves and Eldils: Fantasy and Philosophy in C. S. Lewis and J. R. R. Tolkein*, 79-81, the good remain concealed because the evil expect them to manifest themselves as another power-hungry group like themselves, and cannot perceive the actual ineffectual-seeming members for what they are; the main instance of this is seen in *That Hideous Strength*, 237-8.
2. See e.g. Urang, *Shadows of Heaven*, pp.26-7; Carnell, *Bright Shadow of Reality*, 103-4; Walsh, *The Literary Legacy of C. S. Lewis*, 120; Margaret P. Hannay, *C. S. Lewis*, 99.
3. See the poems 'Prelude to Space: an Epithalamium' and 'Science-Fiction Cradlesong' in Lewis, *Poems*, 56-8.
4. However, 'The war creates no absolutely new situation: it simply aggravates the permanent human situation so that we can no longer ignore it. Human life has always been lived on the edge of a precipice. Human culture has always had to exist under the shadow of something infinitely more important than itself' (Lewis, 'Learning in War-Time' (1939), repr. in *Transposition and Other Addresses*, 46.
5. Mark's nature is a fictional version of that of the modern 'trousered apes' or 'men without chests' Lewis attacked in his *The Abolition of Man: Reflections on Education with Special Reference to the Teaching of English in the Upper Forms of Schools*. On the debt of *That Hideous Strength* to *The Abolition of Man* see Brian Murphy, *C. S. Lewis*, 58-70.
6. See his 'The Inner Ring', in Lewis, *Transposition and Other Addresses* (1949): 'Of all passions the passion for the Inner Ring is most skilful in a man who is not yet a very bad man do very bad things' (62).
7. See also Carnell, *Bright Shadow of Reality*, 98; Carnell even suggests that Lewis's book might have influenced Orwell's, though he prefers a common origin for both in Huxley's *Brave New World*.
8. See on this Lewis, *The Abolition of Man*.
9. Howard, *The Achievement of C. S. Lewis*, 125-39, gives a very full analysis of Jane and her development.
10. For further contrasts between Anne and Mark, and St Anne's and Belbury, see Patrick D. Callaghan, 'The Two Gardens in C. S. Lewis's *That Hideous Strength*', in Thomas D. Clareson (ed.), *SF: the Other Side of Realism*; Richard L. Purtill, '*That Hideous Strength*: a Double Story, in Schakel (ed.), *The Longing for a Form*, 91-101; and Glover, *C. S. Lewis*, 112-18.
11. See Lewis, *Surprised by Joy: the Shape of My Early Life*, 169.

CHAPTER 6

The Great Divorce (1945)

This book can be seen as the culmination of the space trilogy and indeed of the kind of literature that Lewis had been writing about Hell and devils during the period of the war – *The Screwtape Letters* and *A Preface to 'Paradise Lost'*. Insofar as the book is more generally involved with a process of distinguishing and clarifying (see its preface), it belongs too with the clear-cut moral criteria of *The Problem of Pain* (1940), where Lewis's object is to demystify suffering and establish it as in some way morally deserved or proportionate; or to the brilliantly clear, if at times dogmatic, intellectual landscape of *Miracles* (1947), written at the same time as *The Great Divorce*. As we said when considering the character of *That Hideous Strength*, the war was a time of absolute distinctions: there can have been few occasions in history when the contest was so clearly with a form of absolute evil, an evil a Christian could assign directly to the influence of Hell. As much as anything else, incidentally, the polarising influence of the war may well be part of the reason for the literature of Lewis's 'middle years' being full of sharp moral divisions and clear distinctions. In *The Great Divorce* Lewis finally and most widely locates all the divisions in his previous work in the one great split of Hell from Heaven. *That Hideous Strength* ended with the vortex leading down to Hell: in *The Great Divorce* Lewis starts from the bottom of it.

None of these great concerns would for Lewis be belittled by the fact that one of the sources of his book was a Victorian children's fantasy, Alice Corkran's *Down the Snow Stairs, or, From Good-Night to Good-Morning* (1887), as much as it was V.A.Thisted's dark *Letters from Hell* (1884). In this story some naughty children shut in Punishment Land are granted, like Lewis's Ghosts from Hell, a sort of release every year, whereby, if they follow a certain star no matter where it leads, resisting all temptations and enduring all hardships, they will be home by Christmas. On her journey little Kitty has, like every other child there, her good guardian on one shoulder, and on the other her bad self in the form of a little sprite who keeps tempting her: this particularly recalls the lecherous Ghost we will meet in *The Great Divorce*.

Spiritual instruction is the aim of *The Great Divorce*, at a time when Lewis was much involved in apologetic writing. During the war he had regularly lectured on Christianity at R.A.F. bases, and at the Oxford Socratic Society he was the star speaker for Christianity against all comers. There was never anything dull about C.S. Lewis, nor did he have a mania for converting others, but he certainly wanted to share his insights with those who would listen, and in most of his books the reader has a clear idea of his values, and at least has to confront them intellectually.

But the person Lewis is always trying to convert is actually himself. He writes his stories and essays to find out fresh angles from which to believe. That is why they have life: they are essentially explorations. In writing *The Great Divorce* he was trying out a new form for him, one ultimately derived from the many early medieval visions of heaven and hell. When Lewis rehearses old truths, they sound leaden and bullying. He once said himself that nothing was more boring to him than an established truth: one must move on. He did not mean that one should reject one's beliefs, but that one should keep them alive by continually finding new lights in which to see them. One of his favourite devices is to turn conventional wisdom on its head. Suppose you put some of the damned near Heaven, and gave their saved relatives and friends the chance to change them? So if the moral truths in *The Great Divorce* are plain and inescapable, they are certainly not lacking in life.

Lewis's Hell is a wretched urban one, distinctively English in the characters of its inhabitants, somewhere like the further regions of Cowley Road on a particularly dismal day. Some of its character derives no doubt from James Thomson's long visionary poem *The City of Dreadful Night* (1884), but since Wyndham Lewis's *The Childermass* (1928) there had been a vogue in England for writing stories about hell, of which this can also be seen as one further example. Lewis's hell has little to do with fiends and fiery torture, but is a place where nothing happens and no devil is (by day) to be seen. Indeed the fact that there is a story at all in this book is owing to 'a little-known doctrine' called the *Refrigerium*, under which on rare occasions souls from Hell may visit Heaven and have the chance to repent.[1]

The story is told through a narrator who turns out to be a fictional Lewis who travels with the 'Ghosts' from Hell but somehow escapes being damned for his proximity. However, we do not hear Hell mentioned by name till much later in the story, by which time we have been able to guess where these 'people' come from and what they are. 'Lewis' begins in a rainy street a twilight urban slum at a bus stop where the only 'people' visible in the street have formed a squabbling queue. Eventually a great coloured bus, lit with golden light (almost a child's vision of a bus) comes, and all climb aboard. The bus takes off from the ground and after soaring past huge cliffs, arrives at a great plateau of grass, in a light like that before sunrise. (The bus and its journey are taken from E.M. Forster's 'The Celestial Omnibus' (1908).) Disembarking, the passengers find the grass so solid that it pierces their ghostly feet. Towards them then comes a group of shining beings, who turn out to be old friends and relatives, now angels: their object is to encourage the ghosts to want to stay in that country, which is on the borders of Heaven.

The story follows the reactions of different Ghosts to the new landscape, and then portrays a series of interviews, more or less unwillingly overheard by 'Lewis', between Ghosts and 'solid' beings or Spirits. Most of these interviews prove unsuccessful so far as reclamation of the Ghosts is concerned. Towards the end of them, as Lewis wanders about the heavenly landscape, he encounters a redeemed George MacDonald. (MacDonald's work, particularly his *Phantastes* (1858), helped in Lewis's conversion to Christianity.) This MacDonald tells Lewis of the *Refrigerium*, then comments on a number of conversations with ghosts that they both overhear, and discourses on the true natures of Hell and of free choice. He also explains that Hell, which seemed to Lewis a large enough place, and the great cliffs past which the bus ascended to Heaven, is actually a tiny, scarce-locatable crack among many others in the soil of Heaven. Then the fierce blinding light of the rising sun of that country comes, and Lewis hides his face in the folds of MacDonald's gown. Abruptly these folds then turn into those of an old tablecloth that Lewis has pulled about his head in falling of his chair in his room back in wartime England, where it is 3 a.m. and a siren is wailing. His experience has been a dream.

The whole book is an image of the difference between Hell and Heaven, expressed as an opposition between being and nothingness. Of course the precise forms of these places may be quite different from those in the book, but Lewis wants to find a way of talking about the qualitative difference. Hell – though not Heaven – is said to be a state of mind. To those Ghosts who may repent, Hell will become Purgatory. To those Ghosts who choose to remain what they are, Heaven, which bruises them physically and spiritually, is far more of a hell to them than Hell itself. There are some people, particularly English people, who positively enjoy being left alone and miserable. But whether the Hell they know and choose will remain as suited to them as they presently find it is another matter. Reality is in this sense plastic: and as we are to find again in *Till We Have Faces* the past is subject to alteration.

'Hell' is described as a city; 'Heaven' as the country, with grass, trees, birds, rivers, and hills. Hell at first sight seems more definite, certainly recognisable. 'Lewis' had been wandering about for hours in mean streets, where it rains continually and remains twilight, till he comes to the bus stop. The shops in the street are lit, but not yet warm enough to look cheering; time seems to have halted in this dreary twilight, just as his surroundings have never changed:

> 'However far I went I found only dingy lodging houses, small tobacconists, hoardings from which posters hung in rags, windowless warehouses, goods stations without trains, and bookshops of the sort that sell *The Works of Aristotle*. I never met anyone. But for the little crowd at the bus stop, the whole town seemed to be empty.' (*The Great Divorce*, 13)

Shades of Eliot's *Prufrock* or *The Waste Land*; shades too, perhaps more directly of the landscape of Lewis's close friend Charles Williams's *All Hallows' Eve* (1945); anticipations perhaps of the city of Orwell's *Nineteen Eighty-Four* (1949).[2] But then the picture is to a large extent of a wartime city. No fires, no sooty devils or brimstone pits here: only life as we commonly know it at its most dreary. This Hell is unexciting even to some of its inhabitants. They came expecting to meet some great sinners such as those to be seen in Dante's *Inferno* (to which this book owes some affinity), but instead they encountered only the banalities of the Joneses next door.

And that is to be Lewis's point throughout the book: we are dealing with everyday sinners and often seemingly petty or unremarkable sins, but mean though they are, they are as damnable as the more sensational. Lewis wants to show us how easy it is to slip into the habits of Hell. (But he also wants to show that Heaven is an easy place to enter also – in a sense the *Refrigerium* itself is a testimony to Heaven's openness.) In Heaven are found people who did perfectly ordinary acts of goodness – acts that may not have shaken the world, but certainly shook Heaven.

In portraying Hell in urban and Heaven in pastoral terms, Lewis is utilising a familiar preference of country to city, and to some extent we may feel that the identification of urban life – however debased, as here – with Hell, is unfair. But Lewis is also using the city as an image of 'apparatus': it is a product of 'civilisation', now in decay, by which man with his ordering intellect severs himself from the natural and spontaneous 'stock responses' God gave him.[3] The Spirits from Heaven never give reasons for staying there: it is the Ghosts that argue and erect structures. The Ghosts are clothed, and have 'things' with them – one is dressed in gaiters, another puffs a cheroot, another has a bowler hat. But of the heavenly people we are told, 'some were naked, some robed. But the naked ones did not seem less adorned, and the robes did not disguise in those who wore them the massive grandeur of muscle and the radiant smoothness of flesh' (29).

The opposition is in a way between enclosure and exposure, as it was in *That Hideous Strength*: the Ghosts shut themselves in, but Heaven opens itself to be chosen by them. The Ghosts have habits of self-justification that keep their minds shut against influence. But the exposure of Heaven does not mean that we can 'grasp' it. We have a clear and single image of Hell, but Heaven is both enormously 'there' and yet not apprehensible in one act of mind. We are in a grassy place, though we know nothing of its contours or surroundings. At one point we walk beside a river; we find a waterfall with a tree of golden fruit: but these scenes are all somehow rather separated. Only rarely do we have the sense of any further distance, and that is obscure. Lewis can see far off what could be a mass of cloud or mountains, and occasionally makes out forests, valleys and cities on the mountain-tops, but it is all so indistinct and huge that he cannot be certain of what he is seeing (29). (This recalls Ransom's distant views of Malacandra in *Out of the Silent Planet* when first he arrives; the difference is that Ransom eventually gets close enough to see exactly what these are.)

Indeed it is the extent of the mind's inability to grasp it that measures the enormous bliss of Heaven. When the people of Heaven approach, we are told that some were naked, some robed, but it made no difference; and that they seemed ageless, a mixture of childhood and maturity, and vice-versa (29). Again, no sooner have we learnt that people are approaching than Lewis tells us that they were first visible at a great distance, as a bright light. Yet, if this seems indefinite, we are to feel (almost as with Milton's angels) the ground shake beneath their tread, we are to see the vivid detail, all the more vivid for its smallness and distance, whereby 'A tiny haze and a sweet smell went up where they had crushed the grass and scattered the dew.' Heaven is a resolution of opposites, at once vague to us and yet very solidly there. If we think to grasp it, we cannot, unless we become a part if it: but Hell can be grasped, because it is a far simpler and a smaller place, and a place full of graspers.

In Hell there is twilight, while in this antechamber of Heaven we have the morning light before sunrise: each in its way is a world on the point of turning into something else; but in Hell the something else will be night, in Heaven rather the full morning that breaks on the narrator at the end of the story. In Heaven there is a coming together: the whole of the book is taken up with meetings; and of course the people of that country come from afar to where the bus is to help if they can. In Hell there is everlasting antagonism, refusal and isolation. There is fighting in the bus queue and the bus, hatred of one another, and refusal by most of the Ghosts of the help offered to them. What follows during their visit is a steady shrinkage in on the self and an eventual return to the bus. But the self on which each Ghost recoils is a nothingness: the shrivelling that characterises Hell is imaged in that picture of it as an imperceptible crack beside one blade of the grass of Heaven. Appropriately the last one we see before this picture of Hell is a dwarf Ghost that literally dwindles away to nothing during an interview (99-109). Badness, unlike good, finally has no identity, '"Bad cannot succeed even in being bad as truly as good is good"' (113).

One of the Ghosts tries to tell 'Lewis' that Hell is far bigger than he thought. The town in there was deserted because the people in it always argued with one another and moved away to be on their own. The oldest inhabitants of hell are now at astronomical distances from their starting point, and their houses are still moving, like galaxies flying ever outwards (20). Napoleon is one of these, and he is seen pacing up and down in his self-made Empire house continually blaming Marshals Soult or Ney, the Empress Josephine, the Russians or the English (21). However alone Napoleon may try to be, he has taken the whole company of his enemies and betrayers with him in his head: no distance he goes gets him away from them. And in trying to justify himself, in refusing to admit responsibility, he has no self: we hear nothing of 'I', only of 'it' and of others; he has given his identity to them. He cannot be alone, for he refuses any true self to be alone with. In moving away he has not moved at all. In hating one another, in flying apart, the damned souls are actually fused together, their identities collapsed like the crushed atoms of certain stars into a black hole. '"The whole difficulty of understanding Hell is that the thing to be understood is so nearly Nothing,"' says George MacDonald (68).

We often think of Heaven as more vague and 'ethereal' than Hell, but Lewis reverses that assumption here. He shows that, if Heaven can only partially be visualised, it is because it is too solid to be seen, not because it is too indefinite or 'spiritual'. A Ghost that shakes a tree full of golden apples is crushed and wounded by their weight when they fall; and then it is only able to lift and stagger off with the smallest (45-8). Meanwhile the water of the nearby river proves substantial enough to walk on, though its movement and the foam on its surface cause pain. When 'Lewis' comes to a huge waterfall up the river, he realises that his senses have changed in such a way that he is now receiving impressions which they could not normally take in (45). His senses have been expanded, rather than transcended, to take in Heaven. Here Lewis also upends the standard belief that the senses are the source of sin.

In contrast to Hell, Heaven's distances are both real and vast, and movement is not 'away from' but towards, '"Every one of us lives only to journey further and further into the mountains"'; and there each has a self, because each delights in helping others, '"Every one of us has interrupted that journey and retraced immeasurable distances to come down to-day on the mere chance of saving some Ghost"' (66).

It is commonly supposed that to be evil one just lets go, while to be good you have to make an effort to become better. In *The Great Divorce* Lewis shows that the Ghosts need only to let go to enter Heaven, only to open their shut souls to the glory that is theirs for the taking. Nor does this involve changing what they are, only being what they are. They have only to be the selves that God made them, not the false selves they have built up, and which have turned them into Ghosts. For their desperate clinging to their false selves stops them. As one Spirit says to a Ghost, '"you can step out into ... [infinite happiness] at any moment"' (57). The simplest movement of assent will let all Heaven in. A Ghost dogged by a lecherous beast on his shoulder has only to make the smallest gesture of assent and the Spirit he is talking to destroys the creature. For some of the Ghosts it is actually more of an effort to keep choosing Hell. One Ghost that has shrunk by turning its self largely into a self-pitying histrionic actor refuses at last to be reconciled with the Spirit of his dead wife, and 'Lewis' remarks, 'I do not know that I ever saw anything more terrible than the struggle of that Dwarf Ghost against joy' (106).

Being shaken out of self and its rigid little patterns, into the original selves they were given is what all the Ghosts need. Every portrait shows them clinging to what they have always been. An intellectual Ghost deplores the lack of cultural life in Hell. Another sees the journey to Heaven in the same terms as a holiday, objecting to his companions as vulgar trippers of the sort he takes a vacation to avoid (28). A self-righteous villain thinks he has 'gone straight' all his life. A fat liberal-theological Ghost refuses the realities of Heaven for the feebler and more remote abstractions he has always preferred. One who was an artist in real life is obsessed with his continued fame on Earth. Another, who spent his life trying to prove that there was an afterlife, refuses it when he has it, because it means an end to his hobby. A nagging female ghost cannot cease blaming everyone else for her plight. A rapacious wife wishes to get back her husband so that she can continue to manipulate him to her own ends. A husband cannot cease dramatising his self-pity before his transfigured wife. There are Ghosts that come to tell the spirits about Hell, even wanting to give lectures about it. Others still spend their time telling those they meet what a sheltered life they live in Heaven. Many have come to extend Hell, to tell the blessed to rebel against their servitude, or to transform the rough 'nature' of Heaven into cities with roads and railways, or to reveal that Heaven is a delusion. All of them are locked in their old selves, or rather their nonentities, continuing to exist on the premises by which they have lived and died and been damned.

Lewis's skill in presenting the Ghosts and their conversations lies in keeping us in suspense, even with some of the most wretched of them, over whether they might repent. Partly this comes from the sheer feebleness and nonentity of the self-defence each of them puts up: surely, we feel, they cannot believe that, cannot hold to that? That they do shows how empty Hell is. They shut themselves off even when spiritually they are most exposed: whatever truth they are told they will not hear it.

The first interview between a Spirit or 'solid person' and a ghost occurs when one of the Spirits calls to a big Ghost, Ikey, whom he knew on Earth (30-1). We are given something of the nature of Heaven in that 'solid spirit', his face 'at once so jocund, so established in its youthfulness': here is the movement of opposites, exchanging their natures, that constitutes bliss. The Ghost's first words, '"Well, I'm damned,"' are inaccurate slang in one sense, deadly accurate fact in another: the Ghosts have a habit of continually giving themselves away in Heaven.

The Ghosts, like Devine in *Out of the Silent Planet*, always talk slang, language gone slipshod and out of touch with reality: the Spirit is no prig in avoiding such colloquialism, but speaks plainly because he lives in a medium of precision and exactitude. Later the Ghost says, "'I'm not asking for anybody's bleeding charity'" to which the spirit replies, "'Then do. At once. Ask for the Bleeding Charity'" (32).

This Ghost keeps harping on the fact that the blessed Spirit was a murderer in life (here again the book sets out to shock us a little; no conventional standards operate in Heaven). The Spirit tells it that the murdered man, also in Heaven, has forgiven everything; yet still the Ghost continues outraged at the other enjoying bliss after 'what he did'. What we have is a conversation turning into no conversation: through language Lewis shows the gulf opening up between Heaven and Hell. To the Ghost's "'Aren't you ashamed of yourself?'" the reply is one that transforms the inert words, '"No. Not as you mean. I do not look at myself. I have given up myself. I had to, you know, after the murder. That was what it did for me. And that was how everything began.'"

But the Big Ghost simply repeats its view: '"Personally,' [it] said with an emphasis which contradicted the ordinary meaning of the word, "Personally, I'd have thought you and I ought to be the other way round. That's my personal opinion'" (31). The more the Ghost says 'personally', the more it exposes the fact that it has no person left, only a monotonous list of set responses. "'I gone straight all my life. I don't say I was a religious man and I don't say I had no faults, far from it. But I done my best all my life, see?'" It keeps going on about its rights – "'I'm asking for nothing but my rights'" – but the Spirit says he himself has not got his 'rights', for, if he had, he would not be in Heaven. He tells the Ghost that it, too, will not get its rights, but rather something far better. But the Ghost listens only to the statement, "'You will not get yours [rights] either,'" and says, "'That's just what I say. I haven't got my rights. I always done my best and I never done nothing wrong.'"

It is a sad conversation. But it is a deeply convincing one. Here is the Ghost of a man kept stupid by its evil. Heaven offers it all joy beyond its dessert, '"Everything is here for the asking"'; yet the Ghost cannot make that tiny gesture that would save it. Lewis convinces us that it is not Heaven that shuts out Hell, it is Hell that chooses to shut itself out, chooses to go on being Hell.[4] The nearness of everlasting bliss, the seeming ease with which one might enter it, the blank folly that rejects it, these affect us strongly in the book, and thus Lewis persuades us, much or little, to move ourselves as that damned soul has failed to do.

Something of the obtuseness of evil is caught here in the way the ghost continually exclaims and shouts, while the blessed spirit speaks in a quiet, assured syntax that has assimilated pain and reached a simple understanding. In the end the Ghost closes the interview, "'I'd rather be damned than go along with you'"; "'I'll go home.... That's what I'll do," it repeated. "I'll go home. I didn't come here to be treated like a dog. I'll go home'" (34). And to its 'home', to be treated far worse than any dog, it goes.

The next interview we overhear involves a much more educated and polite Ghost, a former theologian no less – in fact a bishop.[5] By using Ghosts of such widely different origins, Lewis is able to show how capacious is the gape of Hell, and at the same time how people so seemingly separate in personality, ability or class are at one dead level of nonentity in sin. It might seem strange that in this book it is the Ghosts that seem to have all the 'personality' – the angry Ghost, the cynical Ghost, the lustful Ghost, the self-dramatising Ghost – and all are met by the same quite self-effacing tones. But of course the fact that they are personalities is a measure here of how much they cling to their old selves, refusing to be born again. The others, the Spirits, are 'Beyond Personality' (the title of one of Lewis's books, also published in 1945), which is to say that in truth they are much more fully persons, or their true selves, than they ever were. Later we see something of this rebirth in the repentance of the lustful Ghost, who gradually 'solidifies' out of his ghostly self into a golden being until we have 'the actual completing of a man – an immense man, naked, not much smaller than the Angel' (93).

In the clerical Ghost Lewis has also dramatised how the most respectable-seeming of intentions can in fact be the worst. This Ghost was on Earth a liberal theologian, who 'demythologised' his Christianity, by reducing the story of Christ to a fable really intended to convey moral abstractions rather than supernatural belief. It cannot accept from its former friend, now a blessed Spirit, that Heaven is real, and that Christ and Hell and damnation are also facts. If we think this is merely an intellectual mistake, Lewis suggests that even intellectual mistakes are not 'mere': they are sins against the light of intelligence (37). Perhaps he would have made this portrait even stronger had he kept to this, so that simple apostasy, from the best-seeming of motives, would be shown earning us Hell: but he is concerned more to show us Heaven being 'fair' or merciful, and he goes on to portray this cleric's intellectual failure to have emerged from moral corruption. Thus his 'advanced' opinions were put forward without any worldly risk to himself (37), and far from being honest beliefs, were the product of a wish to keep up with the intellectually daring while at Cambridge. The Spirit, who on Earth was with him in this, says to the Ghost, "'We were afraid of crude salvationism, afraid of a breach with the spirit of the age, afraid of ridicule'" (38). He likens the ex-bishop's drift away from true belief to a jealous man reaching the point where he can believe lies about his best friend, or a drunkard the point where he thinks another glass will do him no harm (38-9). In these senses the cleric is most certainly 'not innocent'.

Once again we are shown a Ghost's Hell-addicted nature through its refusal to give up old habits of mind. This is imaged in this Ghost's preference for floppy personal relationships, whereby the fact that 'we know one another' is used to produce 'we can agree with one another.' "'My dear boy, I'm delighted to see you,'" this Ghost begins, and goes on to reminisce about the past; but while it refers to the Spirit as 'Dick', the other replies to it only as 'friend'. The Ghost still uses unanalysed phraseology: "'Ah, Dick, I shall never forget some of our talks. I expect you've changed your views a bit since then. You became rather narrow-minded towards the end of your life: but no doubt you've broadened out again'" (35-6). Lewis is not averse to showing us the comic possibilities in the Ghost's attitudes and habits of speech; but here we also think of the 'strait gate' into Heaven, and perhaps of the needle's eye; and later, when we realise how narrow and constricted is Hell, how wide and boundless Heaven, we will see further irony in this Ghost's comfortable 'breadth of mind'.

But the true sin is again the orientation towards self – self-advancement and self-protection – that stems from an evasion of reality. This Ghost would not in real life accept the literal truths of the Bible, not only because he wanted to be in the intellectual swim, but much more because he was frightened by the demands of spiritual reality. A real, suffering Christ – in particular, a real *demanding* Christ, was to be carefully avoided. As the Spirit says, "'We didn't *want* the other to be true. We were afraid of crude salvationism... afraid (above all) of real spiritual fears and hopes'" (38). The clerical Ghost, told that it has come from Hell, is shocked by the vulgar brutality of the word (one recalls the 'soft Dean' of Pope's *Moral Essay IV,* who 'never mentions Hell to ears polite'); ludicrously it says it believes such matters should be discussed "'simply, and seriously, and reverently'", to which the other answers, "'Discuss Hell *reverently?*'" (36).

This Ghost likes arguing and discussing matters rather than doing anything: '"Well, this is extremely interesting,"' it says to a riposte by the Spirit, '"It's a point of view. Certainly, it's a point of view. In the meantime..."' (39). The reply comes that there is no meantime, that action is called for now. But the Ghost prefers to keep the matter at the level of debate: '"I'm not sure I've got the exact point you are trying to make"'; to which the other, '"I am not trying to make any point.... I am telling you to repent and believe."' And so the struggle on the one side and the smug discursiveness on the other continue.

At length the Spirit tells the Ghost, '"What you now call the free play of inquiry has neither more nor less to do with the ends for which intelligence was given you than masturbation has to do with marriage."' The Ghost finds this obscene, but it is exact, for it has been pleasing itself with ideas rather than reality, it is cut off from truth, it is itself an agent of 'the Great Divorce'. Lewis shows us Hell making itself, severing *itself* from Heaven. Most telling is the Spirit's remark of his time on Earth, '"We didn't *want* the other to be true."' It is precisely 'the other', that which is beyond the self, that the Ghosts refuse. All around them is the supremely other (and yet that to which they most truly belong) – the gigantic solidity and richness of Heaven, full of wild love and beauty and joy beyond all compass – yet they will not see it, they will not accept it, they will not put away for one instant the selves that shroud their eyes.

And so the clerical Ghost ends. Unable to recognise Heaven and Hell for what they are, it speaks of a little discussion group in Hell that it is going to address. It thanks the Spirit for giving it some interesting points to consider. It says its lecture will be about the tragedy of the Crucifixion, which cut Christ off before His talents had reached full development, and about how those talents might have grown if they had been given a chance. Still stuck on self, on 'talents' and on speculation away from fact, it turns away, 'with a bright clerical smile', humming softly to itself, 'City of God, how broad and far': it ends on the 'broadness' of view with which it began, shut in, for all its supposed intellectual adventurousness, on the same premises, shut in on self, and going with all its broad views to a place of eternal constriction. The portrait of this Ghost, so like some people in this world, so readily acceptable within our society, is one of the most devastating and convincing Lewis ever wrote. It suggests how some of the most pleasant people we know may be some of the most surely damned.

After this Ghost has moved off, 'Lewis' sets out on his uncomfortable journey walking up the at once solid and liquid river until he reaches the waterfall. There he finds the Ghost that earlier met the redeemed murderer. Here it is trying to conceal itself while it approaches the fruit-laden tree, though there is no evident person nearby to see it. The absurdity of the Ghost's actions is caught in the way 'Lewis' first sees it, 'A hawthorn bush not twenty yards away seemed to be behaving oddly' (46). Until he looks carefully he cannot see the Ghost, whose efforts at concealment thus seem the more unnecessary. The central contrast of the scene is between this furtive Ghost, clutching its identity to itself in the midst of this huge, open, joyous place. The Ghost takes an hour to struggle to the tree, only to find itself unable to reach the fruit; but then a gust of wind shakes some down. The Ghost eventually tries to pick up some of the fruit but cannot, and is finally reduced to taking only the smallest of the apples and staggering away with it. The account of how it is brought to this is a syntactic imitation of shrinkage: 'One could see how his ambitions were gradually forced down. He gave up the idea of a pocketful: two would have to do. He gave up the idea of two, he would take one, the largest one. He gave up that hope. He was now looking for the smallest one. He was trying to find if there was one small enough to carry' (47). As the Ghost moves off a voice speaks from the waterfall, telling it to put down the apple, for it cannot take it with it to Hell; but it painfully struggles on. The scene captures the futility of Hell, the immense trouble taken to keep hold of nothing. This Ghost could have had every apple, every tree that bears them, all Heaven itself, and yet chose with pain to have nothing.

The next scene extends this reductionist theme further. It presents us with a Ghost for which Heaven is merely a 'stunt' organised by a syndicate of 'con-men'. This Ghost sees the whole of Heaven as a piece of real estate that has been overrated by the brochures: '"You can't eat the fruit and you can't drink the water and it takes you all your time to walk on the grass. A human being couldn't live here. All that idea of staying is only an advertisement stunt"' (49). For the Ghost everything comes down to the same thing: it has been to Peking, Niagara Falls, the Pyramids, Salt Lake City, the Taj Mahal, and found none of them worth looking at; and Heaven is just one more on the list. As for Hell, '"It's a flop too. They lead you to expect red fire and devils and all sorts of interesting people sizzling on grids – Henry VIII and all that – but when you get there it's just like any other town"' (50).[6] And Hell and Heaven are run by the same people, who keep up an illusion that there is a war between the two, when if there really were, the strength of Heaven would have swept Hell away long ago (51). Nothing has any individuality because it is all part of a managed trick. Heaven is '"as good as any other park to look at, and darned uncomfortable"'. There is irony in the way the cynicism of this Ghost, its belief in getting hold of the facts, has brought it to the conviction that reality is an illusion.

This Ghost is the seeming opposite of the clerical Ghost, which put screens between itself and reality: this one looks very hard at reality, so hard it goes through to the other side, and sees no more of true Fact than the other. But it is mistaken to stop short at seeing this Ghost as a cynic: it is as determined to refuse reality as the cleric, it has a megalomaniac desire to make its narrow mind the measure of everything. And narrowness of mind is the dominant impression we have of it. Nothing is to be free and itself. Everything, like its own hellish being, must be reduced to a lowest common denominator. It uses past experience and assumptions to obliterate the present. For it nothing changes and all things are the same empty fraud: ultimately Heaven is no different from Hell. This Ghost prides itself on having seen through things: and what it sees is nothing. In that nothing it proudly rejoices, for no one will be able to take it in: but of course it has been taken in – by Hell; and to Hell it returns.

We proceed now to a female Ghost terrified at the shame of being 'exposed' in Heaven to the gaze of the 'solid' people. This Ghost is in one way opposite to the 'hard-bitten' Ghost in being obsessed with itself to the exclusion of all else, in making the self abnormally prominent rather than evading it. And to the extent that it is ashamed, it is just possible it may be redeemed. After this we meet a perpetually complaining female Ghost who is fast on the road towards turning from a grumbler, someone with a self to grumble with, to a mere grumble (67-9). Then we see another female Ghost the complete reverse of the shame-filled one. This one is wanton to excess, and tries by absurd writhings, intended to be lascivious but actually horrifying, to seduce the blessed Spirits.

Thence to the Ghost of a famous artist, who turns out to be another 'reductionist' who has ceased to care about the light that paint tries to capture, and has become interested in paint for itself. This Ghost speaks of itself as 'One': '"One grows out of that. Of course, you haven't seen my later works. One becomes more and more interested in paint for its own sake"' (74). It is obsessed with its continued reputation as an artist on Earth, yet the paradox is that it has lost touch with a self to have a reputation with: '"One must be content with one's reputation among posterity"' (76).

Now we move to a female Ghost determined to get back control over her former husband. Her evil is quite skilfully revealed in the way she starts by portraying herself as a martyr for her husband while on Earth, and ends with bare, unvarnished power lust and hate, "'I must have someone to – to do things to…. How can I pay him out if you won't let me have him?'" (81). Thence to a mother who lost her son and hates God for having taken him: much of her love is selfish ("'He is mine, do you understand? Mine, mine, mine, for ever and ever'" (86). There is some chance for her, since her love once had goodness in it. But both these Ghosts have used husband or son to fill up a deficiency in themselves: if they had only seen that lack and admitted it, they could have had joy.

Next we meet the Ghost burdened with lustful thoughts, who is the exception in that he is prepared in sheer desperation at his plight to make enough of a tiny effort of will towards Heaven for the Angel with whom he is speaking to save him. His lust is imaged in a little red lizard he carries on his shoulder, which is finally destroyed. He is the only 'success' for Heaven that we are shown. This may be because his sin is seen as a perversion of love rather than an act of selfishness or illusion.

The last Ghost we meet is also a 'duo', here of a tragic actor, the false persona of the man, and the little, shrunken, monkey-like Ghost of the man himself. The scene describes the Ghost's meeting with his former wife, now a Spirit. The Ghost is supposedly leading the actor by a chain, but as the scene proceeds and he resists salvation, he shrinks to the point where it can seem that the actor is leading *him*; until finally, he is a mere tiny insect-like thing scurrying up the chain before disappearing.

What we saw as the vanishing of sin in the Ghost with the lizard is here the vanishing of the sinner. Life has been given away to a falsehood. This Ghost will not be itself, only a cliché; and this again is reflected in the language. The real self has shrivelled up to a little, hard, dry nut of a soul: '"You missed me?" he croaked in a small, bleating voice' (101). The actor transmutes such mean little sentiments to what is supposed to be a magnificent gesture, '"Would to God," he continued, but he was now pronouncing it *Gud* – 'would to Gud I had seen her lying dead at my feet before I heard those words. Lying dead at my feet. Lying dead at my feet" (104). The Ghost is almost overcome by the lady's delight in its presence and her welcome of it to Heaven; yet with all that wide bliss beating on it, it still manages to stay shut in itself, throwing out cries of self-pity. Of that absurd struggle to hold fast to its 'death-line', the tragic-actor-mask, 'Lewis' says, 'I do not know that I ever saw anything more terrible than the struggle of that Dwarf Ghost against joy' (106).

Throughout the book there is some patterning behind the sequence of the Ghosts. We start with former friends, and end with former wives, mothers or husbands. We start by looking at faults relating mainly to the self, and move on to faults that involve others. The clerical Ghost has sinned against Fact, true; and he has probably, through his office, corrupted the souls of others: but our attention is directed to the sins of self, the pride that wished him to stand out from others, the moral self-delusion that let him credit himself with honest originality or bravery where he was following a crowd and risking nothing, the inability truly to hear anything but the self. Again, with the 'hard-bitten' Ghost we look at the way it has deliberately blighted its perceptions; or with the artist-ghost we see how concern with personal reputation has lost it its grip on the outer world.

Later Ghosts depend on others. (There is some overlap: the artist Ghost depends on the world for its reputation.) The wife needs the husband to work on, because of a lack in herself. The mother wants her son back. The Dwarf Ghost needs his former wife so that he can bounce his self-pity off her. Even the solitary figure of the lustful Ghost depends on another, for he has come to this place to ask for help: we see him and the Angel working together to destroy the 'third party', the red lizard.

The changeover from one to the other kind of ghost occurs roughly about the point where 'George MacDonald' enters the narrative. In him the narrator himself gains a kindred spirit, one whose works, ideas and spirits have in part entered his own. The later Ghosts put us with the more exclusively personal and private, in the conventional sense of the word – with secret desires, family relationships, the inadmissible horrors that lurk beneath the supposedly closest of bonds. Certainly the atmosphere here seems much more heated and intense. With these we are concerned more with parental or sexual relationships that are still felt and struggled over, where the earlier Ghosts were more complacent in their selfishness. Here the Ghosts follow in a sequence from power-mania (the wife in quest of her husband), through lust, to love degenerate, to love refused. But at the same time, another love pushes itself before us as the Spirits try to help – the giving love of the redeemed, the love that will take all our hatreds and refusals and petty self-pamperings and return the energy of delight and charity. The Spirits are not less caring at the beginning, but by the end their care is in contexts where its workings are most poignantly evident.

There is some development in the narrator 'Lewis' during the book. We may suppose that C.S. Lewis puts himself with the damned in this story to remove any moral superiority he might otherwise have implied by staying outside. Even if, as we later learn, he is dreaming, then the theatre of the action is also his own mind, and the characters are all dramatised impulses, good and evil, of his own soul. This 'Lewis' is no mere recorder of events, but is also shown changing throughout - indeed much as the Ghosts are asked to do. He starts, though for long he does not know it, from Hell with some of its inhabitants, which makes him to some extent a participant in their natures. True, he finds the others an angry lot, and he dislikes their bad treatment of the bus driver. Some of the Ghosts see him as 'a cut above the rest', and start conversations with him. As the bus approaches Heaven, 'Lewis' has light enough to see, and shrink from, the hideous faces of his companions; but then, in a mirror at one end of the bus, 'I caught sight of my own' (25).

In Heaven he sees to his terror that he is a Ghost like the rest. As the Spirits approach and he realises that there are going to be affecting scenes, he has what seems like the decency to 'sidle' off (a sinister verb in this book); but it may be evasion that moves him, for he is ready enough later to record the most intimate interviews. Later we find him 'Not greatly liking my company' (35), which is a stage better than the other Ghosts, who detest only the company of others. 'Lewis' proves able to appreciate the joyousness of Heaven (30,45), but is also responsive to the cynicism of the hard-bitten ghost, 'the kind of man I have always instinctively felt to be reliable' (49) – even though the experience of this Ghost's vision leaves him depressed and distrustful of Heaven (54). Fearful, and wanting 'to avoid open places' – another bad sign, an image of shutting in on the self - he encounters, appropriately enough, a shame-filled Ghost who is terrified of exposure (55). When this Ghost is driven away from its concealment in the bushes, the narrator flees too.

At this point he is stopped by the voice of George MacDonald. He has been driven into 'open country' – that is, he is in a sense more spiritually accessible (59). He is asked the vital question, '"Where are ye going?"' Now he is further into Heaven, away from the bus that brought him. MacDonald has the superior insight that the narrator lacks: but the fact that the latter can be instructed shows that his soul is more open to Heaven. And whatever he learns advances him a little: one great contrast of the book is between himself as learner and the Ghosts who refuse to be in any way educated out of themselves.

At first 'Lewis' had thought that the Ghosts were treated unfairly (54): but now he gradually begins to understand that they, not Heaven, choose their ends. By the time he meets George MacDonald he is ready to be told that he and his companions have come from Hell. He recognises himself in MacDonald's remarks about those who spend their time proving God's existence rather than getting to know Him (65-6). By the end of the story 'Lewis' has a new awareness of the spiritual nature of Heaven and its inhabitants. Initially, when he saw the solid people steadily approaching, he did not much like it, and huddled closer with the other Ghosts (29). But later, in Sarah Smith of Golders Green, former wife of the Dwarf Ghost, he sees the joy, love and charity that shine through her, and how clothes in that world are not disguises as they are in our world, but rather ways of embodying spiritual beauty (97-8, 100). This narrator can now apprehend spiritual realities through physical form.

'Lewis' has seen deeper into the nature of reality, because, unlike the companions with whom he began, he has opened himself to it. Here, perhaps, we may reflect again that it is he who ostensibly gives us this story: without 'Lewis' there would have been no account even of this image of Heaven, for the damned refuse it existence. The very writing of the book thus testifies to his spiritual growth. He ends, thrown out by the, to him, intolerable sunlight of Heaven, but promoted from the Hell he started from to the Earth in which he awakes – albeit an Earth where his cold study room, with its black and empty grate and the siren howling overhead, is not altogether different in appearance from Hell. But we know it is not Hell, and we are glad to be there.

The book has ended with one further flourish of its subversive technique: what we took to be a reality inside the story is now shown to have been a dream, an invention of the narrator's own mind. While this does not entirely remove the reality of the world in which we have been so long immersed, we are left in a mood of uncertainty. But if we look back, we see that the book started by placing us in uncertainty. For, while the *Refrigerium*, the holiday from Hell, is a possibility, it is not known to theology, and is largely an invention by C.S. Lewis. Further, Lewis admits in the preface that the pictures of Hell and of Heaven are 'only' images. Even within the narrative, the events described both do and do not occur. 'George MacDonald' tells the narrator that from his temporal standpoint events may seem contemporary and sequential, but from the standpoint of eternity they have always been done (114-15). Both positions are equally true and false. In time we do have choice; in eternity choice has in a sense been made from the beginning. 'Lewis' is given a vision by 'MacDonald' of little *idola* of individuals enacting on the little silver board of time the inmost and pre-formed natures of giant forms that sit round the board watching them – these forms being their souls.

In itself the book enacts something of the dialectical character of Heaven. It is both an image, and yet one that partakes in the Real; it plays determinism against free will; it lets us believe that what we have seen 'actually' takes place, and then tells us it was all a dream. But its primary object through all this is to disturb our assumptions, to shake us loose from certainties as from ourselves, and to bring us closer to that Otherness which offers itself throughout to the Ghosts. Lewis wants us to be in uncertainty, because we have seen how the practised certainties of many of the Ghosts make them resistant to change. Hence the constant subversions that run through the story. Hell is both a state of mind and a physical place. Contrary to popular belief, there is nothing dramatic or exciting about it. Heaven is the reverse of ethereal, it is more solid than our senses can grasp. This is seen in images that clash with convention: a leaf is 'heavier than a sack of coal' (27); a fall of flower petals 'would have been like the crashing of boulders' (97). Some of the most trivial-seeming sins in life are the most damnable; conversely, those Ghosts that have become monsters through their hatred of goodness '"are sometimes nearer [conversion] than those that know nothing at all about it and think they have it already"' (72). The one Ghost that exhibits most clearly one of the seven deadly sins, lechery, is the one saved.

Endnotes

1. In a letter of 14 Nov. 1962 Lewis writes, 'About all I know of the "Refrigerium" is derived from Jeremy Taylor's sermon on "Christ's advent to judgement" and the quotations given there from a Roman missal printed at Paris in 1626, and from Prudentius. See Taylor's *Whole Works*, ed. R. Heber, London, 1822, vol. V, p.45' (*Letters of C. S. Lewis*, ed. W. H. Lewis, 306)
2. Green and Hooper, *C. S. Lewis*, suggest a source for this dismal infernal city in V. A. Thisted's *Letters from Hell* (English trans. 1885), which Lewis had on his bookshelves; but Lewis could as readily have been influenced by James Thomson's *The City of Dreadful Night* (1874).
3. Compare the similar rejection of the city in *Dymer* (1926), Canto 1, repr. in Lewis, Walter Hooper (ed.), *Narrative Poems*, 7-11.
4. See also *The Problem of Pain*, 106-7,111,115-6: 'The doors of hell are locked on the *inside*' (115). On Hell and Heaven generally in Lewis's writings, see *The Problem of Pain*, chs. VIII, X; *A Preface to 'Paradise Lost'*, ch. XIII; and *The Screwtape Letters*.
5. Green and Hooper, p.227, suggest the then free-thinking Bishop of Birmingham, E. W. Barnes, as the source: he published a book (*The Rise of Christianity*) at the same time as Lewis's *Miracles*, trying to explain away the miraculous element in Christianity.
6. It is the devils that make a similar complaint about the boring littleness of the modern souls they are reduced to catching in Lewis's 'Screwtape Proposes a Toast', repr. in *Screwtape Proposes a Toast and Other Pieces*, 11-12.

CHAPTER 7

The Chronicles of Narnia (1950-56)

Of all post-war English children's books the 'Narnia' sequence is probably one of the most deservedly famous. *The Lion, the Witch and the Wardrobe* has particularly stuck in the public imagination. In these books it is fair to say that Lewis gave back to children's literature some of the 'high seriousness' that – *pace* Kipling, De La Mare and Masefield – it had been largely without since the mid-Victorian fantasy of Lewis's 'mentor' George MacDonald. Certainly, appearing as they did when the vogue for the work of Enid Blyton was still at a peak among British children, the Narnia books came as a welcome relief for parents, librarians and educationalists who had long looked for contemporary books for children which would not pander to the 'baser literary instincts'.

But this would have meant nothing and the books would have gone the way of many a tract for juveniles in the past, had it not been that they actually delighted children themselves. Lewis's particular skill lay in teaching almost 'without meaning to'. He tells a 'straightforward' story of children entering a fairyland and meeting all sorts of delightful creatures and exciting adventures, and then, before the reader knows what has happened, he or she has traversed the central story of the Gospels. And this is the Gospels not as a story of someone two thousand years in the past, but as one set in the immediate present of school holidays and railway stations, which makes the reader feel not just that the story is being brought up to date but that it is recurrent.

Why, in the middle of his fiction and theology for adults, did Lewis turn to writing children's books? The first reason must be that he had been meeting children during the war, when his home The Kilns had taken in several evacuees. Prior to this, the only significant mention by Lewis of children in his writings had been the comparatively unhappy and fear-ridden childhood of John in *The Pilgrim's Regress*. Yet in the Narnia books Lewis suddenly found an enthusiasm for childhood, akin to the early happiness he had experienced before his mother died. In making a fantasy realm that worked, he was once more making a little world like Animal-Land or Boxen, as he had with his brother Warren all those years ago at Little Lea in Belfast. Late in the 1940s Lewis found again the pleasure of making for making's sake that he had known then.

The second reason for the change in literary direction is probably that Lewis felt his earlier books had been too argumentative and morally explicit. His essays on writing for children emphasise either the need to conceal moral content, or else maintain that he simply happened on the spiritual cores of his stories in writing them, so that they are not imposed and do not jut out. His own views and his love of dispute had sometimes obtruded too much, whether in the continual discussions in *The Pilgrim's Regress*, the great debate among Ransom the Lady and the Un-man in *Perelandra*, the spiritual analyses of Mark Studdock in *That Hideous Strength* or the direct teaching of 'George MacDonald' in *The Great Divorce*. Lewis sensed that he had let his own views trample over the mysterious images from which most of his stories began, and he needed to get the mystery back, for that was at the core of what he was about. Nevertheless Lewis could not simply cut off the intellectual, hortatory and Christian sides of himself. There was no way in which he could write simply as a mystic. He had to get the other sides in without their drawing attention to themselves.

Then, sometime in the late 1940s, Lewis re-discovered the fairy tale. He was at once drawn to it:

> I fell in love with the Form itself: its brevity, its severe restraints on description, its flexible traditionalism, its inflexible hostility to all analysis, digression, reflections and 'gas'. I was ...enamoured of it. Its very limitations became an attraction; as the hardness of the stone pleases the sculptor or the difficulty of the sonnet delights the sonneteer.[1]

In other words, through trial and error, and that meant all his previous stories, Lewis felt he had now found the perfect medium in which 'I must write – or burst'.[2] It would not be altogether easy, for he would continually have to resist the temptation to revert to the old approaches, but nevertheless it was the form that best suited his vision.

And although he would be writing fairy tales for children, he would not be writing for children only, for he believed that the fairy tale is for all generations. He could still put his own vision across, but now less directly, through a story apparently about something else. He had always felt that people froze at the mention of the Bible or of Christ –

> But supposing that by casting all these things into an imaginary world, stripping them of their stained-glass and Sunday school associations, one could make them for the first time appear in their real potency? Could one not thus steal past those watchful dragons? I thought one could.[3]

This may not be quite what happened, for Lewis had a way of remaking his own past to fit with the present – as witness his autobiography *Surprised by Joy: the Shape of My Early Life* (1955). Moreover he had already stolen past such watchful dragons in writing the story of an averted fall in *Perelandra*. All his main essays on his writing appear from 1952 to 1958, and it is noteworthy that while he was still lauding the fairy tale as the only form in which he wanted to write, he was writing a highly intellectualised myth in the form of a novel for adults, *Till We Have Faces* (1956).

Lewis's idea of his literary creations was that he always started with a strange and haunting image; then he built up a world and a story inside which this image would be believable; and finally adjusted the story and the world to fit a Christian vision. The last stage is crucial, because it not only alters the means of expressing the mysterious image, it also to a greater or lesser extent draws attention away from mystery to a named way of seeing the world. The Christian will always be troubled by the imagistic approach, for it always risks the reader experiencing it in ways that are not Christian at all: of all Christian fantasy writers only George MacDonald was brave enough to let it speak for itself. The issue comes down to whether you are prepared to let your work operate on a mystic basis alone, or whether you feel called to step in and name some of the parts, even if indirectly. And that is an issue that Lewis never quite overcame, even in his Narnia books.

Lewis was also probably drawn to writing for children because in the years following the war children's literature was becoming once more a genre for which there was a ready market and demand. The whole atmosphere after the war was future-oriented to such an extent that society in the 1950s was often almost utopian in outlook – particularly in regard to the benefits of scientific advance. Children, and later teenagers, were becoming increasingly valued for themselves in society: the liberal Benjamin Spock was replacing the old brutal behaviourism in child rearing. And children's literature was becoming more widely popular among children, particularly through Enid Blyton, whose many books were being read with the frenzy now given to those of J.K.Rowling. Lewis also felt that fantasy for adults was difficult to place and sell, and while this in no way troubled him in terms of prestige and financial reward, he wanted to share his mystic vision with as many people as possible.

Lewis had always read widely in children's literature, and one can trace the influence of several contemporary writers on his work. Enid Blyton's *Five On a Treasure Island* (1942) and *Five on Kirrin Island Again* (1947) may have suggested the idea of a group of children with their own secret world which is under threat; and Blyton's young Georgiana, who owns Kirrin Island and will not at first take her cousins to it, is a little like Edmund in *The Lion, the Witch and the Wardrobe* with Narnia. In all his previous fiction Lewis had his protagonists travel by themselves, but in his children's books we have an interactive group, all with different characters, which allows him to dramatise ideas rather than present them directly.

Most debts are more incidental. We know for instance that Lewis got the idea of the wardrobe from E.Nesbit's story 'Whereyouwanttogoto' – though he could also have got it from Enid Blyton's *Five Go Adventuring Again* (1943). The account of the oddly-titled books Lucy finds on Mr Tumnus's shelves in *The Lion* is very like those that Judy sees in the Lord Salmon's bookcases in Beverley Nichols's *The Stream That Stood Still* (1948) – *Sharks in Shrimps Clothing*, *Songs by a Sardine* or *My Life Upstairs* by Laura Goldfish. In *The Lion* Lewis may well also be indebted to Nichols for the characters Mr and Mrs Beaver and the seemingly beautiful witch who enchants Jack (the latter also in *The Silver Chair*).

At this stage in his writing Lewis felt rather more assured in the presentation of his beliefs. This shows itself in the way that his aim is less to prove that God and Heaven exist and are just, as in his previous books, and more to show them interacting with mortals, whether in saving them from a White Witch, or in bidding them believe in them when they are not present. In *The Pilgrim's Regress* John follows what in the preface Lewis calls 'an ontological proof' of God, and in the 'space trilogy Ransom learns about the divinely-based reality of the universe. But now it is not so much the existence of Aslan that is proved or found out, but rather the existence of men and women, in the form of the 'Sons of Adam' and the 'Daughters of Eve' long prophesied as the rescuers of

Narnia. Aslan does not wait to be found out, but rushes into the story. After *Miracles* the character of Lewis's apologetics changes, in that he no longer argues towards something, but away from it: the Christian vision is now more of a given for him.

Much of Lewis's fiction had already valued the child-like, without stating it to be such. John in *The Pilgrim's Regress* must shear away all the modernist, worldly and philosophical clutter that obscured his originally pure childhood desire, till he can find the naked truth and return as a true adult to the place of his boyhood, which is nearest to God's house. The innocence of the Lady in *Perelandra* is child-like, for she accepts every new experience that comes to her, and she remains like this even when she is made 'older' and realises that she has free choice. Ransom in both *Out of the Silent Planet* and *Perelandra* learns to undo his adult suspicions and inhibitions and open himself to strange new worlds. Mark and Jane Studdock in *That Hideous Strength* must rediscover a childlike – not a childish – yielding of themselves to better directors than themselves of their confused lives (which is partly why the term 'Director' is used of Ransom in that book). In *The Great Divorce* the Ghosts will not undress, that is, remove the adult illusions about themselves and others that they have built up over their lives, and so open themselves to the glory all about them.

Lewis is very far from believing children incapable of depravity, or that childhood is an innocent condition, as will be seen with Edmund in *The Lion, the Witch and the Wardrobe* and with Eustace in *The Voyage of the 'Dawn Treader'*. He seems rather to have felt that evil in children was less deep-rooted, less hidden beneath long-constructed trappings of adult rationality and evasion, and therefore might be more readily removed. In making children his protagonists, Lewis is using them only as an image of a child-like state that adults too could attain if they would. Lewis vowed that he never 'wrote down' to children, and denied that his awareness of them as a specific age-group seriously conditioned his writing: 'I was... writing "for children" only in the sense that I excluded what I thought they would not like or understand; not in the sense of writing what I intended to below adult attention.'[4] In other words, like his mentor George MacDonald before him, he wrote for the child of any age.

However there are certain problems in using children as images of a child-like quality that can be found in people of all ages. It is, for example, a little hard to take the image of children fighting in battles or becoming kings and queens as they do in *The Lion, the Witch and the Wardrobe* and *Prince Caspian*. As Sons of Adam and Daughters of Eve, and the long-prophesied heroes who will help rescue Narnia from the White Witch and fill the empty thrones at Cair Paravel, they are portrayed at once as children and as 'grown-ups' in relation to Narnia, and it is difficult to reconcile their grand roles with their everyday reality as English children. It is similar when Edmund's yielding to the Turkish Delight offered by the White Witch and his betrayal of his siblings are seen both as the acts of a thoroughly naughty boy and as primal treachery requiring the ultimate sacrifice on Aslan's part.

Of course, for Lewis, mere size is nothing, and 'proportion' alien to the Christian view of reality. For him the smallest act may be of enormous significance. (His use of Reepicheep the mouse as hero in the Narnia books is almost symbolic of this.) But that is not quite the same as viewing the act two ways at once. Frequently in the narrative of *The Lion* we feel the uneasy juxtaposition of children and child-adults: quite what are we doing except in wish-fulfilment with a child who leads an army into battle? By contrast, in the children's books of one of Lewis's favourite writers, Edith Nesbit, the children remain children wherever they are: in *The Story of the Amulet* (1906), for example, the children continue, despite their visits in a time to a great number of past civilisations, to behave precisely as their normal and often comical child-selves, and take on no other role. In asking us to accept his children both as children and as adults, Lewis is sometimes in danger of forfeiting our belief in them as either.

An important issue in considering the 'Narnia' series is the sequence of the seven books. In order of publication yearly from 1950 to 1956 they are *The Lion, The Witch and the Wardrobe, Prince Caspian, The Voyage of the 'Dawn Treader', The Silver Chair, The Horse and His Boy, The Magician's Nephew* and *The Last Battle*. So far as the history of Narnia goes, however, *The Magician's Nephew*, which describes the creation of Narnia and its Talking Beasts, belongs chronologically first. Then comes *The Lion, the Witch and The Wardrobe*, where we are first introduced to the Pevensie children Peter, Lucy, Susan and Edmund, and Aslan the Lion undergoes a voluntary sacrifice to the White Witch for Edmund's sake, after which he rises again. After this is *The Horse and His Boy*, which takes place during the time, briefly summarized at the end of *The Lion*, when Peter and the others reigned as Kings and Queens of Narnia before they returned home.

Then in *Prince Caspian*, the children return to Narnia to restore the rightful king Caspian to the throne of Narnia. In *The Voyage of* the *'Dawn Treader'*, Edmund and Lucy, together with their unpleasant cousin Eustace Scrubb, find themselves in Narnia aboard a ship on which Caspian is voyaging to find some of his father's banished friends and perhaps discover Aslan's country far to the east. In *The Silver Chair* a reformed Eustace and his friend Jill Pole have to carry out a task appointed for them in Narnia by Aslan. Finally in *The Last Battle* a battle in Narnia is the prelude to the final destruction of that world by Aslan and a journey by the central characters, via progressively more 'real' Narnias, towards Aslan's country, or Heaven.

It might seem perhaps more reasonable to consider the books in this chronological order, rather than that of their publication: but the benefits of reading them in their published order outweigh such ordering.[5] In any case, accidental though the sequence in which the books appeared may have been, for Lewis as for his protagonists 'there is no such thing as chance or fortune beyond the moon' (*Perelandra*, 135). But, this apart, to read them simply in the narrative sequence would impose something of a grid on the series, just as it would ruin *Paradise Lost* to read it in chronological order. To open *The Lion* and suddenly come upon the magical world of Narnia and encounter its inhabitants without prior explanation of whys and wherefores quite simply heightens wonder and increases our sense of the individuality of the world.

Mystery and strangeness are of the essence. In *The Lion* the children have to go through the process of variously doubting Narnia's existence; then they encounter its strange inhabitants, find out why it is always winter there, and are told of and meet Aslan, and so on. Often the Narnia books themselves are structured to heighten mystery. Part of the pleasure of *Prince Caspian* comes from the gradual realisation by the children that the island ruin to which they have been transported is the remains of their old castle of Cair Paravel when they ruled in Narnia, and that though they have been absent only a year in their world, a thousand years have passed in Narnia. The whole story of how they came to be called into Narnia is then gradually unfolded for them by a dwarf messenger – so that the narrative sequence is deliberately jumbled, and we stop present events to hear of separate and past ones that led to them.

The jumbling of sequence here and across the entire Narnia series may have a deeper motive still. In eternity all acts are eternally co-present, and the last exchanges its nature with the first: may not this violation of sequence in the Narnia books be an imitation of precisely that? Not that that has always been so in Lewis's work: the three books of the space trilogy move from a beginning to an end. But in Lewis's view of reality, arguing from past to present events is futile, where 'All is new.' Certainly these children's books mark as radical a departure in literary genre from his space-novels as they in turn did from his allegory, and his allegory from his poetry – and as *Till We Have Faces* (1956) will from everything before it. 'We operate, mostly, in sequence, but sequence is not all.'[6]

THE LION, THE WITCH AND THE WARDROBE (1950)

This story describes how, while on holiday in a professor's rambling old country house, four children discover a door into a strange new country called Narnia. First Lucy, then Lucy and Edmund, and finally Peter and Susan too, get there through the back of an old wardrobe they find in an empty spare room. Narnia, they find, is in the power of a tyrannical White Witch who has caused the country to be gripped in a perpetual winter, and has reduced its inhabitants, a variety of Talking Beasts, to servitude and fear. As in fairy tales, there is one way the Witch may be overthrown, and this is by the enthronement of two 'sons of Adam' and two 'daughters of Eve' on the four thrones in the castle of Cair Paravel. The arrival in Narnia of the children, who as humans are sons of Adam and daughters of Eve, promises to bring this about. The children are as magical to the Witch as she is to them; and to the Narnians they are also magical in being of the human race (which is of far greater antiquity than Narnia). Thus Lewis cleverly suggests that all worlds are in their own way full of magic; though it has to be said that in other books he does not make our world seem so, usually portraying it as a place of tedium, whether going to or stuck at school, from which removal to Narnia is a glad release.

The Witch, realising that the four children threaten to bring about the prophecy, tempts one of them, Edmund, into putting his brother and sisters into her hands. The perceptiveness of some Talking Beasts with whom the others are staying forestalls this, and the arrival of the also long-foretold lion Aslan, bringing spring with him, prevents it. But the Witch demands Edmund's life as forfeit to her under the ancient Law, since he has been guilty of treachery. Aslan acknowledges her right in this, but offers to substitute himself for Edmund, and is duly slain by the Witch, who tells him that she will kill Edmund anyway. But after his death Aslan rises again, by a 'Deeper Magic' from before the dawn of time. The powers of the Witch are defeated, and the children enthroned at Cair Paravel. After they have ruled for a number of years, a hunt they make one day in pursuit of a White Stag leads them to the forest where they entered Narnia. They then return through the back of the wardrobe to their own world at exactly the same time as they left it all that seeming time ago.

The very title of the book, *The Lion, the Witch and the Wardrobe*, suggests that it is a kind of amalgam of different things. And this indeed proves to be the case. There is a sense in which at least three separate crystallisations of the imagination have occurred in it, in the forms of Aslan, the White Witch, and the strange means of conveyance into Narnia. The book is a compendium of different figures and motifs. Even the children are dealt with less as a group, as in later books, than in separation from one another. Lucy goes into Narnia on her own first, and is not believed by the others. Then on another day Edmund follows Lucy through the wardrobe and goes his own way and meets the Witch; then all four enter, but soon divide into two sets of adventures, as Edmund leaves the others at the home of the Beavers to tell the Witch about them. The two girls remain near Aslan at his death, and afterwards go with him on his risen body to the palace of the Witch, to release the creatures of Narnia imprisoned in stone there. Later they return with Aslan to the boys, to help them in their desperate battle with the forces of the Witch.

Throughout the book we are moved from a Faun to talking Beavers, from Father Christmas to sacrificial death, from Turkish Delight to Ancient Magic, from snowdrops to resurrection and from fur coats to fir trees. It is as if Lewis delights in the juxtaposition of as many different things as he can, and in refusing us any settled view or position. The book is almost a cornucopia, or, in other terms, rather like a Christmas stocking, full of various and mysterious objects all held together by one container. Indeed the presence of Father Christmas with his diverse gifts, from a magic cordial for Lucy to a sluice-gate for Mr Beaver, may not be the anomaly in the story that some have found it. This is to some extent a story about gifts – the gift of Narnia to the children as an adventure (if later more demanding); the gift of Aslan to Narnia in turning winter to Christmas (always so exciting for children) and then to spring with its flowers; the gift of Aslan's life itself in place of Edmund's; the gift of the four children as the long-promised human rulers of Narnia, topping off the 'unfinished' hierarchy of the Talking Beasts. Indeed it is in the light of its being a box of increasing delights that the book is perhaps best appreciated – even if some of the delights are to be won with difficulty or through grace. It is in a sense a story of Paradise Regained.

One of the recurrent motifs of the story is the relation of fiction to reality. What kind of reality does Narnia have that it has a lamppost in it? Or, for that matter, a Faun whose behaviour when Lucy meets him is distinctly reminiscent of the White Rabbit when Alice first sees him, a Witch who has evidently come straight out of the pages of Hans Andersen, beasts from Beatrix Potter and Kenneth Grahame, and a

Christ-figure from the Bible? For the Narnians, man himself is fictive: the Faun Tumnus has among his books such titles as *Men, Monks and Gamekeepers: a Study in Popular Legend,* and *Is Man a Myth?* Edmund and the others at first think Lucy's Narnia is a fiction. At the end, as they become translated into Kings and Queens and described by use of the 'high style' of romance, the children become fictionalised in relation to us. And in the old prophecies having come true, what was fiction is also turned to fact. In the book Aslan becomes a fictional version of Christ: yet in a world of talking animals, it is not right that the image of the King of Beasts should offer himself in sacrifice for man? (In *The Last Battle* the children see that Aslan has other images than that of a lion.) And all of this raises the question of whether our own world is more or less real or fictional than Narnia, a question answered in *The Last Battle* when both are shown to be of equal (un)reality. By re-enacting a fiction, that is the pattern of the story in the Gospels, Aslan accomplishes a fact.

Throughout the story it is impossible to settle to any one level of reality. There is always something further beyond what appears. The unprepossessing wardrobe in the bare spare room with the dead bluebottle on the window-sill is a doorway to Narnia.[7] The charming Faun is a deceiver. The Talking Beasts are concealed. The Witch deceives Edmund. The beasts at the Witch's castle seem to Edmund alive, but are actually stone – and in one case, vice versa (ch.9). The winter of Narnia is a false one, though felt as real enough. When Edmund has been rescued from the knife of the Witch and we feel him safe, the Witch returns to claim his life by a 'Law' we could never have supposed. Then, when all seems hopeless, Aslan offers himself and the Witch thinks *she* has won. And then, by the deepest Law of all, Aslan rises again and overthrows the Witch and her schemes. What seemed dead flesh to the children becomes a miraculously risen Lion. Then, after the 'children' have become Kings and Queens, they are suddenly returned one day from Narnia to their former selves in their old world. We move through the story, 'farther up and farther in' to deeper and deeper levels of reality. In a sense the wardrobe itself is a symbol of this: as the children go into it they find they do not come to its back; Lucy goes through one row of coats, then another, then, wondering at the size of the wardrobe, finds a crunching under her feet which eventually reveals itself to be snow, while the coats become fir trees. The wardrobe gives a smoothness of transition between one reality and another. Other shifts in the story are more abrupt, forcing us more violently out of previous assumptions and expectations.

The book has a pervasive theme of awakening. This motif is, incidentally, seen in others of the Narnia books, particularly *Prince Caspian*, where Caspian has to waken the absent powers of the first Kings and Queens of Narnia,[8] and bring the Talking Beasts of Narnia from their hiding places, while Aslan rouses the trees, the gods of water and of nature generally. But awakening is particularly marked in *The Lion, the Witch and the Wardrobe*. There the land is woken from winter to spring. The long frozen stasis gives way to motion. Ice and snow turn to water, the hard ground thaws and flowers appear, time moves on in a land that, like the Sleeping Beauty or the world of Dickens's Miss Havisham, has too long stood still. (Lewis here might well have been inspired by the long, hard, snowbound British winter of 1947).

And with the overthrow of the Witch the frozen statues of animals in her castle are returned to life by the breath of Aslan:

> I expect you've seen someone put a lighted match to a bit of newspaper which is propped up in a grate against an unlit fire. And for a second nothing seems to have happened: and then you notice a tiny streak of flame creeping along the edge of the newspaper. It was like that now. For a second after Aslan had breathed upon him the stone lion looked just the same. Then a tiny streak of gold began to run along his white marble back – then it spread – then the colour seemed to lick all over him as the flame licks all over a bit of paper – then, while his hindquarters were still obviously stone, the lion shook his mane and all the heavy, stone folds rippled into living hair. Then he opened a great red mouth, warm and living, and gave a prodigious yawn. And now his hind legs had come to life. He lifted one of them and scratched himself. Then, having caught sight of Aslan, he went bounding after him and frisking round him whimpering with delight and jumping up to lick his face. (*The Lion, the Witch and the Wardrobe*, 152-3)

This passage incidentally, shows some of Lewis's strengths. The analogy with the newspaper at once roots the magic in the everyday and literally makes the scene 'come to life' for us. The sentences, short at first, spread in length as, like a flame, life expands; then they shorten themselves again as the lion collects himself before the last longer one, in which all of him comes to life and he bounds after Aslan, trying to lick him as he breathed on him. A fine touch is 'all the heavy, stone folds rippled into living hair': the heavy, stone folds feel heavy because each word is separated by comma or consonantal disjunction, and each has a similarly sonorous and weighty stress; then the 'rippled into living hair' reads like lyric, with trochaic metre, light, open sounds and a rising rhythm.

The whole passage also stands in counterpoise to the earlier passage when Edmund came to the castle and on seeing the stone lion thought at first he was alive (88). There what seemed alive was dead stone, here what seems 'dead' comes to life. But of course the great awakening in the story is that of Aslan's resurrection itself, through which these later awakenings are possible. He seemed to be dead, reduced on the slab first to a helpless, bound, static thing and then slain, but the next morning he is back, literally larger than life and twice as natural and supernatural (147), to dance and romp with the children.

What of other awakenings? The Talking Beasts are roused from their torpor. Aslan returns to Narnia at the same time as the children enter it to change all things. The evening scenes that characterise the early visits to Narnia, Mr Tumnus, and the Beavers, change to morning, as time begins to move and winter moves on to Christmas (98). There is to be one other night, the dark night of the soul of Aslan's death, but after that no more, and with these changes the moon imagery associated with the Witch (85, 125, 136 – perhaps symbolic here of coldness and sterility) gives way to sunlight with Aslan's resurrection: 'the red turned to gold along the line where the sea and the sky met and very slowly up came the edge of the sun' (146).

The transformations of the book are also from monotony to variety. The Witch is a tyrant. Her evil is her selfishness. What she does with it is never clear. She simply spreads herself over all Narnia in the form of a dead white frost, allowing nothing else independent life: the unchanging monotony of winter is her symbol. When she and Aslan talk together (the suggestion of familiar discourse driving them more surely apart), 'It was the oddest thing to see those two faces – the golden face and the dead-white face – so close together' (128). When her power goes, colour and variety return to Narnia, imaged in the 'zoo' of different creatures brought to life by Aslan in the castle courtyard:

> Instead of all the deadly white the courtyard was now a blaze of colours; glossy chestnut sides of centaurs, indigo horns of unicorns, dazzling plumage of birds, reddy-brown of foxes, dogs and satyrs, yellow stockings and crimson hoods of dwarfs; and the birch-girls in silver, and the beech-girls in fresh, transparent green, and the larch-girls in green so bright that it was almost yellow. And instead of the deadly silence the whole place rang with the sound of happy roarings, brayings, yelpings, barkings,

squealings, cooings, neighings, stampings, shouts, hurrahs, songs and laughter. (153)

Corresponding to all this, the reigns of the children when they become Kings and Queens are full of variety and activity in contrast to the profitless stasis of the Witch's reign. They root out the remaining evils, drive back marauding giants and make alliances with surrounding nations that enable Narnia to enter from isolation into a community of countries. They make just laws, keep the peace, preserve the forests and above all promote the freedom of the individual which the Witch has so long suppressed (166).

The Witch, as the daughter of Lilith, is a vampire, a drawer of life from things to herself, and one who lives only with the unnatural and the deformed – with Hags, Werewolves, Minotaurs and the like. She drains the vitality from Narnia, literally 'bleeds it white', and she would with her dagger do the same to Aslan. But where she can only take, Aslan delights to give. The contrast between the two is caught in different passages describing them surrounded by their followers. This is Aslan:

> Aslan stood in the centre of a crowd of creatures who had grouped themselves round him in the shape of a half-moon. There were Tree-Women there and Well-Women (Dryads and Naiads as they used to be called in our world) who had stringed instruments; it was they who had made the music. There were four great centaurs. The horse part of them was like huge English farm horses, and the man part was like stern but beautiful giants. There was also a unicorn, and a bull with the head of a man, and a pelican, and an eagle, and a great Dog. And next to Aslan stood two leopards of whom one carried his crown and the other his standard. (115)

And this is the Witch:

> A great crowd of people were standing all round the Stone Table and though the moon was shining many of them carried torches which burned with evil-looking red flames and black smoke. But such people! Ogres with monstrous teeth, and wolves, and bull-headed men; spirits of evil trees and poisonous plants; and other creatures whom I won't describe because if I did the grown-ups would probably not let you read this book – Cruels and Hags and Incubuses, Wraiths, Horrors, Efreets, Sprites, Orknies, Wooses, and Ettins. In fact here were all those who were on the Witch's side and whom the Wolf had summoned at her command. And right in the middle, standing by the Table, was the Witch herself. (136-8)

In the first passage we start with Aslan; in the second we end with the Witch. Life radiates outwards from him, but it is all drained and funnelled towards her. It is our first meeting with Aslan, and in a sense he needs no introduction: he is what the children have long known in their deepest hearts (65), he is *Yahweh*, 'I am'; his name is an act and he is all the creatures that emanate from him in the passage. His followers have arranged themselves about Aslan in order, 'in the shape of a half-moon' whereas the Witch's followers are simply a crowd about the Stone Table; and there is no living centre to their group, only stone. The beasts in the first passage have gathered voluntarily about Aslan, but those around the Witch have been summoned at her command. She knows nothing of freedom or individuality.

The creatures in the first passage are also portrayed in a hierarchic order. We move through a chain of being from the Dryads and Naiads, spirits of the trees, to the centaurs, half man, half animal, then to a fabulous animal (the unicorn) and to a man-bull, and then to the (still faintly symbolic) Dog; there is some reminiscence of the beast of *Revelation* 4, 6-7, here. Then the passage ends as a circle, symbol of perfection, taking us back to Aslan, who as it were surrounds and embraces the whole. The leopards who heraldically bear his standard remind us that here to be a beast is to be also far more than a beast, and that hierarchy can also involve equality: the idiom of Narnia is one in which the animals rejoice to embrace whatever intelligence or spirit they may. (In *The Last Battle* the Talking Beasts who do not go to Heaven lose the ability to talk and become mere beasts as they pass into Aslan's shadow.)

In the passage describing the Witch there is no hierarchy. Ogres (level of 'men') are followed by beasts (wolves), then by beast-men, then by spirits of trees, then by plants. What was a beast becoming human, the man-bull, in the passage with Aslan, has become a man turning to a beast, a creature with head of brute and body of man, the Minotaur. There is a sense of perversion in the poisonous plants. Finally whatever the reason Lewis politely gives, the effect is of sinking away to evil as nonentity, a matter of obscenities: we know only intermittently anything of that list of 'Cruels and Hags and Incubuses, Wraiths, Horrors, Efreets, Sprites, Orknies, Wooses, and Ettins'.

It is not without significance that the 'good' are continually surrounded by a variety of objects – the very detailed description of the interior of Mr Beaver's house with all its furniture and tackle hanging up and even the tea things (66-72) is an emblem of this – while the

Witch in her spiny castle seems to have nothing about her in her empty rooms, apart from the white statues of the creatures she has frozen by her magic. All she can do is reduce things – the living to frozen, life and colour to one dead white, time to stasis, Aslan to a dead corpse, even herself to a mere stump (125). Or pervert them, as she tries to cheat the laws after holding Aslan to them (140-1). Aslan is treated as more than a lion by the 'good', but as less than one by the followers of the Witch, as they cut off his mane before his death and speak to him as a mere cat, '"Puss, Puss? Poor Pussy.... How many mice have you caught to-day, Cat?... Would you like a saucer of milk, Pussums?"' (139; it will be an ironic undercutting of their ignorant insults that mice will come to bite away Aslan's bonds (144-5)).

The end of the narrative involves an opening out, a removal of the enclosure of evil that previously gripped Narnia. The Witch's castle, hemmed inland between two hills, is invaded and broken open to release the reawakened statues. The castle of the new Kings and Queens is by the wide sea with its wild enchantment. At their coronation, 'through the eastern door, which was wide open, came the voices of the mermen and the mermaids swimming close to the shore and singing in honour of their new Kings and Queens' (165). The sea looks towards Aslan's land, far to the uttermost east, and the sunrise. During their reign the children open up Narnia to contact with other countries.

It is in keeping with Lewis's portrayal of the good that they have most of the attention in the book. We do not see the evil figures very much, apart from the White Witch. Her dwarf is anonymous. There is a brief vignette of her chief of police, the wolf Maughrim, but that is about all. The characterisation of the Talking Creatures is striking by comparison. First there is Tumnus the Faun, superficially a nice furry person asking Lucy to tea, but actually a deceiver, and then a deceiver ashamed of himself. Then we meet Mrs Beaver, very motherly, and so concerned with the little things that she can ignore the large, and can even contemplate taking her sewing machine with her when they have to flee from the grasp of the White Witch. Later we meet such individuals as the amiable but stupid giant Rumblebuffin, or the over-excited lion who has to be 'steadied' when woken by Aslan. And of course the arrival of Father Christmas, the waking spring with its sudden profusion of flowers, and the gradual uncovering of Narnia itself, all add to this sense of diversity.

As for Aslan, he is Lewis's finest 'creation' (if he can be called that, since in a way he is 'traditional'[9]), a creation of such quintessential lionhood that he becomes far more than lion. The Witch is in plain view from the outset, but Aslan is long anticipated and heralded through Father Christmas and growing spring. And when he comes and is seen, he is purely himself: 'Aslan stood' (115). Yet no simple, single thing he: he contains and reconciles some of the most energetic opposites. 'People who have not been in Narnia somehow think that a thing cannot be good and terrible at the same time. If the children had ever thought so, they were cured of it now. For when they tried to look at Aslan's face they just caught a glimpse of the golden mane and the great, royal, solemn, overwhelming eyes; and then they found they couldn't look at him and went all trembly' (117). Nor is Aslan a good that is hidden or remote from creatures: he is actively among them, helping, enlivening, fighting, dancing and rolling with the children after he has risen from his death; and all this even while, in thus being the 'nearer', he is also the 'farther'. He can be shamed, his lionhood stripped from him, and he reduced to a bald helpless thing for all his divinity, and yet in his offered shame the glory of his true pride is validated.

The children, too, are well individuated. Lucy, the youngest, is the kindest and most generous of heart: she wants to help the Faun, she suffers Edmund's early jeering over her 'belief' in Narnia, she is quick, perhaps too quick, to help him when he is wounded in the battle (163). She is the first to find Narnia: she is the most spiritually perceptive; not for nothing is her name Lucy, from lucidity or *lux*, 'light'. Peter often relies on her for decisions: he feels that she has more insight. He himself is brave, considerate, practical and steady – hence with him, too, 'Peter', from 'a rock'.

Susan, however, changes during the narrative. She is a slightly impatient teenager, a little concerned to look after herself, and rather unwilling to take things as they come: one of her most frequent questions is '"But what are we to do?"' (49,54,62,134). Susan is also rather inclined to give up at difficulties (57, 78). And, less perceptive than Lucy, she thinks at first that the mice about Aslan's dead body are mere vermin (144). But by the end it is she who sees before Lucy how Edmund must be spared the knowledge of how Aslan gave his life for him (163); she has grown, if only for now.[10]

Edmund at first is jeering and rather malignant: he finds nothing wonderful in life and disbelieves in Narnia at once until he finds it himself. His greed for the sweets of the Witch expresses something of the insatiable need of evil to fill itself by devouring; and he is to devour others, to draw even his own siblings towards the Witch. Only the shock administered to him by his experience of evil, and Aslan's subsequent mercy, save him. He is no simple villain, for his conscience revolts against what he is doing (83). Perhaps the cruel treatment of him by the Witch, and his extraordinarily difficult journey to her castle through the cold and snow (84), express not so much what is being done to him by others as what is being done to him by his own soul, and his gradual movement towards a spiritual change that otherwise might seem rather abrupt.

The different characters of the four children – perhaps their moral characters rather than their personalities as such – always come over well. When they first see Mr Beaver beckoning at them from behind a tree in the forest, they have a range of reactions:

> 'The question is,' [said Peter] 'are we to go to it or not? What do you think, Lu?'
>
> 'I think it's a nice beaver,' said Lucy.
>
> 'Yes, but how do we *know?*' said Edmund.
>
> 'Shan't we have to risk it?' said Susan. 'I mean, it's no good just standing here and I feel I want some dinner.' (62)

Peter is concerned with action and Lucy with instinctive feeling. The calculating, cynical and cowardly nature of Edmund at this point is well expressed: his emphasis is on knowing rather than trusting, which reflects both on the foolish trust he gave to the Witch and on his own present incapacity to 'know' goodness when he sees it. Meanwhile Susan, like Edmund, does not trust Mr Beaver as Lucy does, but is prepared to take a risk, not because it is better than standing still but because she is hungry.

Always one feels with the 'good' side of the book that one is finding out more about the nature of reality. First there is Narnia itself behind our world; then, Narnia itself changes from winter to spring, and at the end from land to seaside. The rules seem to alter continually: the story almost depends on continual breaking of expectations. The Witch has only one notion of reality – a frozen world and a threat contained in a prophecy about four humans: she clings to this and her knowledge of the law myopically. She is shut in her castle, confined to the limited consciousness of her frozen realm, while Aslan walks free over many realms, taking many forms, and in Narnia is always seen on the move, having 'no fixed abode'. By his death Aslan puts down a taproot to a deeper and more universal reality than the Witch could know.

Then, the seemingly random is found to have a pattern behind it, and yet somehow remains itself. The children come to Narnia 'by chance' it would seem, simply happening to use the wardrobe as a hiding place in a game of hide-and-seek and then finding that they could go through its back. It could have been any children, surely? And any time? Yet when they are in Narnia they gradually find out that there is a prophecy concerning two sons of Adam and two daughters of Eve arriving to overthrow the Witch and take the four thrones in Cair Paravel: clearly they fit it, children though they are, and their arrival itself is in one way predetermined. There is another prophecy too, concerning the return of Aslan: again, only gradually do we and the children come to see that the two prophecies are not coming true separately, but are bound up with one another.

Yet still, no prophecy is a determinant: acts of choice and will have still to be made. Aslan finds dying no easy matter: the choice is hard, the pain of the soul very real, the shame and indignity very great. Nor do we see that his death will at best do any more than save Edmund – and even this is denied by the Witch in her last malicious words to him (140-1). Later we see the deeper reality of which Aslan knew but perhaps could not feel at the time. Peter and Edmund are nearly overwhelmed in battle and later badly wounded. Death and danger are real enough, however much one may be part of a pattern of prophecy. This interplay of freedom and the foreseen, of the random and the patterned, also contributes to the dancing variety that is goodness in the story. *The Lion, the Witch and the Wardrobe* may have its uneasy moments, but as a work of full and various vision it is a marvellous beginning to the Narnia series.

PRINCE CASPIAN (1951)

In this story, the same four Pevensie children we met in the first book are at a railway station on their way back to their various boarding schools, when they find themselves suddenly pulled by a strange force back into Narnia. They are in what they later realise are the ruins of Cair Paravel, their royal seat. They rescue a dwarf messenger who has been sent to them but was intercepted by enemies. He explains to them that they are in Narnia one thousand years after they left it, since when it has been invaded by men from the neighbouring land of Telmar. The present ruler is a usurper called Miraz, who has seized the throne from his nephew Prince Caspian and forced him to flee for his life. Caspian has succeeded in awaking many of the long-dormant Talking Beasts of Narnia (warred on and suppressed by the Telmarines, who detest all wild things). He has enlisted them on his side in a battle currently being fought around the hill at Aslan's How, a hill cast up above the stone table where Aslan was killed, and now honeycombed with tunnels. Caspian has in his possession the magic horn of the High Queen Susan, which she left behind her on leaving Narnia (an accident again with a purpose): it is said that when the horn is blown at need, the first Kings and Queens will return to Narnia; and this is what has happened to the children. Caspian knew that they would arrive at one of three places particularly associated with them, of which Cair Paravel was one, and dispatched messengers to meet them.

The rest of the story describes the journey of the children with the dwarf, Trumpkin, towards Aslan's How. The landscape has changed since their time, and though Lucy has a view of Aslan inviting them to follow him, the others decide to ignore this, and soon find themselves out of their way. Eventually, however, they reach Caspian, save him and his loyal followers from a *coup* by a renegade dwarf Nikabrik who has leagued himself with evil powers, and overthrow Miraz and his forces. Thereafter Narnia is liberated from various forms of Telmarine tyranny. The Talking Beasts and all the gods and spirits of Narnia are restored to freedom. Caspian is enthroned, and the Telmarines are given the choice of returning to the realm (actually on this Earth) from which they originally came, or joining with the new Narnian society. Then the children once more return home, or rather to the railway station from which their adventure began.

In some way the story is similar to that of *The Lion, the Witch and the Wardrobe*. The same children are brought to Narnia to save it again in its hour of need. A tyrant has usurped the throne of Narnia, and the Talking Beasts have long been silenced and driven into hiding. Caspian's struggle with the army of Miraz is going against him until Aslan and the children come, just as happened with Peter and Edmund in their battle against the forces of the Witch. Under the influence of Caspian and Aslan, the Talking Beasts and the natural powers of Narnia are roused, as they were by the children and Aslan in *The Lion, the Witch and the Wardrobe*. The duel between Peter and Miraz is to some extent paralleled by that between Peter and the Witch. The story also ends with the establishment of a true King and a feast.

In a sense this story reiterates at a practical and immediate level what was realised more spiritually in the first book. There, Peter, Edmund, Susan and Lucy were made Kings and Queens after defeating a force of much more metaphysical evil: the White Witch's nature is categorically different from the fairly bumbling wickedness of Miraz. In becoming Kings and Queens the children as it were established Kingship in Narnia: the prophecy of the Talking Beasts had long looked to the arrival of two Sons of Adam and Daughters of Eve to sit in the thrones at Cair Paravel and complete the unfinished hierarchy of being in Narnia by the addition of men and women. But since the children disappear from Narnia, the thrones remain vacant until a new human king appears. This king eventually comes from a people called Telmarines, actually pirates from our world, who find a way into Narnia and establish a royal line. In this line Caspian is to be the tenth of his name. When the children return, Narnia has changed historically and geographically over a thousand years, and they themselves have sunk once more to the status of legends. They restore Narnia to something of the spiritual condition it had at the end of *The Lion,* but in this story they are establishing not themselves but another as king. The story has moved from a symbolic context of the establishment of the First Things to the more directly secular levels of politics and sociology, in an everyday world where issues are a little more confused.

But the confusions and uncertainties of the story come not just from its changed context, but also from the fact that the throne of Narnia has been usurped. Since the general view of the Narnia books is that the kingdom reflects its ruler, a king who is not the king will turn the very air of Narnia to uncertainty. Because Miraz is king *de facto* but not *de jure*, the country is turned to confusion. This is a very Shakespearian view, whereby the macrocosm reflects the microcosm, and a Macbeth who supplants the legitimate king Duncan makes a realm where 'nothing is, but what is not.' It may well be that Lewis had Shakespeare's plays about usurpation – *Hamlet, Macbeth, Richard II* and *Henry IV Parts I and II* – in mind when writing *Prince Caspian*.

Confusion is in fact one of the motifs of the story, if not always to reflect realism. Even when the children are first taken to Narnia their sense is one of bewilderment as they are whirled from the station platform. When they arrive they cannot be sure they are in Narnia; and the place where they are is so overgrown and geographically altered that they cannot for long recognise it as Cair Paravel. Even more confusing for them is to be the dawning knowledge that they are in Narnia one thousand years beyond the time when they left it a year previously.

Meanwhile Caspian has also been finding the world more complex than he supposed. His tutor Dr Cornelius (another 'confusion', for he looks like a small man but is later to reveal himself as part-dwarf) has told Caspian that his uncle Miraz has usurped the throne that is rightfully his. Cornelius has also disclosed that Narnia is actually inhabited by Talking Beasts, as Caspian's nurse once told him and his uncle punished her for so doing. And later, when Miraz has at last succeeded in begetting a son, Cornelius tells Caspian that his uncle's previous favour to him as eventual successor will now cease and that he must flee the court, which he does. In the forest, symbol of uncertainty, to which Caspian eventually comes in his flight, he loses his way and knocks himself out on a tree branch. On waking, he sees a strange man approaching him, only to realise with a shock that it is a badger. The world here is always showing itself more multiplex and disorientating than supposed.

In fact, finding one's true bearings in it is also one of the issues in the book, as the children try to find their way to where Caspian is, and continually lose themselves or become sidetracked. Narnia itself has lost its own true bearings, as the Talking Beasts have been suppressed and as the true King has now been banished. When Caspian winds Susan's horn to call back the legendary Kings and Queens to Narnia, he does not know which of the three possible places in Narnia they will arrive at, even supposing they hear his call. Even Trumpkin the dwarf finds reality steadily more confusing than his practical commonsense mind would have supposed, and has to accept that what seem to be mere children are in fact the High King and his companion King and Queens, and that Aslan is a real and immediate being. As for the children, they themselves are given only individual or uncertain views of Aslan on their journey, and doubt and disobey him: in the medium of this world it seems, he will not at first appear plainly, though as all clears at the end, he does so.

Nikabrik the dwarf is a striking example of confusion. His no-nonsense practicality has changed to a hard-bitten contempt for Caspian's trust in the First Kings and Queens, and that to a readiness to compromise with the evil, even the White Witch, to gain the ends for which they all seek. "'They say she ruled for a hundred years: a hundred years of winter. There's power, if you like. There's something practical'" (*Prince Caspian*, 145). Another example of confusion is seen in Miraz, who is tricked by his lords into agreeing to a single combat with Peter. He thus himself becomes involved in an uncertain world, and is overthrown by it.

True, at the end, all confusion is removed. In a journey that owes much to that of Princess Irene and Curdie and their strange retinue of creatures into the city of Gwyntystorm at the end of George MacDonald's *The Princess and Curdie* (1882), the girls and Aslan and their Bacchic followers enter the Narnian capital Beruna and scour it. People then reveal themselves for what they are. In one school a pupil who can see Aslan joins the 'invaders', while the remainder, including their teacher Miss Prizzle, are driven out; in another (and it is still typical of the book to refuse us simple responses to reality) it is the teacher who is saved and the pupils all turned to pigs (170-3). Then there is a division among the Telmarines. Those who wish to make themselves one with the new Narnia stay, while the others go back to the 'other' country from which they came, through a magic doorway set up by Aslan. Last, there is a separation of one King from others, when the children go home leaving Narnia to Caspian.

Yet one feels, despite this general and very real movement from confusion and uncertainty to order and clarity, that the ambiguities of the world as we have experienced them are somehow more native to it than they were in the last book, and that we have been in touch with a harder, more resistant Narnia than before. This is actually portrayed through the emphasis on the Narnian environment, and the much closer contact with it. The first thing the children find when they are transported to Narnia is that they are 'standing in a woody place – such a woody place that branches were sticking into them and there was hardly any room to move' (12). Then, when they have struggled out of the wood they find themselves on a seashore. The shore is very physically described: they smell the sea, wade in it, walk on 'the dry, crumbly sand that sticks to one's toes'; then they explore the beach, walking along it till they find another shore opposite them, but though the two grow closer they never meet, and eventually they realise they are on an island. There follows the discovery of a stream, and they walk up it as far as they can until they are forced to 'stoop under branches and climb over branches, and they blundered through great masses of stuff like rhododendrons and tore their clothes and got their feet wet in the stream' (17). And so on, forcing their way through crowding trees into a ruin, making a fire out of sticks and cones, suddenly realising that they are in Cair Paravel, locating the door of what should be the treasure room behind the thick ivy, cutting away the ivy in great clumps with Peter's knife and then, when it breaks, Edmund's penknife, pulling the rotten wood of the door to pieces and exposing the dark, dank and draughty place behind.

In *The Lion, the Witch and the Wardrobe* there was less sense of this contact with the environment. One felt it most in evil contexts, as when Edmund struggled through the snow and beside the frozen stream to the Witch's castle, or when the Witch found the runners of her sledge stick as the thaw increased. In *Prince Caspian* it is pervasive. During his exile Caspian goes literally underground, first in being taken to the badger Trufflehunter's sett, and then in putting his army inside the hill of Aslan's How. The whole long journey of the children and Trumpkin towards Caspian is a trek over a series of natural obstacles – the sea, a creek, a forest, a precipice along which they force a way before having to return, a difficult descent, a river crossing, a climb up a path over a precipice, and so to Aslan's How. All this makes us have a strong sense of Narnia as a particular and solid place.

There is also much less sense of perspective over whole areas than there was in *The Lion*. Here there are so many forests that we could not have that anyway. Narnia, which seemed a relatively small realm in the first book, has as it were grown over time into its true size and self: distances have become very real, and the doings and nature of one part can be radically separate from those of another – Beruna here, Cair Paravel there, Aslan's How far off. The narrative describes a slow convergence of all the participants through this 'bigger' Narnia. What we feel throughout the story is a growing sense of the complex 'personality' of Narnia.

Throughout the emphasis is on nature's power. The civilised castle of Cair Paravel has been reduced to an ivy-covered ruin, surrounded by an orchard gone wild and a forest. What was a promontory on which the castle stood has been turned over time to an island. As we have seen, during the children's journey they are constantly thwarted by natural objects and lost in a changed landscape. Caspian is as it were taken into the earth in the badger's sett. He chooses to lodge his army inside a hill. The Telmarines first came to the world bordering Narnia not through an artifice (a wardrobe, a picture), but through a 'natural' cave in a mountain on a South Sea island on Earth (184-5).

Partly this emphasis on nature is thematic. The Telmarines have established the rule of man in Narnia to the exclusion of all other living things. They have built towns, roads, bridges. They have disinherited the Talking Beasts of Narnia. They will have nothing to do with raw nature: they cut down trees wherever they can and are 'at war with all wild things' (60). They are particularly afraid of the wildness that is Aslan, and, knowing from the stories that he comes from over the sea, they have let the coast become impenetrably wooded so that none may reach it. Yet they have not defeated nature, only increased its terror. '"Because they have quarrelled with the trees they are afraid of the woods. And because they are afraid of the woods they imagine that they are full of ghosts. And the Kings and great men, hating both the sea and the wood, partly believe those stories, and partly encourage them"' (53).[11] This is another example of the confusion in Narnia. In a sense, the Telmarines have severed themselves from the land itself, which '"is not the land of Men"' but '"the country of Aslan, the country of the Waking Trees and Visible Naiads, of Fauns and Satyrs, of Dwarfs and Giants, of the gods and the Centaurs, of Talking Beasts"' (50).

This is one reason why the 'good' are put so closely in contact with the land, for Narnia is everything that is in it, even its earth and its water (which themselves come to prominence and some life at the end). The children have to struggle with their environment; they have to eat the raw meat of a wild bear. Caspian, taken into the ground, comes to see that as man he has no higher status necessarily than the creatures for which he should care (especially when they are *talking* creatures). Nikabrik refers to him as '"this Human"' and speaks of not letting 'it' '"go back to its own kind and betray us all"' and Trumpkin retorts, '"It isn't the creature's fault that it bashed its head against a tree outside our hole"' (63); 'creature', 'it', 'its own kind' – suddenly Caspian, no longer in control, is being treated like an animal himself. What was a sense of hierarchy with the creatures looking up to man in *The Lion, the Witch and the Wardrobe*, has become more of a sense of corrective equality here. (In *The Lion* the beasts had no men to 'round them off'; here the men have shut out the beasts.)

And the wilderness that the Telmarines shut out is to return. Aslan, long feared by them, comes back. At his great roar the wildness of Narnia is set loose in the awakened trees, and its very essence returns in the frenzied dance of Bacchus and Silenus and their Maenads (135-8). The trees smash Miraz's army (167-8). Then Aslan, the two girls and Bacchus and his Maenads approach the river Beruna and beyond it the town. The river god rises and asks Aslan to loose his chains: under Bacchus's influence ivy spreads over the bridge and pulls it down (169-70). The town is invaded and most of its inhabitants flee. The dancing crowd go out into the country and break all bonds: 'At every farm animals come out to join them. Sad old donkeys who had never known joy grew suddenly young again; chained dogs broke their chains; horses kicked their carts to pieces and came trotting along with them' (171).

All the works of man seem swept away, and his civilisation with it. This perhaps may give the impression that building bridges or towns is a bad idea, which is unfortunate: the only real intent here is to show wildness reasserting itself, righting the balance of its excessive neglect. Since the direction of the narrative has been to make Caspian king, we are not ending with some primitivist manifesto. The Telmarines may have built bridges because 'they all hated and feared running water just as much as they hated and feared woods and animals' (179), but bridges built to help society remain goods, as does civilisation when it does not exist at the expense of all other creatures. At any rate all thereafter gather together to feast – men, beasts, dwarfs, trees, gods and Aslan – and Narnia once more belongs, as it did long ago, 'to the Talking Beasts and the Dwarfs and Dryads and Fauns and other creatures quite as much to the men' (182). It is the inclusiveness that matters.

The journey of Caspian himself has been one to incorporate and bring back with him all these other levels of being. He has followed the pastoral movement of a departure from the court or city to the wildness of nature and then back again with new and redeeming power, as we see it in Shakespeare's *As You Like It* or *The Winter's Tale*. His journey itself imparts to him a regality he could not otherwise possess:

> 'To sleep under the stars, to drink nothing but well water and to live chiefly on nuts and wild fruit, was a strange experience for Caspian after his bed with silken sheets in a tapestried chamber at the castle, with meals laid out on gold and silver dishes in the anteroom, and attendants ready at his call. But he had never enjoyed himself more. Never had sleep been more refreshing nor food tasted more savoury, and he began already to harden and his face wore a knightlier look' (76).

The movement of the story is one towards increasing meeting and community. At first separated from the court, Caspian meets in the forest with 'his various strange subjects' (76). The children journey to join with him. From being alone he becomes increasingly surrounded by friends (and enemies too). At Aslan's roar all Narnia starts into life. The group of different children and the dwarf Trumpkin form an emblem of relationship and – to some extent – cooperation. What is fighting Miraz is not Caspian, nor even his army, but the whole tormented nature of Narnia itself. At the end, the harmony of king and country is re-established.

Presiding over it all is the promise contained in the rare conjunction of the stars that his tutor Dr Cornelius shows Caspian one night in Beruna before telling him the truth about Narnia, '"Their meeting is fortunate and means some great good for the sad realm of Narnia. Tarva, the Lord of Victory, salutes Alambil, the Lady of Peace"' (49; see also 72). Cornelius describes the meeting of the stars as a dance, and dances pervade the narrative. There is the circling dance of the Fauns in the forest, in which Caspian takes part, and the 'Great Chain' of dancing trees that Lucy sees by night during the journey of the children (122). Then there are the dancing tree people and Bacchus and Silenus round Aslan (136-8) and the dancing invasion of Beruna and its environs (170-4). At the end, there is the dance of Bacchus, Silenus and the Maenads, which creates the fuel and the food for all beings, even down to the various Narnian soils that nourish different tree peoples (180-1).

There remains one other recurrent motif in the book. It concerns faith in the unseen.[12] It is perhaps a symptom of the very solidity of the world of Narnia that this should be a central issue. The Telmarines and Miraz refuse to believe in the existence of the Talking Beasts. Trumpkin finds it hard to accept the children as Kings and Queens of Narnia. At the edge of the gorge Lucy sees Aslan beckon her, but the others do not believe her, and all are led out of their way until they trust blindly. Nikabrik the dwarf does not believe in the magic power of the horn Caspian blows to summon the Kings and Queens back to Narnia, and he comes to lose faith in any possibility of success against Miraz except through the use of evil powers. 'Seeing' is the crucial image here: if one looks with 'commonsense', or with sloth or evil, one will not see, only if one's imagination and love are awake and ardent. When Lucy sees Aslan in the forest, 'She never stopped to think whether he was a friendly lion or not, she rushed to him. She felt her heart would burst if she lost a moment' (122-4).

Even Caspian is for a time spiritually blind through his sinful Telmarine heritage. When Nikabrik brings two sinister creatures into his council in Aslan's How, it is only gradually that Caspian is able to see the evil for what it is, and in doing so perceive plainly the identities of these others: '"So that is your plan, Nikabrik! Black sorcery and the calling up of an accursed ghost. And I see who your companions are – a Hag and a Werewolf!"' (147). Perhaps even the debate between Caspian's good and bad counsellors just before this is a debate within his head – certainly the imagery of the closed room in which it takes place is suggestive: and one has felt something of a 'faculty psychology' at times elsewhere in the narrative, in the various relationships of the children and Trumpkin (the gorge they come to and the response to Aslan there reminds us of the allegory of John and Virtue offered the help of Mother Kirk at the gorge in *The Pilgrim's Regress*).

Prince Caspian is in large part an exploration of Narnia, opening it up for us and extending and thickening our awareness of it. At the end of *The Lion, the Witch and the Wardrobe*, Narnia remained a fantastic realm. The children returned in a sudden jerk from their grown-up, Narnian personalities, described in high style, to the colloquial world of holidays in the Professor's house in a country they had for 'decades' forgotten. At the end of *Prince Caspian* the children have been in Narnia for far less time; they know they are going back to their own world before they do so; and they change back into their school clothes while still in Narnia. When they have arrived back through Aslan's door at the railway station from which their adventure started, Edmund's first words are '"Bother! ... I've left my new torch in Narnia,"' as though Narnia were as real as a holiday cottage or a bus – or home.

THE VOYAGE OF THE 'DAWN TREADER' (1952)

Here Lewis turns away from Narnia itself to give us the story of a voyage by three children, Lucy, Edmund and their cousin Eustace, together with the warrior-mouse Reepicheep, to the Uttermost East and Aslan's Country. (At the end of their last adventure Peter and Susan have been told by Aslan that they are now too old to return to Narnia.) Searching for a plot for his story, Lewis happened this time on the tradition of the adventurous sea journey, from Homer's *Odyssey* or the eighth-century Irish *Voyage of Bran* to John Masefield's *The Midnight Folk* (1927). He also revisited his unpublished poem of 1930, 'The Nameless Isle,' for the long episode of the Island of Voices in the story.

Lewis in fact starts with an episode from Masefield's book. Edmund and Lucy have been staying with cousin Eustace Scrubb, who has been brought up by 'progressive' parents and is thoroughly unpleasant. Eustace has just been deriding the picture of a ship on the wall of Lucy's room as a mere fiction, a piece of wishful thinking, when the fiction becomes fact. The ship, which proves Narnian, comes alive and sails out of its frame into an English bedroom, where the three astonished children now struggle in an ocean until they are rescued and brought aboard.

On the ship, the *Dawn Treader* they find King Caspian, the former Prince of *Prince Caspian*, who, after having established his reign, has set out eastwards to find seven lords, friends of his father, who were sent away over the sea by Miraz. The fighting mouse, Reepicheep, who has come with him, has larger ends in view: he wants to sail to Aslan's land, which he has long desired. After a series of adventures, during which Eustace's unpleasantness is largely cured by his being turned into a dragon, and it is found that three of the lords are dead, and the other four variously enchanted, the ship journeys on to the very end of the world and near to Aslan's country.

There Reepicheep leaves, and the children receive an inner prompting to go too. Caspian also wishes to land, but is dissuaded by Aslan, and returns home to rule Narnia. What happens to Reepicheep is not revealed. The children come ashore through a great, stationary wave to a flat grassy place where the sky meets the earth. There a lamb meets them, and feeds them with fish roasting on a fire. The lamb then becomes Aslan, and tells them that they will be returning to their own world. Edmund and Lucy are told that they will not come back to Narnia because they are now too old. When Lucy wonders how they can live without Aslan, he tells them that he is in all worlds, though in different guises. In their world "'I have another name. You must learn to know me by that name. This was the very reason why you were brought to Narnia, that by knowing me here for a little you may know me better there.'" Aslan then 'opens' the sky and returns the children to the room from which they started their adventure.

This book is distinctive in the Narnia series for its episodic structure. There is a central line of progress, from Narnia eastwards to the world's end, but along the way a series of incidental adventures occurs, quite separate from one another at the narrative level, and each highly individualised – as is common in voyage stories. On an island Eustace suffers his transformation to a dragon through unwittingly sleeping on its hoard, and has to be helped by Aslan to make a painful repentance and return to human shape. Another island has on it a pool that turns everything that enters it to gold. On another is a collection of bizarre monopods called Dufflepuds, and a magician Coriakin whose spell book tempts Lucy to knowledge and power. On the sea itself the voyagers encounter a giant sea serpent, and a huge area of darkness in which they discover and rescue one of the seven lost Narnian lords, who has long been confined on an island there, at the mercy of nightmares. The last island on the journey is that of another magician, Ramandu, where the three remaining Narnian lords are found in enchanted sleep. The children learn that only a spell brought back from the world's end will wake them. The final part of the journey enters a great sea of clear sweet water which eventually becomes covered by lilies, until the *Dawn Treader* reaches water too shallow to go on save by rowing a boat.

In many ways it would seem that Lewis has exploited the loose structure of his narrative to create little islands of the imagination *en route*. True, they are not without spiritual meanings: the changing of Eustace into a dragon accomplishes his moral transformation, and the experience of the spell-book 'develops' Lucy a little too. There are also those who maintain that the whole idea of a directional journey implies a spiritual journey in the book:[13] and it has been argued that Caspian in particular develops throughout.[14] But there is not very much evidence of this. True, he is impractical in going ashore on one island early on with only a few companions (*The Voyage of the 'Dawn Treader'*, 38), for he is captured and sold by slavers: but an advance in common sense is hardly the same as a spiritual progress. And when he is tempted by greed and the gold-making pool (111), so are the others, for magic is also at work on them. At the end Caspian is still impetuous in his – quite natural – desire to go to Aslan's land, and has to be corrected by Aslan himself. These moral moments really do not make much of a connected sequence, nor do they show much development: Lewis seems rather to happen on a failing at one point than to have thought more widely in terms of growth. All we can say at the end is that Caspian has had an exciting and faintly questionable holiday from his royal duties, to which he is then returned.

Is there any pattern at all then behind the narrative? There is something of a hierarchic movement after we leave the last known or Lone Islands, where Gumpas the Governor and a crowd of pirates and slavers are overcome. For thereafter we meet first a dragon, then a Sea Serpent, then the stupid Dufflepuds, the man reduced to terror on the dream-island, the sleeping men in Ramandu's land and some sea-people. And as far as magic is concerned, we progress from a transforming dragon's hoard, to an alchemical pool, to the magician-cum-former star Coriakin (who is confined to his island undergoing some kind of purgatory for past sins), to the 'good' star magician Ramandu; and thence to the Great Magician, the Lamb Himself, who has been present throughout the story as Aslan as much as at the end. We thus move from 'ordinary' to more and more mystical forms of magic action.

Then, in another way, the islands may be symbols of selfishness, cut off from one another. The ship and its crew provide an image of the relatively cooperative organic body. But on most of the islands life has in some sense degenerated, or can be perverted. The slavers on the Lone Island treat people as beasts; the dragon hoard reduces people to dragons; the magic pool turns people to dead gold; the Dufflepuds are devolved dwarfs whose clumping forms express their nature; the lord on the island of dreams has been worn ragged by his experience; the slumbering lords at the table of Ramandu are covered by their own hair. Selfishness is found everywhere. Eustace for long shuts himself off from the rest of the community of the ship, refusing to co-operate. The slavers and pirates of the Lone Islands, a Narnian dependency, prey on others for gold; and Gumpas, the Governor, considers himself no longer responsible to his homeland. Caspian brings the islands back into the Narnian commonwealth. The dragon's hoard turns the would-be thief to a dragon: Eustace comes upon it at the fog-shrouded centre of an island, remote from the wide and 'connective' sea, when he has fallen into an enclosed gully, symbol of the isolated self (71-3). The gold-making pool on the next island awakens greed and discord in all who see it (111-12). The temptations of Lucy by the magician's book on the island of the Dufflepuds all relate to dilation of the self (131-4). The lord on the island in the darkness has been shut in on the dark self of his dreams; the lords on Ramandu's island have been locked in slumber ever since they quarrelled. At the end Caspian abandons his royal duties in his desire to go to Aslan's land.

By virtue of the very journey it makes, the *Dawn Treader* brings connection to the scattered selves of these places; and almost every enchantment is broken or overcome. The effect is one of a general release from captivity of the shut-in self: the slave markets of the Lone Islands (aptly-named) are removed, Eustace is released by Aslan from far inside his dragon body; the *Dawn Treader* itself escapes from the closing coils of the sea-serpent's body: the Dufflepuds are at least able to move off the island to play on the sea, though there is no escape from their stupidity; the Narnian lord is taken from his dark island and the others will be released from their slumber.

There are other patterns. One is the increasing awareness of the presence of Aslan. He is not in evidence until almost halfway through the story, in Eustace's reported dream of him when he is released from his dragon form. He comes to Lucy after she has used the magician's book of spells. In the form of an albatross he saves the *Dawn Treader* from the darkness surrounding the island of dreams, though only Lucy knows this (158-9). He interviews Caspian directly in his cabin after his wilfulness about going to the world's end. Finally he appears to the three children in his own country. His appearances in this book are much more restricted than in the previous two (though there has been a progressive 'wind-down' from *The Lion*, where only he himself could intervene). Here the characters are journeying 'towards' Aslan (insofar as he is in any place) rather than he coming in to Narnia. They are in effect travelling in a mystic progression towards a clearer and clearer sight of him. The operative text is 'For now we see through a glass, darkly; but then face to face.' As the voyagers come nearer to Aslan's country, the sea becomes so clear that the bottom is plain many fathoms down, the sun is far larger, and they all seem to move in excess of light (185-6). This is in sharp contrast to the slumber and darkness that characterised their immediately preceding adventures.

But clarity of detail, especially in the bright, elemental descriptions of the *Dawn Treader* and the sea, has been a leitmotif throughout of the almost heraldic world of this book. Failures of clarity are seen as evils from the start. Eustace's parents blur their identities by allowing Eustace to call them by their first names. Eustace in his diary falsifies his experience aboard the *Dawn Treader* into one of unmixed misery; and persists in believing that Narnia is an ordinary place with a British Consul somewhere to whom he can complain. Gumpas, the Governor of the Lone Islands, is a man of bureaucratic evasions and verbosity. The Dufflepuds cannot think connectedly, but are forever contradicting themselves or uttering tautologies as though they were discoveries, and have therefore fittingly been made invisible, or 'unclear'. Even the Sea Serpent assumes without looking that its tightening coils will have crushed the *Dawn Treader*, and is left peering along its body for the wreckage, with what seems to be 'a look of idiotic satisfaction' (104).

As befits the character of this book and its creation of so many strange worlds, the accent is on the imagination. Among his other defects, Eustace suffers from a lack of that faculty: 'He liked books if they were books of information and had pictures of grain elevators or of fat foreign children doing exercises in model schools' (9; that word 'foreign' is unfortunate). Characteristically of this book he is thrown into Narnia via a work of imagination, a picture, which comes to life – and a picture, at that, of a wholly 'fictional' ship. For the rest of the adventure he is living inside a fiction, a story, which he comes to accept as a fact. And then, during the voyage he is turned into a creature of 'fiction', a dragon. He is eventually led to see that the world of the imagination is at least as true as the world of 'facts', and indeed often more so.

Nevertheless Lewis shows Eustace's grasp of the 'real world' being a real help at times to the others (108-10). By contrast the strange Dufflepuds met on the later Island of Voices are portrayed as utterly impractical, washing up plates and cutlery before dinner to save them doing it afterwards, or planting boiled potatoes to save cooking them when they dig them up (141). The Dufflepuds, like Eustace at first, are almost totally lacking in imagination; but in themselves they are brilliant creations of the comic invention of a wizard - and beyond that of the imagination of C.S. Lewis who made the magician, and beyond that of Pliny and his picture in the *Natural History* of the Monopods.... There they lie in afternoon slumber on the sunlit grass, each with its gigantic foot held aloft as a shade, images of fantasy without any belief in it.

The dark island the travellers next come upon is an island of the tormented imagination, where bad dreams come true. Here the imagination is seen as dangerous if not controlled and kept pure. The implicit distinction here is perhaps that of Coleridge between the imagination, which embodies significance, and the far wilder fancy, which does not. This may be why as we move through the adventures the imagination becomes less purely inventive, and more symbolic: it begins to draw on images of spiritual significance. The sea of lilies over which the *Dawn Treader* glides is an image of dying into a new life, and of purity (seen also through the sunlight and clarity of the water). The lamb that meets the children beyond the upreared wave is the Lamb of God, the same God who divided the Red Sea for the Israelites. When he tells the children, "'Come and have breakfast,'" and offers them fish roasting on a fire, he is the risen Lamb of God appearing to his disciples in John 21, 9-13. And when he now turns from a Lamb into a Lion, we recall those reconciled images of lion and lamb (even Old Testament God and risen Christ) that are long hallowed in Christian tradition. Then, looking back, we begin to see that the whole narrative, in journeying eastwards, has been journeying to the sunrise of the everlasting day (perhaps the boat's name, *Dawn Treader*, coming into its own at last).

The changing landscapes of the book are also suggestive here. We have left islands and come to a continent. We seem to have come to the increasingly horizontal: the first islands are more or less hilly, but Coriakin's island is flat, that of Ramandu is gently undulating (befitting in part the slumber on it), the sea thereafter is flat with lilies, and the place where the children meet the lamb is a flat area of grass. Yet heaven, or Aslan's land, finally defies the imagination: try as we may we cannot put together the pictures of a giant, still wave, a grassy area with the sky coming right to the ground behind it, and yet at the same time include those huge far-off mountains that the children sea as part of this land. In a sense throughout the book we have moved into the increasingly imaginative – a heroic sea-journey, a dragon, Sea Serpent, Dufflepuds, Ramandu – and beyond, to the point where imagination turns to paradoxical vision.

Of all the Narnia books this one is shot through with what Lewis called the 'dialectic of Desire', *Sehnsucht*. Every move the boat makes further to the east is a pull on our imaginations, all the more strong for the fact that each stage has put the last totally out of sight, whether by storm or darkness, or by simple endless travelling. Before us is the pull of that great name, the World's End (Lewis once said that the title itself of Morris's *The Well at the World's End* was almost enough without the novel[15]). When will we reach it? What will it be like? When we join the *Dawn Treader* it has already left most of the known lands east of Narnia, and has only the Lone Islands to come. And beyond them – what? The mind ranges freely here, tipped off the edge of the world.

In the first two books the objective soon became known – the establishment of the first Kings and Queens, the defeat of the White Witch, the restoration of Caspian. But here the goal is mysterious: no one can know of Aslan's land, none along the route have anything but vague hints to give of what lies further to the east from their immediate locations. Every island and experience we reach seems charged with mystery, as a station on the way: how near, we wonder, are we to the end? Will this place provide a key to it? Lewis whets the desire finely with the marvellous variety of the places and behaviours along the *Dawn Treader's* route. It was a fine touch, for instance, not to have a simple increase of mystery but to mix with it an element of the comic and even the grotesque, in the pictures of Eustace trying to write with his dragonish claws in the sand, or of the stupid Sea Serpent crushing in its coils a ship that is no longer there, or of the ludicrous Dufflepuds on an island of deep moral magic. Even at the end Lewis is still doing this: Ramandu's island is sublime, and the misfortunes of the three lords are real, but their appearance even then is grotesque, with their hair so overgrown that they are 'nearly all hair' (165).

The longing in the story is partly raised by a desire for the unknown, but it also comes from the knowledge that the unknown is the wholly 'other': no simple magic realm or wondrous place lies at the end of this quest; rather these are all passed on the way. Something whose mystery and simplicity transcends and includes them all lies still further, and still beyond the sight of all save a few – and even then what we see is not the heaven that Reepicheep presumably finds. In a sense we learn as we move that though like Tolkien we may have desired dragons with a profound desire, they are not the end of all desire; and so with all the other wonderful places we visit. Though the breath of the numinous is strong throughout the story, romantic yearning becomes altered to a more mystical longing as Aslan is more in evidence and the magicians become more his executives; until finally, as the rowing boat crosses the last of the seas of lilies,

> suddenly there came a breeze from the east, tossing the top of the wave into foamy shapes and ruffling the smooth water all round them. It lasted only a second or so but what it brought them in that second none of those three children will ever forget. It brought both a smell and a sound, a musical sound. Edmund and Eustace would never talk about it afterwards. Lucy could only say, 'It would break your heart.' (206)

Here Lewis has realised, if in a romantic context, something of that journey in search of the source of desire that he portrayed in more self-conscious form in *The Pilgrim's Regress*. Of course, the images, and the picture such as we have it, of Aslan's land, are all inventions. The whole story is a fiction, the creation of one C. S. Lewis. How can these possibly touch any reality? But that is the question that Lewis, like George MacDonald, is asking us of the creations of the imagination. Where do they come from? If they move us, are they not more than personal? To confuse the images themselves with the source of the desire is certainly a mistake: that is why Lewis has led us from one to another throughout and still left us with a mystery, even till the last, when metaphor becomes replaced by paradox, and image and truth become closest. But still they carry the mystery, as the breeze carried that nameless something to the children. In his earlier Narnia books Lewis made us see, and perhaps some of his child readers believe a little in, the Deep Magic of God: here, more surely than anywhere else in his work save *Perelandra*, he makes us feel it. He does it without drama, without the heavy romantic cadences of a Dunsany, with his imagination balanced by intellect and common sense, and with those pictures from beyond the world anchored in everyday reality. As the voyagers pass over the clear water on the way to the World's End, Lucy sees a black thing under the boat continually expanding and diminishing in size, and then realises what it is through a remembered likeness:

> It was like what you saw from a train on a bright sunny day. You saw the black shadow of your coach running along the fields at the same pace as the train. Then you went into a cutting; and immediately the same shadow flicked close up to you and got big, racing along the grass of the cutting-bank. Then you came out of the cutting and – flick! – once more the black shadow had gone back to its normal size and was running along the fields.
>
> 'It's our shadow! – the shadow of the *Dawn Treader*,' said Lucy. 'Our shadow running along on the bottom of the sea. That time when it got bigger it went over a hill. But in that case the water must be clearer than I thought! Good gracious, I must be seeing the bottom of the sea; fathoms and fathoms down.' (186)

Later, as the *Dawn Treader* crosses the sea of lilies, we find the practical sailors wondering how lilies could grow in such deep water; and have it explained to us that an 'undersea' girl Lucy saw, and who dropped quickly astern, did so because she was not in a current, about forty feet wide, in which the ship is being driven (199, 200). No better way could have been found to bring us close to the experience: but that way is part of Lewis's nature.

THE SILVER CHAIR (1953)

The children in this story are Eustace Scrubb and Jill Pole, a bullied girl he befriends at the 'Experimental School' they both attend; all four Pevensie children have now gone, too old to enter Narnia any more. Aslan draws this pair into his land to tell them to carry out a task. They are to go in quest of Rilian, son of the now old Caspian, who has been captured by an enchantress. She, in the form of a huge green serpent, slew his mother; and he has been lost to Narnia for ten years.

Aslan gives Jill four signs to remember to help them on the way. First Eustace will meet an old friend in Narnia and must greet him to secure help. This sign is missed when the children see Caspian and let him take ship in search of his son without greeting him. Then they must travel north to the ruined city of the ancient giants. Helped by a creature called a Marsh-wiggle on their journey, they go in the right direction; but encouraged by a lady dressed in green whom they meet, they aim for an existing city of giants called Harfang and for what they think will be comfort there, and actually pass through the ruined city in a storm without noticing it. The third sign Aslan gives them is writing which is to be found on a stone of the ruined city: they are to do what it tells them. From Harfang the children can the next day see the ruined city they missed, and a giant stone with the inscription 'UNDER ME' on it. Though detained by the giants, who plan to eat them, they manage to escape; but they are pursued into the ruined city and have to crawl into a crack under one of the stones.

This crack, however, leads inwards and eventually they find themselves sliding down a steep slope a mile or more into the earth. At the bottom they are met by a crowd of gloomy goblin-like Earthmen, who take them a long journey to meet their Queen of Underland. But she is absent, and at the command of a knight in black armour the Earthmen leave the children and the Marsh-wiggle with him to await her return. This knight, who does not know his own name, tells them he is bound for one hour every day in a silver chair by order of the Queen (whom he reveres), supposedly lest he become a devouring serpent. He warns the children not to release him when this happens, however he begs. Now the fourth sign given by Aslan was that the children would know the lost prince Rilian by his calling for help in Aslan's name. When, locked in the silver chair, the Black Knight does this, they release him and he proceeds to destroy the chair.

But then the Queen, the green serpentine Witch who slew Rilian's mother and abducted him, enters. With magic charms and incantations over a fire in the room, she almost succeeds in putting them all into a trance of disbelief in any world outside themselves. Finally it is Puddleglum the Marsh-wiggle who, by stamping on the fire puts out its hypnotic smoke, restores the children to their senses and enables them to destroy the Witch, who has now reverted to her serpent form. They all now escape towards the surface through a tunnel: the Witch had been organising the Earthmen to dig a tunnel up to the 'Overland' to invade it and make Rilian king, and this tunnel was all but complete. But on their way the group find the Earthmen, previously enslaved by the Witch, now rejoicing at their freedom. A giant crack has opened in the floor of Underland, revealing the fires of their native land Bism, from which they were taken long ago: now they return and the crack closes. Meanwhile the end of the Witch's magic has started a rising flood in Overland and the travellers reach the final route to the surface just in time. When they break out, it is to find they are in Narnia. The rest of the story describes the last meeting of Rilian with his father Caspian (who then dies). Then the children journey back to Aslan's land, where they find a rejuvenated Caspian. Finally they return to Experiment House, their school on Earth, where with the help of Caspian and Aslan, their erstwhile bullies are terrified and punished.

There have been several excellent accounts of this story,[16] and only a few points will be made here. First, this is a highly 'literary' story. It has been pointed out that the Witch is a lamia and is related to Lilith; but she can also be linked with the evil Geraldine who enthrals Christabel in Coleridge's 'Christabel'. The idea of the Earthmen tunnelling through the ground towards Narnia to invade it probably owes much to George MacDonald's account of the goblins mining upwards beneath the Princess Irene's castle, and the subsequent flood, in *The Princess and the Goblin* (1872). The man-eating giants of Harfang may come as readily from MacDonald's 'The Giant's Heart' (1867) as from 'Tom Thumb'; and a group of owls in a tower perhaps from Peake's *Titus Groan*. The journey into the underworld is evidently traditional, but Lewis has added a twist by making the deepest part, Bism, a place of fiery joy and fecundity. The journey of the children from the high places of Aslan's land and down into the deepest regions before a return to the heights follows the romance pattern of the initiation of a hero.[17] It has been well shown that the silver chair came from a similar chair in the cave of Mammon in Spenser's *Faerie Queene*, Book 2; and that the serpentine

Witch is also related to Spenser's Error in Book 1.[18] Doubtless there is much more. This literary derivation is perhaps not inappropriate in a world where the relation between appearance and reality is a constant theme; and where Aslan asks of the children attention to certain signs which will appear in a predetermined pattern.

Nevertheless the story is one of the most lively and poised that Lewis wrote. He is dealing with two fairly ordinary children and letting them make mistakes and fail without too much blame, which permits relaxation; and he delights in incidental creation along the way, from the owls in the tower (ch.4) to the Marsh-wiggle Puddleglum with his cheerful gloom, or from a group of giants vacantly hurling rocks at a target, to the giant porter of Harfang offering Puddleglum a drink in a salt-cellar, "'You needn't mention it over at the House. The silver *will* keep on getting over there, and it's not my fault." (*The Silver Chair*, 95).

The Silver Chair is in marked contrast to *The Voyage of the 'Dawn Treader'*. Where *The Voyage* dealt with episodic adventures with little narrative connection among them, this book insists on narrative pattern right from the outset: Aslan has chosen the children for a specific task and he tells them the route to be followed and the sequence of signs to be looked for. *The Silver Chair* also goes in the opposite direction from that of *The Voyage*: here, instead of going towards the east and a place of greater and greater clarity, we go to the west and places of increasing obscurity (storms, darkness, underworld gloom). Obscurity is what characterises the Witch: she operates by deceptive appearances and tries to cloud the existence of an external world to the travellers, literally by using drugged smoke.

In a way – a modest way – the book follows a dark night of the soul, journeying in doubt and uncertainly, looking for signs and failing to see them. This is, of all the 'Narnia' books, the one in which Aslan plays least part. From the time he blows the children out from his country until the end, he does not appear, and the powers of the Witch have increasing sway, as the travellers move deeper into 'enemy territory'. And as they do so they go down and down. What was a 'horizontal' progress in *The Voyage* is here a vertical descent. Nevertheless, for all that he does not appear, Aslan is not wholly absent. The very existence of the signs shows that the patterns of the world are embedded in him. And the children's success testifies to his grace: for they failed the first three requirements, and only 'luck' found them a way underground that turned out to lead them to their goal.

What is the significance of the Marsh-wiggle? It may seem an odd question to ask, since he is so obviously a comic character with his perpetual glooms: "'I don't suppose we shall ever see the King back in Narnia now that he's once set off for foreign parts; and he had a nasty cough when he left. Then there's Trumpkin [the dwarf regent]. He's failing fast. And you'll find there'll have been a bad harvest after this terrible dry summer. And I shouldn't wonder if some enemy attacked us'" (67). Even the black smoke from his pipe falls to the ground and trails drearily along it: it is glum tobacco.[19] The children by turns find him comical and exasperating.

Yet Puddleglum is by his very gloom prepared for anything that reality may throw at him. He is not in fact disillusioned or a cynic (like Nikabrik in *Prince Caspian)*: he is simply made more ready to deal with disasters by postulating their existence before they occur. And about several of them he is right. Caspian is in fact dying. Trumpkin is too old for his job; and the travellers are attacked. Later, when they meet a beautiful lady with the black but silent visored knight, Jill ludicrously suggests that the knight said nothing because "'he was shy.'" Puddleglum, however, wonders whether there may have been a skeleton inside the armour, or even "'nothing at all'" (82): and nothing at all is indeed to turn out what Rilian has been almost reduced to by the Witch. Puddleglum always finds bedrock: much of what he says may never occur, but he will not be taken in by false appearances. He sees through the false Witch before Harfang and in the Underland; he recognises the ruined city of the giants as they pass. He is the one who finds it in himself to resist the attempts of the Witch to portray the Sun and Earth itself as illusions: he has his feet on the ground, so much so that it is one of them he uses painfully to stamp out the Witch's charm in the fire.

When he does so, Puddleglum reveals a rather happier self than we have known: he says to the Witch,

> 'Suppose we *have* only dreamed, or made up, all those things – trees and grass and sun and moon and stars and Aslan himself. Suppose we have. Then all I can say is that, in that case, the made-up things seem a good deal more important than the real ones. Suppose this black pit of a kingdom of yours *is* the only world. Well, it strikes me as a pretty poor one. And that's a funny thing, when you come to think of it. We're just babies making up a game, if you're right. But four babies playing a game can make a play-world which licks your real world hollow. That's why I'm going to stand by the play-world.' (156)

He is prepared to opt for an illusion rather than the Witch's 'reality'. But it is not just that: he wants that which gives happiness rather than misery. After this avowal, he is subtly changed. When he sees the flood rising in Underland he says, "'Not much danger of being burnt. That's the bright side of it'" (166); and later he tells the others that "'there's one good thing about being trapped down here: it'll save funeral expenses'" (182) – though it must be said he resorts to glooms again at his farewell (197). In parallel with his 'change', the Earthmen, far more truly dismal than he, are transformed by delight at the breaking of the enchantment and the opening of their home Bism for their return.

It is 'keeping in touch with reality' and the signs contained in it that Aslan has asked of the children. Every loss of contact involves people more heavily in the Witch's world of deceptive appearances. She deceives Rilian into her power by appearing to him as a beautiful woman clad in thin green; actually she is the serpent who stung his mother to death. She makes the children head for Harfang and supposed comfort instead of attending to their quest for the giants' ruined city; and in Underland she tries to make them believe that the world is an illusion. The giants of Harfang seem very welcoming but are in fact preparing to eat the children at their Autumn Feast. The children cross a strange flat area of odd squares and ridges in the storm as they struggle towards Harfang; they fall into a stone trench that goes in several directions with dead ends: only later, looking back from Harfang in clear day, do they see that what they traversed was in fact the ruined city they were supposed to be aiming for, and that the trench was one of the 'E's of 'UNDER ME'. The Black Knight is Rilian, and his 'reptilian side' is not the real one. The Earthmen are not really hostile, nor naturally gloomy: they are under the influence of the Witch. Nearly every deception is the result of a perversion of something, whether the perverted ('turned away') vision of the children, or the distortions of reality presented by the Witch. By contrast, in Aslan's country, things take on their proper forms: the old, dead Caspian, through a drop of Aslan's blood, is transformed to the young, vital prince whom Eustace knew (202-3).

A theme of lost and found identity also runs through the book. In the Underland, Rilian, enchanted, has never heard his name or that of Narnia. The Witch tells them all that the sun and the world do not exist and are mere mental extensions of things seen down below: she bids them sleep; she is here a solipsist. The Underland is itself a place without identity: even time, which distinguishes events, has gone to sleep there (128). Merely to go there is for the children to lose contact with the world from which they have come; at the end that contact is re-established via the hole by which they escape into Narnia, and the Narnians can then visit the Underland themselves. There is a kind of devolution of being, a dwindling of identity to absolute zero during much of the children's journey towards the Witch. In Narnia they fail to greet Caspian, and speak to no other human; owls take them into their avian society and then one of them takes them to the Marsh-wiggles. From the Marsh-wiggles they descend to the stupid or brutish giants and thence to the etiolated monotony of the Earthmen in their faintly troubled darkness.

In the Underland being seems to shrivel towards nonentity. The second cavern the travellers are led through

> was full of a dim, drowsy radiance, so that here they had no need of the Earthmen's strange lantern. The floor was soft with some kind of moss and out of this grew many strange shapes, branched and tall like trees, but flabby like mushrooms. They stood too far apart to make a forest; it was more like a park. The light (a greenish grey) seemed to come both from them and from the moss, and it was not strong enough to reach the roof of the cave, which must have been a long way overhead. Across the mild, soft, sleepy place they were now made to march. It was very sad, but with a quiet sort of sadness like soft music.
>
> Here they passed dozens of strange animals lying on the turf, either dead or asleep, Jill could not tell which. These were mostly of a dragonish or bat-like sort; Puddleglum did not know what any of them were (125-6)

The style flops, like the scene. The radiance is uncertain; the moss is of 'some kind'; the shapes are 'strange' and no sooner tall and tree-like than they become mushrooms; they do not quite make a forest; the source of the light is unclear and it cannot reach the roof; the place is 'soft' and 'sad'. The animals are 'strange'; Jill cannot tell whether they are dead or asleep; they are either bat-like or dragonish; Puddleglum does not know what any of them are. This is life tending towards entropy. The Earthmen have reduced speech to empty saws, "'Many sink down, and few return to the sunlit lands.'" Their vague city has few lights, they are noiseless even when in crowds, they take no interest in the travellers; even their cakes are flabby and tasteless (130). Increasing darkness accompanies the journey downwards through cave after cave. The Earthmen lead them to one golden light in the place, but it is a fraud, for it is in the Witch's lair. Inside it the Rilian they find is a mere gesturing husk (133-9).

Yet the way down away from the light is to prove the way up. Perhaps the story follows a fundamental Christian rhythm in this. It is when Puddleglum's foot touches bedrock that the charm is broken: for in thrusting his foot into the Witch's fire he has as it were touched the fiery element of Bism, the bottommost and true world of the abyss. Things then take their proper shapes, the Witch turns to a serpent, Rilian knows suddenly who he is, and the Earthmen are their true selves again. The world turns back to a place full of life and identity as the travellers make their way out of Underland into Narnia with its many different creatures all taking wild part in their Great Snow Dance (185-6).

There are other patterns behind the story. The imagery of descent from heights relates to the Fall;[20] though one must be careful not to draw the links too tightly here. A son of Adam and daughter of Eve have to go down from the vast height of Aslan's land to Narnia. They fall by several acts of disobedience and are saved through grace. But Rilian is perhaps the fullest expression of man bound in the chains of his sin by the tempter or serpent. His wish to avenge his mother's death on the serpent (there was something she tried to say to him before she died, and it was probably that he should not seek vengeance) has led him to find the green-clad woman and fall to her wiles in the very place of his mother's death; his flesh has rebelled against him. As Lilith, the succuba, the Witch has drained life from him. But when Rilian asks for Aslan's (Christ's) help in his need, he is eventually given it, and is saved and redeemed, and rises to take his true kingship in the country of his inheritance. So too, when the children trust to Aslan instead of their own resources, they are able to achieve their quest and to save another. This quest we may note, is for a 'treasure' of giving, not getting. Yet all would still have been lost without that further act of Christ-like sacrifice on the part of the Marsh-wiggle, curiously the more Christ-like for his comic and ungainly nature.

The story moves towards increasing enclosure – usually a bad sign in Lewis's books. We begin with the huge aerial perspective Jill is given over the world as she travels to Narnia, then the children journey to the flat lands of the March-wiggles, become closed in by the mountains, shut in a storm, imprisoned in a giant castle, trapped in underground caves and finally in a single room in which is a chair on which a person has to sit bound every day. The evil of the Witch is like a black hole: she sucks beings in and tells them nothing else exists – hence the "'few return to the sunlit lands'" of the Earthmen. The journey of the children and Puddleglum effectively unlocks these cages. Rilian is saved, Underland flooded, Bism opened to its inhabitants and the way to the Overland opened.

Thereafter the story becomes circular. We return to Narnia, to Aslan's land and to Experiment House in reverse direction from the way we came in. The symmetry of the story, its circular structure, is perhaps an imitation of the perfection of the sphere of Heaven. In a sense the narrative is 'enclosed' by this circle, but such enclosure is in stark contrast to that of the Witch, which diminishes all things to a point where the other expands like an open cone.

Last but not least, the story seems to contain a celebration of identity that counters the Witch's drive to nonentity. For at every phase we are reminded of the four elements, the basic constituents of being. There is the air of Aslan's breath, of the great distance down from the precipice, of the sky through which Jill flies, the cold air of Narnia when they break through from the Underland. Then there is the water of the sea, of the underground lakes and of the (purgative) flood released at the overthrow of the Witch. Earth appears in the Underland and the Earthmen themselves, and in the very muddy and rocky nature of the journey before that. Fire is found at the children's first meeting with the Marsh-wiggle, there is a blazing fire in the giant Porter's lodge, and then we have the Witch's fire, the joyous flames of Bism, and the firelight in the cave where the travellers are taken on their first return to Narnia. As these elements recur and intertwine with one another, they celebrate the very roots of being that the Witch denies. The Narnian Great Snow Dance amid which the travellers return seems in this light not only an ending but a symbol of something that has been happening all along.

THE HORSE AND HIS BOY (1954)

This story has little directly to do with Narnia, though it takes place at the time of the rule of the great Kings and Queens of Narnia (Edmund, Peter, Susan and Lucy) and they come into the story a little. It is set in the land of Calormen, where a boy Shasta lives with a poor fisherman he knows as his father. Actually this fisherman found him in a boat that ran aground nearby and brought him up as his own. One day a Tarkaan, or aristocratic warrior of that country, passes and offers to buy Shasta. While he and the fisherman are endlessly haggling over a price, Shasta moves some way off where the Tarkaan's horse is tethered. To his astonishment the horse speaks to him. For in fact it is a Narnian Talking Horse called Bree who has been sold aboad, but has never revealed his identity. Both he and Shasta are thus 'displaced persons'. The Horse offers to take Shasta to Narnia with him, the boy agrees, and they escape by night..

On the way they fall in with another Talking Horse, Hwin, a female, on a similar journey, carrying a well-to-do Calormene girl Aravis who is fleeing from an arranged marriage. In the Calormene city of Tashbaan they overhear Rabadash, son of the ruling Tisroc, plot to invade neighbouring Archenland to provide a base from which to strike at Narnia. Rabadash goes to gather two hundred mounted warriors, and Shasta and Aravis race across the desert and by a hidden pass reach Archenland to warn King Lune of that country of the approaching threat. At several points during the story Aslan appears, sometimes as an apparently wild lion, to drive or shepherd Shasta and Aravis forward. Lune, warned, takes to his castle, and Shasta goes on to Narnia to enlist help, returning with King Edmund and Queen Lucy at the head of an army. They lift the siege and overcome Rabadash's army. King Lune then recognises Shasta as his long-lost son Cor, stolen long ago (and brother to Corin). Cor is the rightful heir to the throne and becomes king on his father's death. He eventually marries Aravis; we are told however that the two horses Bree and Hwin, though happy in Narnia, do not marry.

This story is again well told, with a fine sense of humour. Here Lewis shows a capacity to enter fully into a culture that might have seemed alien to his temperament (though actually he had long been fascinated by it) – that of a quasi-Arabic society. The story owes something to the eighteenth-century oriental tale and the *Thousand and One Nights*, and the idiom of its discourse could also be traced to George Meredith's *The Shaving of Shagpat* (1856), Edward Fitzgerald's translation of 'The

Rubaiyat of Omar Khayyam' (1859) or James Elroy Flecker's play *Hassan* (1922). Here Lewis shows a readiness to go out of his usual preference for 'northern' and heroic romantic societies, and we will see this again in *Till We Have Faces*. Here, at one point, it is the northerners who are seen as strangers, when Shasta sees his first Narnians in Tashbaan (54).

The book is also different from the other Narnia stories in its resistance to flights of creative imagination. We move through a realistic landscape in a 'believable' society. Nothing radically new is done to the world, as in the other books. Though Shasta is to turn out the son of the king, we do not deal with him as a king in the narrative. Aslan intervenes from time to time to hurry the travellers along to warn King Lune, and now and then to give a moral scratch or nudge, but his presence has little of the numinous significance or metaphysical import that it has in the other books: there is no sense, for instance, of cosmic finalities such as resurrection or Aslan's land here. In most of the other books there is a death (or near-death, in the case of Digory's mother in *The Magician's Nephew*): but this story is much lighter. Rabadash, who sets out with bloodthirsty intent against Narnia, is not killed, but left dangling in disarray in a hook on which he has been caught. Then, transformed temporarily to a donkey by Aslan, he ends his days as Rabadash the Ridiculous.

This is the most 'local' of the Narnia books, in that it concerns the doings of a few private individuals. While there are wider issues in the conspiracy of Rabadash against King Lune - and even that is his own scheme, not openly backed by the Tisroc – the main emphasis is on the Horses and the two children. No 'epic' or 'national' significance hangs on their escape. Indeed the plot with Rabadash is to some extent grafted on to give such meaning to their journey as it proceeds. This is unfortunate, for it removes our attention from the earlier issue of the relations among Bree, Shasta, Aravis and Hwin, and instead involves us in mere exciting narrative with the occasional spiritual reminder - which makes the end of the story rather a gabble of events and resolutions.

If we consider the 'Narnia' books looked at so far in a line, we can see that they have followed a movement towards the more local. *The Lion* involves cosmic finalities of good and evil and the Deep Magic of death and resurrection within Narnia. *Prince Caspian* portrays the re-establishment of a full society in Narnia; *The Voyage* portrays a royal expedition to discover Aslan's land; *The Silver Chair* occurs outside Narnian society, in a search for a missing prince; and then this one.

The two preceding have also involved journeys beyond Narnia, to the World's End, and to Underland. But only in this book has Lewis gone out of his way to create a different society from that of Narnia. It may be one from which the central figures are escaping, but it is one given considerable reality and a certain amount of love. Calormen is, we have to recall, as much a creation of Aslan's as is Narnia or any other realm. But the fullness with which it is described helps to thicken the reality of Narnia too: far from being an island world created in a vacuum, it is joined on to other lands of different characters. This does not make it, for Lewis, of the same importance as other countries: the journey of the travellers towards it across inhospitable territory, and the fact that it is home to the horses – not to mention that it is the prime target of the Tisroc and of Rabadash's expedition – make it a focus, growing ever more real throughout. One commentator, Peter Schakel, has seen Narnia here and the longing for it by both the Horses and Shasta, who has always wished to go there, as an image of the desire of the soul, journeying through enemy territory towards its own 'far-off country', as Lewis called it. Doubtless too as Schakel says it has some roots in the story of Joseph's exile by his brothers and the journey of the Israelites across the desert to the Promised Land.[21] While such larger readings should not be over-emphasised, they too add density, as it were, to Narnia.

The story seems simple, and traditional: a peasant boy who turns out to be of noble parentage, a journey across a hostile land to a goal. Certainly it is fairly relaxed: we do not for much of the time feel that great issues hang on the escape of the travellers, and are more concerned with how they escape, and with the society they move through. Lewis delights in the description of the island city of Tashbaan. Even if certain crucial events occur there, we are left with a very full impression of the streets and houses and gardens, the smells and sights, and orotund, polite discourse of the Grand Vizier or the Tisroc, the languor of the aptly named society girl Lasaraleen. In such a context it may seem inappropriate to emphasize patterns of significance behind the narrative. Nevertheless, such patterns, however lightly, are there. Several have been pointed out by Peter Schakel.[22]

One theme is that relating to identity. Shasta realises that he is not the peasant's son; and he could be said to be searching for his true identity in the story – though his discovery is made more a justification for leaving the peasant than a motive for finding out about himself. During the narrative he proves himself in various adventures, to the point where he has shown himself to be of nobler birth than appears. At one point he is mistaken by the royal Narnians visiting Tashbaan for his brother Corin. However it is not until the dénouement where both brothers come together publicly, that he can be correctly identified.

Meanwhile Aravis has been proud and disdainful towards Shasta – though this diminishes through the story as she realises his inherent worth (not his rank). Her insistence on self is a measure of her lack of a true self. She refuses (if rightly) to go through an arranged marriage and escapes; she is frequently in disguise; she is literally leaving her self behind because alone of the group she is leaving her own country.

As for the Horse Bree, he is so insistent on his superiority of blood, prowess and insight that he makes numerous mistakes and has to be brought down several pegs to a plain view of himself: the Hermit just inside Archenland tells him, "'You're not quite the great Horse you had come to think... But as long as you know you're nobody very special, you'll be a very decent sort of Horse, on the whole'" (*The Horse and His Boy*,129). Rabadash also values himself more highly than he should, insisting on his identity as descendant of Tash even to Aslan (182); and the doom of his transformation to an ass thus falls on him. The law of the story seems to be that those who takes themselves for less than they are may find that they are more, and vice versa. But as well as finding his royal self, Shasta also finds something of his true identity in Christ or Aslan, who meets him and guides him on the road into Narnia. When he asks who Aslan is, he is told, three times, "'Myself'" (139; the word goes back to the 'I am' of Yahweh in Exodus 3, 14).

Other lesser themes of the story concern freedom and slavery, and apparent luck and providence. In escaping from Calormen the travellers are leaving a place of severe constraint for one of easy freedom. Shasta's fisherman 'father' is a tyrant to him, and the first act in the novel is his selling Shasta as a slave. Aravis is escaping from an enforced marriage. If the Narnian visitors do not accept Rabadash's proposal of marriage to Queen Susan she will be made his wife, or slave, by force. The Tisroc detests Narnia because it is 'free' (97, 99). The Narnians as seen by Shasta on first meeting them in Tashbaan are a complete contrast: 'instead of being grave and mysterious like most Calormenes, they walked with a swing and let their arms and shoulders go free, and chatted and laughed. One was whistling' (54). They have come to Calormen to enter into free alliance with that country through marriage; and they regard it as equally a matter of free choice to decide against that marriage if it is not agreeable to their Queen. But the Calormenes think always not of the free marriage of individuals, but of the absorption (and cancellation of identity) of one by the other – of the wife by the husband, of all other countries through the conquest by Calormen. The 'marriage-plots' and the Rabadash and war-plots are thus different faces of the same coin.

There is also a theme of luck and providence in the story, whereby what seems to be pure accident bringing the travellers through their dangers is often – probably always – the result of interventions by Aslan (139).[23] The Hermit says, "'I ... have never yet met any such thing as Luck'" (126). Such submerged patterning, by which every act, however random-seeming, is actually arranged, is in a way something of a parallel to the patterns of significance that are to be found hidden in the apparently casual details of the story itself. Such arrangements are not constraints on action of the Calormene kind: choice is still free, even if choice is foreseen, and even if the acts presented to choice are pre-arranged. Aslan may alter acts, for instance when he makes the Horses of Shasta and Aravis come together at night (28-33), but he leaves choice free. In a sense he combines and transcends Calormene constraint and Narnian freedom. We are not always to find the freedom of Narnia simply a good: when Shasta first arrives there to warn them of danger he finds that many of the creatures are rather 'head-in-the-sand', and talk more than act: 'For the truth was that in that golden age when the Witch and the Winter had gone and Peter the High King ruled at Cair Paravel, the smaller woodland people of Narnia were so safe and happy that they were getting a little careless' (145).

There is some growth of society throughout the story. Shasta at first is alone; then Bree joins with him; and later Aravis and Hwin. But though together they are still apart, for Bree and Aravis are variously snobbish. In Tashbaan they separate. Shasta finds poignantly temporary society with the Narnians, but they have taken him for the prince he is not, and he leaves them when the rightful prince returns. Aravis finds that her friend Lasaraleen is far more shallow that she has previously had occasion to notice. When she comes together again with Shasta she is now more amenable, and the ride across the harsh desert binds the group more closely. Yet again in Archenland they are separated and Shasta must go on to Narnia, whence he returns with help in the battle against Rabadash. With his recognition as prince he finds family and society at once; and Aravis stays and later marries him. Bree and Hwin find their kind in Narnia.

Yet this pattern of increasingly 'social' emphasis does not perhaps come over as strongly as it might: there is a frequent sense of isolation in the story. We do not really see much of Aravis getting to know Shasta: it is more a statement of humble intent by her than a developing relationship. In a way the closest bond Shasta forms in the story is with Aslan during the night of his dangerous journey to Narnia. Otherwise, for most of the story he is the lonely peasant boy, forced to leave Narnian society in Tashbaan, snubbed by Aravis and enduring a night of isolation at the tombs outside the city. Aravis herself is rootless, having left her family, and finding her friend a broken reed: even the great ruler of her country turns out to be murderously treacherous, when she accidentally overhears his midnight conversation with Rabadash. Rabadash too is a curiously lonely figure. The Tisroc his father regards him as a rash fool who may serve his purposes but from whose exploits he will dissociate himself; and he ends his life as a figure of fun. The Horses Bree and Hwin do not marry. Throughout the travellers are alone in a hostile land, which is largely uninhabited. Just inside Archenland they come to a hermit, a solitary. Many scenes take place by night – the selling of Shasta, the meeting with Aravis and Hwin, the meeting of the Tisroc and Rabadash, Shasta's vigil at the tombs, the escape across the desert, the journey to Narnia. The desert itself is a symbol of loneliness. This story largely concerns how one manages 'on one's own': the others have all had schemes arranged by Aslan or a larger social unit in them. It is in many ways as much a book about coming to terms with one's essential isolation as about coming together with others.

 Other themes lie in the differences between Calormen and Narnia. The Calormene people conceal things. Their orotund, polite language, is used to cover violent reality. We see this right from the start in the whining language of the peasant selling Shasta to the Tarkaan. The Narnians, by contrast, are open and informal. The Calormenes enclose things too. Their crowded city Tashbaan is on an island: it is as though all the population of the country shrank into it, since much of the land about it seems empty.

 By contrast Archenland and Narnia seem to have no cities – though there are castles, such as that of King Lune, in which Rabadash and his army shut him up. But when Shasta first encounters King Lune he is out hunting in the country with his courtiers. There is no absorptive centre here. We are in two different but friendly kingdoms; Narnia has not one but four Kings and Queens, and is populated as much by talking animals as humans; the travellers themselves are temporarily split up between the two kingdoms. But Tashbaan's gates are regularly closed: it is inward looking, inwards up progressively less dirty streets to a centre.

And at the centre squats a scheming Tisroc who lives only for himself, indifferent even to his no less savage children.

Shasta's Calormene nature at first leads him to hide things: not knowing 'how noble and free-born people behave', he will not tell the Narnians in Tashbaan the truth about himself or ask for their help (66-7); after this, and a piece of suspicion concerning Aravis (75-6), he finds himself outside the locked city, exposed to terror of the tombs. Now he no longer shuts himself in or conceals things. Later in the narrative he goes out of himself in helping others, such as Aravis or Archenland; and in the dark on his way to Narnia he opens his story to a strange Voice - which already knows it and simply asks for it so that Shasta may learn to give it up (138-9). After that he is able to reveal himself to the Narnians as the boy who in Tashbaan let them take him for Prince Corin (150).

The Calormenes are a divided race. There is division throughout between high-born and low-born in the story of Aravis and Shasta. The first episode of the book is the meeting of the contemptuous knight or Tarkaan with the grovelling peasant fisherman. In Tashbaan there is clear division of high from low in literal terms of elevation of streets. Lasaraleen boasts of how she mixes with the palace people and the Tisroc; but she is actually terrified of the Tisroc when she sees him (89, 92). And there is sexual inequality – no coming together of equals as with Shasta and Aravis at the end, but rigid suppression of the female by the male. In Calormen as said there is a split between extreme politeness of manners and discourse on the one hand, and savagery of intent on the other. This is imaged in the landscape itself, in the generally beautiful city amid the wild desert and beasts outside it. Calormen is a place of little integration with nature. In Narnia men and Talking Beasts live together, while in Calormen the beasts are shut out and savage; even Aslan here appears as a wild lion. The Calormene notion of vertical division between one order and another, whether through class, sex or species, is in Narnia answered by one of equality.

But not just in Narnia: and here perhaps we come to at least one reason for Lewis's having written a story about the escape of both Horses and humans. The Horses are not mere 'horses': they are Talking Horses, full citizens of Narnia with rights equal to those of humans. This is what both Shasta and Aravis have to learn on their journey. At the same time the Horses, or rather Bree, have to come down from their excessive valuation of themselves and learn to accept others on their own merits. The whole journey then becomes an education in equality, in which each contributes his or her part to their success – the Horses their speed, Aravis her knowledge of Rabadash's plans, Shasta his bravery at need. That is why the title of the book, *The Horse and his Boy*, is peculiarly appropriate as an ironic inversion. It says much for Lewis that in all of this there is not a single overtone of Swift's Houyhnhnms and their condescension towards man.

One still wonders, though, at the choice of horses in particular as companions. Doubtless, of course, for their ability to carry the humans: yet one recalls that in the Renaissance the horse was a symbol of the passions and was thus ironically used by Swift as the exemplar of reason. And Lewis was well aware of the significance of the centaur to which he gives such pride of place in Narnia.

THE MAGICIAN'S NEPHEW (1955)

This story describes the creation of Narnia. Two Edwardian children from different families, Digory and Polly, find that Digory's Uncle Andrew is a magician who has discovered a way of travelling into other worlds using magic rings. This Uncle Andrew manages to trick the children into making the journey so that they can tell him what it is like. Their first journey takes them to a dying world called Charn, where they inadvertently bring to life the statue of a beautiful but cruel woman. She is Jadis, destroyer of Charn, who is later to be the evil White Witch in Narnia. Despite the children's efforts, she comes with them back to London where she creates havoc, before they once more succeed in using Uncle Andrew's magic rings to take her into another world. This world proves at first to be quite dark and rocky; but soon they hear singing, stars come out, grass and trees cover the land, and then all manner of creatures, including Talking Beasts, are created by a great singing Lion. The Witch throws an ineffectual missile at the lion and flees.

When the creation of Narnia by Aslan – for that is what it is – is complete, Digory is asked by Aslan to help protect the country from the Witch he has brought there. He is to journey to a walled garden in the mountains of the far Western Wild to pluck and return with an apple from the tree he will find in the centre of the garden. Besides Digory, Polly and the Witch, there have also been brought into Narnia a cab-driver and his horse, commandeered in London by the Witch. The horse is transformed by Aslan into a Pegasus, and flies Digory and Polly to the remote garden. Once there, Digory must go in alone. When he has plucked an apple, he is met by the Witch, who has already eaten one and bids him do so too. Her main temptation however is directed at Digory's love for his very sick mother back in London, for she tells him to take her an apple that will cure her. Digory refuses and takes the apple back to Aslan, who then tells him to throw it into the Narnian earth.

Then Aslan makes the cab-driver Frank and his wife Helen (the latter now brought by special magic), into King and Queen of Narnia. After this, the apple Digory threw is found to have grown into a tree bearing fruit, which as long as it stands will keep the Witch far from Narnia. Aslan now gives Digory an apple for his mother and sends him home with Polly. The apple cures Digory's mother, his father comes back rich from abroad, and the family go to live in a big country house as Digory has always wanted.

The structure of travel in the book, the London context, and especially the drama of the Witch's invasion of London are all close to the method of E. Nesbit's *The Story of Amulet* (Lewis used the same idea of an Atlantean source of magic material for the rings in his story),[24] but the creation story and the presence of Aslan and the Witch are quite outside E. Nesbit's idiom. The work of George MacDonald, fairy tale, science fiction (for the picture of Charn), Milton for the creation (*Paradise Lost*, Book VII)[25] and the garden, these are some of Lewis's other sources. He has welded them as does Aslan into a marvellous new creation that, so far as its laws go, rings true at every point.

Nevertheless this is also one of the most restless-seeming of the Narnia books. No sooner are we in one world or situation than we are whisked into another – from Edwardian London to the dead world of Charn, back to London with the Witch, off to a strange dark place which Aslan turns into Narnia, then on a journey to a magic tree, and finally back to London again. In *The Voyage of the 'Dawn Treader'*, where there is also continual change of context (though the *Dawn Treader* itself is a constant) the journey was much more directional than here: we knew the voyage was in quest of Aslan's land; but here we do not know for long where anything is leading.

This restlessness in *The Magician's Nephew* may suit with the idea of creation, of being woken up, that informs the book. But it also gives a sense of contingency. This sense is incidentally furthered by the way the death of Charn, so strikingly described, plays against the creation of Narnia; or even in the way that the open nature that is Narnia (the first thing Digory does is fly out into its furthest reaches) is contrasted with the shut-in realm of Charn (name an inversion of Narnia?), which seems one continuous built up area, and where there are few perspectives. Each undercuts the other.

Both of the last books of the Narnian series (the other being *The Last Battle*) are full of the sense that reality can in the next moment be quite otherwise than it is. This is one reason why it is appropriate that these books should come at the end of the sequence, for they remove the previous security of being. Narnia, thickened and made more steadily 'there' up to *The Horse and His Boy*, now seems to shimmer before us, whether into being or nonentity, pointing us to the deeper and more true Narnia in heaven with which the series is to end.[26] In both the last books there is a variety of settings. In *The Magician's Nephew* there is a kind of magical airport between worlds, a strange wood full of little pools of water: if one jumps into a pool with a certain colour of ring on, one comes to a new world (or equally can return to one's own). Edwardian London, the wood between the worlds, Charn, Narnia: all interpenetrate; people and objects from one world are moved into others; the boundaries of things are not hard and clear-cut. Most of the many worlds appear in the first half of this novel, while in *The Last Battle* they come at the end, as Narnia begins to be turned into something else: the one has them on the way 'in' the other on the way 'out', as suits with their dealing respectively with First and Last Things.

The sense of contingency in *The Magician's Nephew* is increased by the impression that much happens by accident. Of course, in Aslan's universe, nothing happens by chance: but we are usually given some hint of the fact – or, as with Shasta in *The Horse and His Boy*, overtly told that what seemed random was in fact Aslan all the time (139). Here the sense of the accidental is heightened, without any such explanation being offered: even if we do find an explanation, the strangeness is still there. The children meet one summer: it is raining, so they must play indoors. Polly has made a secret place of a corner of the attic of her house in the terrace in which they live. Once there Digory sees that there is a gap which might make it possible to squeeze through from one attic to another along the whole line of houses. There is an empty house beyond Digory's, which is next door to Polly's, and the two resolve to explore it. They carefully work out the number of rafters they will have to step over to get there, but when they reach where they think the empty house starts they find a closed door in a brick wall. This turns out when they enter it to be Uncle Andrew's study. The children assume they have made a mistake counting the rafters and must still be above Digory's house, but one cannot be sure. In the study they are caught by Uncle Andrew, whose secret magical researches have reached a point where two children are '"just what I wanted"' (*The Magician's Nephew*, 19). This is the first coincidence.

When Uncle Andrew has tricked the children into using his magic rings, they find themselves in the strange wood between worlds with pools in it, out of one of which they have emerged. They work out that each of the pools must be the way to a world, and jump through another chosen at random. Once through, they find themselves in a ruined city world called Charn. Polly wants to return, but Digory encourages her to explore, telling her that they can return home at any time using their magic rings. They take a building in the city at random and wander through it as fancy chooses, through halls, courtyards, and rooms until at length they come to two huge doors, slightly ajar. (It may be that the whole city is constructed as a maze, so that whatever direction is taken always ends at this point; but this is never hinted.)

Inside the doors is a great room full of people who are actually statues. They are sitting in a line, the first looking good and happy, but growing progressively more solemn and then evil-looking as the line proceeds. There is a little table in the centre of the room and on it a little hammer and a golden bell. On the golden hoop that holds the bell is written, *'Make your choice, adventurous Stranger;/Strike the bell and bide the danger,/Or wonder, till it drives you mad,/What would have followed if you had'* (50). Polly does not want the danger, but Digory says the act must be done: he does not want to go mad thinking what might have happened. The deed does not at this stage seem particularly *wrong*: it is an act of mere curiosity, it seems, and that is all. But it wakes the evil Witch.

The children try to flee back to their world without her. They think that if they put on their magic rings she will be left behind: but in fact, so long as she has hold of a part of the children she will come too, and she has her hands twined in Polly's hair. Accident and the contingent seem to rule. They all find themselves in the wood between worlds, where the Witch loses much of her strength. Realising now that the Witch must not be allowed to touch them at all, the children break free of her and jump into the pool to take them home. But still the Witch has managed to seize hold of Digory's ear at the last moment, and thus she is brought to London. Eventually the children are able to use the newfound attributes of the rings to remove her from there back to the wood. They arrive there with her on the back of a hansom cab-horse she had taken over, together with the cabman and with Uncle Andrew. The horse, tired after its exertions, wanders over to a pool to have a drink. Digory has his hand on the Witch's ankle, Polly is holding Digory's other hand and Uncle Andrew holding Polly's, while the cabbie has his hand on the horse: the result is that all of them fall through the pool into a new world. They have arrived in what is to be Narnia by apparent complete accident, and with a number of accidental companions and even objects (the Witch with a torn-off piece of lamp-post; Digory with some toffees). At this point they hear the singing that is to bring this world to creation. Have they stumbled on an act that was about to occur anyway? Or has their arrival triggered it? For the time at least we think the former: the sense of the contingent is at its strongest.

After this, by contrast, everything is highly planned and organised by Aslan. The Witch is powerless and soon flees. Aslan makes the world, he appoints a place in it for the cabdriver, he sets Digory a task and transforms the horse so that it may carry him to it. Digory returns with the apple, the coronation is organised, the tree grows. Digory is given the apple and returned home. The whole narrative has become much more directed. The curious thing about this change from the 'accidental' to the organised is that it occurs exactly halfway through the book, when we reach Narnia.

Now, we can say that Lewis is letting life be as real and random as it likes before showing that it observes a pattern, just as (in a different way) Oedipus's unwitting wanderings in fact brought the details of a hideous prophecy to pass. Or one can say that events have, as with the experience of Ransom on Perelandra, being 'caught up into the larger pattern', where 'the whole distinction between things accidental and things designed' is seen to be 'purely terrestrial', and 'there is no such thing as chance or fortune beyond the Moon' (*Perelandra*, 135). It is probable that this is the intended meaning behind the shift in *The Magician's Nephew*, and that this in a sense is its deeper significance: but Lewis has chosen here to do it without any direct statement or underlining, so that we have to feel our way – if we do at all – beyond the bafflingly accidental for ourselves.

The ruling metaphor of the book is one of growth. The first growth is seen in the kinds of magic seen at work. The children's play adventure becomes more and more a real one. They embark on an exploration of a house that turns into discovery of Digory's supposedly crazy uncle. But the uncle proves to be more than crazy, a magician. Then by means of his magic rings and laws of magic the children are able to visit strange worlds. A magic bell then releases the Witch, and she comes back to life. She is a far greater magician than Uncle Andrew: she long ago destroyed Charn using the 'Deplorable Word'. Her whole objective is domination and destruction. But when she reaches Narnia her power is as nothing against the Lion, and she flees. Like the stars spreading in the dark sky, or the grass spreading over the bare earth, so the magic of the book has finally dilated to this Deep Magic of creativity. (The pattern is not unlike that of the magic in *The Voyage of the 'Dawn Treader'*.) The Witch can only pervert things already made: here we see them in the making.

Yet the deepest Magic is perhaps that which we would not think magical at all: the free choice of a creature to walk in its creator's will, as Digory does in resisting the temptation to take the apple from the garden for his mother and in bringing it back to Aslan. It is true that the apple was needed for Narnia, to protect it against the Witch: but that was only part of the truth. The deeper truth was that the creator was giving his creature the chance to work some of the magic for itself: Digory is contributing to the making of Narnia. And what he is contributing is not only the apple but the moral strength he exercised to bring it back.

Then there is also a growth in perspective throughout the book, in a way that recalls the gradual extension of view in *Out of the Silent Planet*. First we are in the narrow places of the attic, and then this opens into the light of Uncle Andrew's study; from the study the children go into the wood between the world; then to a world they can walk through, Charn. But still there is a sense of enclosure, if a diminishing one, in the close air of the wood and the confining buildings of Charn. And so back to London where the street and the behaviour of people rather cramp the Witch's style. Thence to Narnia, which as the light comes and creation begins, gradually extends and comes to life before them. In Narnia the children make their first real journey over distance. Finally, back in England, Digory's family can leave London for the country.

As the growth of view has proceeded, so has the understanding of the children. At first they do not have an accurate view of how the rings work, or the wood between the worlds, or the bell in Charn: they find these out by experiment. They thus have knowledge, but not insight. Though they can control where they go, they cannot control what happens there. Nor have they any larger vision of consequences. They, and Uncle Andrew, are all in their way responsible for the introduction of the Witch into Narnia. In Narnia however the children learn to think no longer locally or for the moment. They are given a task, and a meaningful framework in which to carry it out: and they know it is a task with great consequences. What were previously acts forced on them, or ignorant choices, or choices frustrated, or events for which they had to find a remedy – Uncle Andrew tricking them into use of the rings, their going to Charn, releasing the Witch, trying in vain to escape her, taking her out of their own world – become fully free and knowing choices, the choice to go to the Western Wild to pluck the apple, the choice not to take more than one apple, the choice to resist the Witch and take the apple back to Aslan, and throw it as he asks in the mud. Then, living freely in the idiom of Aslan, the children need no more apparatus of magic, no more rings: in Aslan's world magic is done by singing.

The children grow morally as they become more able to control their lives. Magic is associated with curiosity. It is Digory who suggests to Polly that they explore the attics, and thus brings them to Uncle

Andrew. Uncle Andrew plays on Polly's vanity before encouraging her to look at and touch the magic rings. Curiosity makes Digory decide to try to enter another world before returning to their own. Once in Charn, he persuades Polly against her will to stay and explore. In the room of people they eventually come to he is the one who cannot bear the thought of not knowing what would have happened if he did not strike the bell (Aslan's view is always that the 'would have' is much less important than the 'is'). In a sense Digory can be seen, however ignorantly, to have eaten of the tree of knowledge; and it is he therefore who must go to a new garden of Eden in Narnia, and cancel his sin by plucking an apple for Aslan. On the golden gates to that garden there is a magic rhyme which answers that in the hall in Charn, asking care for others and not for the self (146).

If we think Digory's sin small, perhaps the image of the Witch's bell in Charn may provide an answer: it is a tiny bell in all that huge room and city; it might seem that to awaken the great Witch some vast gong might be more appropriate; but when that little bell, corresponding to Digory's little sin, is struck, its tone grows louder and louder till its sound not only wakens the Witch but brings all Charn to final ruin. In Lewis's universe, the smallest act can have the greatest implications:[27] this motif pervades the story, so that tiny grains of dust in the rings give them their power, the singing of a 'mere' lion creates a whole world, a cab-driver and his wife become a King and Queen, a cab-horse is changed to a Pegasus and a child brings a single fruit that will save all Narnia from the Witch. So here, as the evil spreads outwards and eventually enters Narnia. The way the Witch keeps hold of the children despite their best efforts perhaps shows that she is a part of them. But it is not so simple as this, for Digory feels sorry for the Witch when she asks them not to leave her to suffer in the wood between the worlds, and it is this pity which also allows her to seize hold of him (66).

After this there is a steady moral advance. At first the children simply wanted to get away from the Witch. In London, however, their object becomes one of saving their world from her by removing her from it: but whatever world she goes to she will try to wreck, and their good intentions are still undermined by the initial act of releasing her. It is when Digory brings himself to confess his sin in Charn to Aslan, and he has been forgiven, that a new start can be made. The act that Digory must now carry out is one of obedience. His errors before were of self-will: he would determine the future and bring it to pass. That is the temptation he is faced with in the garden: why should he trust Aslan, why should he not take another apple for himself, why should he not use the apple he has plucked to help his sick mother rather than take it back for Aslan's uncertain purposes? He refuses: he gives himself back into Aslan's hand: he chooses not to follow himself and his personal wishes, but rather a far deeper wish, which is to obey out of love. And in doing so he gains all that he could have taken for himself, and much more.

If the children grow, the Witch declines. She sits at the end of a steady devolutionary line of people in the hall in Charn. At first she seems just faintly ambiguous morally. Her destruction of Charn by the use of the Deplorable Word is reported rather than seen. In London she is a giant figure, exciting no doubt ignorant amazement. Lewis is careful to avoid any facile attraction for her as a colourful primitive disturbing grey respectability: but still, even in her absurdity – and there are ludicrous clashes between her understanding of the world and the reality – she comes over as almost human. The children have to manage her like some dangerous relative. But once in Narnia she is, as it were, thrown out of solution. She hates the Lion on sight and tries to kill it. She turns into the Evil One in eating the fruit and in her temptation of Digory. She becomes a dreadful creature of night. And finally she, who was surrounded by people throughout, from the people in the hall at Charn, to the children, their relatives and London society, is seen setting off alone towards the north.

Uncle Andrew, with his feebler depravity, does not follow quite this journey. He is punished within the story. He, who thought to use others to further his schemes with magic, finds himself overpowered by the forces he has raised. The Witch treats him with contempt as a meddling fool. In Narnia he cannot experience the broadening vision of others: in his darkened mind he cannot understand the speech of the Talking Beasts as anything but the noises of plain beasts; nor can they understand his language. They treat him, albeit with some affection, as a lower creature. At first they think him a tree, and try to plant and water him; then they see him as some kind of unhappy animal and cage him and try to feed him with their foods. (The cage is a good symbol of Uncle Andrew's narrow view of reality.) But, however mistakenly, they love him as a pet: he is made any unwilling part of their society, just as at home in London he is still a part of the family and husband to the delightful Aunt Letty, who knows how to put him down. At the end there is some reform. 'Uncle Andrew never tried any magic again as long as he lived. He had learned his lesson, and in his old age he became a nicer and less selfish old man than he had ever been before' (171).

In the story characters often have fixed notions that are challenged. The Witch cannot believe that any but a great magician could have released her, and tells the children to take her to meet Uncle Andrew, who she thinks must be the source of their power. This is partly her pride: she cannot believe that she, a great enchantress, could be released by a mere child. She lives by the sublime: she is to suffer the ridiculous. Aunt Letty, faced by the Witch, can see her only in her own terms, as either a "'Shameless hussy'" or drunk, and then, when the Witch has thrown her across the room, as "'a dangerous lunatic'". The people in the street jeer at her claim to be the Empress Jadis, admire her strength, demand her imprisonment for theft, and become enraged at her when she uses violence on them. The joy of the Lion cannot enter the Witch or Uncle Andrew. Uncle Andrew treats the Witch as a naughty woman who has caused him immense trouble (98); he cannot see her for what she is any more than he can see Narnia for what it truly is. Digory himself has his 'idée fixe' concerning his sick mother: he nearly lets it determine what he does with the magic apple, but learns to give apple and idea to Aslan to do with as he pleases. The world cannot be known truly unless one comes out of one's ready-made ideas of it – which ultimately means growing out of oneself.

Growing out of oneself here involves growing towards one's true self, a process that is never ended in this world. The cabbie, in Narnia, loses his sharp city ways and recovers his open, country nature; the horse, Strawberry, is given wings and called, appropriately, Fledge; Uncle Andrew is given a false self by the Talking Animals and there is evidence that later in life he grew nearer a true one. Digory brings his mother back to health and her natural self; the family returns to its proper roots in the country, in their former house.

When one grows aright, one's growth serves others: it is caught up into a larger pattern. Digory is to grow up to be the Professor Kirke in whose house the children of *The Lion, the Witch and the Wardrobe* are to find their way into Narnia. The core of the apple he gave to revive his mother, when planted in the garden of a London house, grows to a fine apple tree: when one day a storm blows it down Digory has a wardrobe made from its wood; and it is that wardrobe, made of 'Narnia-seeking' wood that transports the Pevensies to Narnia. In this way the story in *The Magician's Nephew* literally grows into that of *The Lion*.

Like Narnia, which opens out, truth goes far beyond the boundaries that we give it. The creation of Narnia, described in terms of continuous movement – Aslan walking as he sings, the stars coming into the sky, the grass and trees growing in a wave, the animals starting from the ground - is an image of the essential plasticity of the self in God's hand. Charn, the world of dead rigidity, is the antitype. It is the Witch who, eating one of the magic apples, becomes finally locked into herself: Aslan says, "'length of days with an evil heart is only length of misery and already she begins to know it'" (162).

In no other of the Narnia books does Lewis allow adults so much space. The Witch herself plays a continuing part throughout the story, as does Uncle Andrew. There are Aunt Letty, and the people in the London street; there are the cabbie and his wife; and there is Digory's mother, framing the whole. Digory's mother is to some extent a symbol of Digory himself: she is ill for much of the narrative until he has come 'right' with himself. With adults about, we are more aware of children as the new generation, which fits with the theme of creation and growth. We are also being shown how adults are more inclined than children to become shut in on themselves, as Uncle Andrew is shut in his study with his secret. And adults who seek to manipulate children, forfeit all claim to respect, and are indeed themselves more childish than children. The presence of the adults Frank and Helen among the creatures of Narnia makes it more of a family, and it is with a family that we end as Digory's is restored to him.

Perhaps the deepest theme of *The Magician's Nephew* is how out of evil is grown a greater good. The magical meddlings of Uncle Andrew set in chain the whole process that is to end in Narnia. Digory's curiosity sets loose the Witch: but in a sense it also initiates the creation of Narnia. Always the lesser becomes the greater, and some better thing is made. Even the broken piece of lamp-post turns into a whole shining lamp-post that is to light the way back to this world in *The Lion, the Witch and the Wardrobe*. If Charn dies, Narnia is born. Out of beasts come Talking Beasts. Out of a cab-driver comes a King, out of a cab-horse a Pegasus. Out of an apple got in obedience comes a whole tree to preserve Narnia. Out of an act done for another comes the act most desired for the self. The whole book unfolds like creation itself. It is in the end an exhibition of divine power and love still more than it is a chapter in the history of Narnia.

THE LAST BATTLE (1956)

This book begins in the west of Narnia, in 'the last days', with a Talking Ape called Shift and a stupid donkey called Puzzle. Shift uses the donkey to carry out uncongenial tasks for him. One day they find an old lion's skin and Shift has the idea of dressing Puzzle in it and making it known that Aslan, who has not been seen in Narnia for a long time, has now returned. The trick works only too well on the Narnian Talking Beasts, especially since the disguised Puzzle is shown to them only at a distance and in poor light, normally keeping to his stable. Various orders imputed to 'Aslan' are conveyed by Shift to the credulous Narnians. They are to work for new Calormene masters, to cut down Narnia trees for timber. Warned by a Dryad, King Tirian of Narnia comes from his far-off country retreat, but he is captured and his crown hidden by a Calormene, before he is bound a prisoner near the stable. As Tirian watches the presentations by night of 'Aslan' to the Narnians, he sees the deception that is being practised.

In his despair Tirian calls on the help of the great Kings and Queens of Narnia, and has a vision of them all seated together in England. They see him too, but neither can communicate. Immediately after this, two of the children, Eustace and Jill Pole (the others are too old) appear beside Tirian and release him. It later transpires that they were planning to come anyway, by using two of the magic rings we saw at work in *The Magician's Nephew*; but while they were travelling by train to meet Peter and Edmund, who had found the rings, they felt a bump and found themselves in Narnia.

With Tirian, they discover the disguised Puzzle in his stable and take him away. But their enemies, who now include a Calormene Tarkaan and a Talking Cat, are too cunning for them, and their hopes of proving to the Narnians that Shift has deceived them are frustrated, because their enemies produce another story before them. The Ape tells the Narnians that a donkey dressed as Aslan has been going about the country in his name, and has been devoured by him; now, angry at this deed, Aslan will no longer come from the stable. In this way the falsehood may be preserved and the Narnians remain subjected.

However, Shift has now admitted many Calormenes to Narnia under licence to use the Talking Beasts to cut down Narnian timber in return for cash. The Narnians cannot understand how Aslan could authorise this, particularly since the Calormenes have a hideous vulture-like god called Tash who is the opposite of Aslan in every way. To answer them, the Ape tells them that Tash and Aslan are actually the same God under different names, and that Aslan should now be known as Tashlan. Thus invoked, the dreadful god Tash himself eventually appears in the stable: invited by these corrupt means, corruption comes; the children and Tirian smell the death-reek as he stalks like a cloud past them on his journey (75-7). When the plotters stage a demonstration of Aslan's continued 'presence' by having a specially picked member of their group volunteer to enter the stable, the place is far from empty as they supposed. Tirian and the children now attempt an attack, supported by some of the Narnias, but Calormene reinforcements overwhelm them and they are driven through the stable door.

There they find not Tash, but a great, open, sunny place, and in it all the other people who have entered Narnia throughout its history. Aslan appears, and standing at the stable door he looks out on Narnia and brings towards him all its creatures for a final judgment, before he causes the end of that world and then has the door finally closed. The children are bid to travel 'farther up and farther in': and as they do so they realise that the country they are now in is a new and more real Narnia. They meet all the old friends of previous adventures, and gradually journey through progressively more 'real' Narnias till they are on their way to Aslan's land. There, as they approach, Aslan meets them and tells them they will not be going home as they are all dead, having been brought to Narnia via a railway accident that killed all of them and their parents, whom they now see coming towards them over a neck of land from a more real England. Then Aslan changes, and they begin 'Chapter One of the Great Story which no one on earth has read: which goes on for ever: in which every chapter is better than the one before'.

The most striking feature of this moving story is the way we begin with a mere Ape and Donkey in an obscure part of Narnia and end with the destruction of the world and with heaven. To say the least there seems a certain disproportion, and this sense prevails right through most of the Narnian doings when they are compared to the later ones. Further, there is the contrast of tone. Never before in Narnia have we had to deal with such vulgar events. Where is the beauty of Narnia when we are reduced to a nasty Ape with a dirty scheme? It is the pettiness and absurdity that strikes us too. The story begins with the Ape, 'merely' an unpleasant creature, deceiving his friend Puzzle into carrying out the more tiresome activities of life for him. If water is to be got, the Ape fills the skin bottles, but Puzzle has to carry them; when food has to be brought, Puzzle brings it back in heavy panniers. Then the best things are eaten by the Ape, who says, '"You see, Puzzle, I can't eat grass and thistles like you, so it's only fair I should make it up in other ways." And Puzzle always said, "Of course, Shift, of course. I see that"' (*The Last Battle*, 7). Life seems to have shrivelled down to the nasty and mean. The drifting lion's skin which at the risk of his life Puzzle recovers for Shift from Caldron Pool seems at first mere garbage: it is hard to take seriously Shift's plan to disguise Puzzle as Aslan, or to believe that he can possibly succeed in deceiving the Narnians with so grotesque a travesty – especially as 'A good deal of Puzzle's grey nose and face could be seen through the open mouth of the lion's head. No one who had ever seen a real lion would have been taken in for a moment.' But that, it seems, is the point: no one in Narnia seems to have seen Aslan, let alone an ordinary wild lion, for a very long time; and thus, 'if someone who had never seen a lion looked at Puzzle in his lion skin he might just mistake him for a lion, if he didn't come too close, and if the light was not too good, and if Puzzle didn't let out a bray and didn't make any noise with his hoofs' (14-15).

But in fact this Ape, with his mean nature and his tawdry, scarce-credible little plan, is an image in some degree of what Narnia has sunk to: the extent to which the Narnians will believe in his deception is a measure of their own degradation.[28] So too is the long absence of Aslan and even that of ordinary lions from Narnia. This is Narnia, we are told on the first page, in its 'last days', on its last legs.[29] As the story proceeds, it is progressively less even this Narnia: the woods are felled, the place gradually filled with Calormenes until a sea attack takes Cair Paravel. Life has shrunk to the periphery, and the Talking Beasts of Narnia have been gathered about a fraudulent hovel on the kingdom's skirts rather than freely about their king.

Meanwhile the King himself is alone, without parents, siblings, wife or children: he wanders about the country as a displaced person; his only refuge and source of arms is a damp tower. We first meet him in a hunting lodge, a 'low, thatched building', where he has retired as is his wont in spring, to live at ease away from 'the state and pomp of Cair Paravel, the royal city' (17). Cair Paravel is taken in his absence. In a way he has half-abdicated. He is listening to news of 'Aslan' but doing nothing. When he has direct evidence of the death of Talking Trees, he rushes off to deal with the matter accompanied only by Jewel, a unicorn; torpor is followed by unthinking activity. When he finds two Calormenes driving a Talking Horse he kills them in a rage, and then, at the thought that they were unarmed, is ashamed at himself. He thinks that he has gone against Aslan, who, the Talking Horse tells him, has commanded that the Narnian beasts work as they do; and he gives himself up to the Calormenes. But then, when later he sees that the Ape Shift is a fraud, he shouts the fact to the Narnians and is silenced and tied up. All his actions seem futile. He is eventually released by the children, for the Narnian beasts, frightened of 'Aslan', will do no more than feed him. Tirian now plans with the children another foray, to release Jewel the unicorn: but it takes Jill to think of finding out about 'Aslan' while they are about it, and then leading Puzzle away. Tirian later releases a group of Dwarfs from their servitude to the Calormenes, but they are so degenerate that they believe he wants to use them as the Calormenes did. He then plans to reveal the true nature of 'Aslan' to the Narnians, but his plot is forestalled. Finally he is reduced to fighting a battle against superior odds which results in his being thrown through the stable door, supposedly to feed Tash.

As for the Narnian Talking Beasts, many of them are dupes. The Ape has all the degenerate intelligence going. Of course it is right for the creatures to trust Aslan and follow his commands: but they never hear them out of his mouth, only out of that of the Ape; and these commands are remote from their understanding of Aslan's nature. The Lamb does question the Ape, but is answered (34). The creatures are well-meaning; they try to do their best: but they are confused and spiritually blinded. They have in a way given up much of the intelligence, the clarity of thought, that once made them Talking Beasts: now they are only poor, superstitious creatures. Some give help to Tirian – the dogs, particularly, out of a native friendliness to a master – but most are evasive or even plain hostile.

If the beasts are deluded by blind faith, the Dwarfs are equally deluded by lack of it: like the cynical Ghost in *The Great Divorce* they refuse to be taken in by anything, and the result is that they are 'taken in' by nothingness. They say Tirian does not look like the King, that he has designs on them no different from the Calormenes; they will not believe in either Aslan or Tash when they realise the Ape's trick. If the Narnian beasts accept something as far more than it is, the Dwarfs reduce everything to far less than it is. Hurled through the stable door, six of them sit in a huddled circle, refusing to accept the reality of the open world about them, insisting that they are still in a filthy hut; and seeing the rich foods and wine that Aslan gives them only as turnips and dirty water (131-5).

But the reason for this unhappy state of affairs is not really a moral one: we are not really to waste time blaming the Narnians. The real cause is a kind of ontological decrepitude in Narnia. In its last days the life in it has become tired and worn down, to the point where a fraudulent Ape can be the centre of things, and Aslan can be reduced to a skin on a stupid donkey. This decrepitude shows itself most in a theme of uncertain identity that runs through the book. The Ape makes an image of Aslan to ape the real one and deceive the Narnians. He is rightly called Shift. He even tries to alter his own identity by telling the beasts that he is not really an ape at all, but a very old, and 'therefore' very wise man (32). He tells the beasts that Tash and Aslan are the same, and renames Aslan as Tashlan, causing further confusion. Thus the boundaries of divine identity are, for the Narnians, broken down, as are those of their country as the Calormenes invade. Meanwhile Talking Trees are being reduced to mere timber; Talking Horses are used as mere horses. And the King loses a good part of his identity when he surrenders and his crown is taken from him.

When Tirian calls on the children he can only appear to them in England as a ghostly figure, unable to communicate, who then fades away (45, 49-50); when Jill and Eustace come to him they 'simply appeared from nowhere' (46). Even they are not quite sure how they got to Narnia; they were on a train and felt a bang, and that was all; later they wonder whether if they are killed in battle in Narnia they will also be dead in England (88). Tirian and the children disguise themselves as Calormenes to approach the stable to rescue Jewel the unicorn. The false Aslan in the stable is reduced to no Aslan at all when Puzzle is removed. When Tirian and his friends find the truth about 'Aslan', it is driven out by fresh falsehoods. The identity of the 'supernatural' is reduced by the Calormene Rishda Tarkaan, the Cat and the Dwarfs: the first two believe neither in Tash nor Aslan but use them as devices to keep the Narnians in subjection; the last refuse to believe in anything they do not see.

All this confusion spirals down through lies and falsehoods to final destruction. The very fact that all the children from every stage of Narnia's history are present prefigures this ending. In a terrifying sequence Aslan brings about the systematic annihilation of Narnia. First the creatures are brought to judgment and divided, then huge saurians devour the Narnian vegetation and a gigantic wave immerses the land; last the huge figure of Time or Death reaches out a great arm to crush the heat and light of the dying sun 'as you would squeeze an orange'. Then, in total darkness and freezing cold, the uncreation of Narnia meets its terminal point.

But if Narnian reality is winding down, other realities are coming nearer. By the very act of exploiting Tash and Aslan for their own ends, the evil brings them closer. What was a theatre designed to put over a fraud, becomes the platform for truth: the theatrical analogy is used at length (93). When the Cat goes to 'see' the angry 'Aslan', expecting to find nothing, he is met by the horrifying Tash. At this point true Realities begin. Tash is the reality behind the corruption of Shift and Rishda Tarkaan. Aslan is the Reality behind the noble Calormene Emeth's search for Tash, for Tash is a horror of evil, and Emeth (whose name means 'truth') sought purity under Tash's name only. Out of the decrepitude and final destruction of Narnia its inhabitants are to meet their final realities of Heaven or Hell at their Last Judgment.

The stable is the focus: in a sense all life has come to a point here, for in this book all events occur about this one place. The Ape, the Cat and Rishda Tarkaan pretend that Aslan (also as Tash) is inside it: the pretence is to come true. The story is like an egg-timer, with the neck at the stable door. Life shrivels before that door, including all Narnia as Aslan extinguishes it, but beyond it it opens out. The trivial, nasty world of the Ape opens into a vast, open new Narnia, which opens out further and still further. The stable proves as large as the universe: supposed to be empty, it is full of all Reality. When Digory says that the inside of the stable is bigger than its outside, Queen Lucy observes, "'In our world too, a stable once had something inside it that was bigger than our whole world'" (128). We are reminded that a stable once admitted God into our world just as another now admits another world to God; that one held a child and a new beginning, this one is the centre of a world that is ending. At the Last Judgment the creatures suddenly become truly revealed for what they are, and go into Aslan's shadow or through the door. Beyond the door the motif becomes 'farther up and farther in': all have to move further into the land in which they find themselves, and then beyond that.

The idiom is one of paradox and reversal. What was a process of being sucked backwards towards a centre of annihilation becomes a progressive journey ever upwards to fuller and fuller life. What began with the skin of a dead lion washed down the Great Waterfall at Caldron Pool becomes the ascent, against 'nature' and mortality, of the children and their Narnian companions up it (156-7). They rush at great speed through this new Narnia and over the Western Wild to the garden where Digory plucked the apple in *The Magician's Nephew*. Yet just as with the stable, the garden contains a bigger world than the one they have just left. Lucy is told by the Faun Mr Tumnus, "'The farther up and the farther in you go, the bigger everything gets. The inside is larger than the outside'" (162). As Lucy looks at the garden she sees that it is the whole world, another Narnia, and says, "'I see.... This is still Narnia, and, more real and more beautiful than the Narnia down below, just as *it* was more real and more beautiful than the Narnia outside the stable door! I see... world within world, Narnia within Narnia...'" To which Mr Tumnus replies, "'Yes... like an onion: except that as you go in and in, each circle is larger than the last'" (162-3).

At the 'end' we have traversed the infinite distance from the fraudulent locality of the Ape with which we began to the ever-dilating cosmic and yet human reality of Aslan. The old world has a beginning and an end (153): this one has neither. This book has a close, but God's story is never done. The night and darkness in which they left the old Narnia has given way to everlasting day. Aslan tells them, "'The dream is ended: this is the morning'":

> And as He spoke He no longer looked to them like a lion; but the things that began to happen after that were so great and beautiful that I cannot write them. And for us this is the end of all the stories, and we can most truly say that they all lived happily ever after. But for them it was only the beginning of the real story. All their life in this world and all their adventures in Narnia had only been the cover and the title page: now at last they were beginning Chapter One of the Great Story which no one on earth has read: which goes on forever: in which every chapter is better than the one before. (165)

Endnotes

1. Lewis, 'Sometimes Fairy Stories May Say Best What's To Be Said', *Of Other Worlds*, 36-7.
2. Lewis, 'On Three Ways of Writing for Children', *Of Other Worlds*, 28.
3. Lewis, Sometimes Fairy Stories May Say Best What's To Be Said', 37.
4. Ibid, 37-8.
5. There is something of a similar strain put on Tom's greed for Mrs. Bedonebyasyoudid's sweets in Kingsley's *The Water-Babies* (ch.6).
6. Charles Williams, *He Came Down From Heaven and the Forgiveness of Sins* (London: Faber, 1950), 92.
7. The idea of the wardrobe with no back might have come from the backless cupboard, opening on a tunnel, down which a strange shadow comes in George MacDonald's *Phantastes* (1858), ch. VIII (Stephen Prickett, *Victorian Fantasy*, 195 n.57); however as Green and Hooper say (250-1), a more probable source is E. Nesbit's magic Bigwardrobeinspareroom in her 'The Aunt and Amabel' (1909). One general source of *The Lion, the Witch and the Wardrobe* is Roger Lancelyn Green's unpublished fantasy *The Wood that Time Forgot*, which Green gave to Lewis to criticise: see Green and Hooper, 239-40.
8. Actually when we have read *The Magician's Nephew* we find that they are not the first kings or queens or even humans in Narnia after all – for there an Edwardian cab-driver Frank and his wife Helen are made first rulers of the newly-created Narnia after they have 'accidentally' been brought there.
9. See Kathryn Lindskoog, *The Lion of Judah in Never-Never Land: God, Man and Nature in C. S. Lewis's Narnia Tales*, 48-60, on the Old and New Testament uses of the lion as symbol.
10. In *The Last Battle*, however, we are to learn that Susan relapsed as she 'grew up' and put away what she considered the childish things of Narnia; so that she does not return with the others at the end of things in Narnia (ch.12).
11. Miraz, we learn, 'disapproved of ships and the sea' (54). This dislike of the sea is ironic in view of the very name 'Telmarines', and the fact that these people are descendants of a race of pirates (184-5).
12. See on this Schakel, *Reading with the Heart*, 36-43 and Glover, *C. S. Lewis*, 145-6.
13. Schakel, 49-63; Glover, 149-57.
14. Schakel, 51-2.
15. Lewis, 'On Stories', *Of Other Worlds*, 18.

16 Particularly John D. Cox, 'Epistemological Release in *The Silver Chair*', in Schakel (ed.), *The Longing for a Form*, 159-68; and Schakel, *Reading with the Heart*, 65-80.
17 Schakel, 68-80; Cox, 164-8, prefers the notion of onion-layers of reality to the vertical concept.
18 Cox, 162-4. Cox also cites the chair to which the Lady in Milton's *Comus* is enchanted (221n.4).
19 Green and Hooper, 122-3, say that Lewis based Puddleglum on the lugubrious gardener Fred Paxford at the Kilns (Lewis's Oxford home).
20 This pattern, and a subsequent redemptive ascent, is argued by Glover, 163-4.
21 Schakel, 81-5.
22 Schakel, 85-96.
23 See also Schakel, 93-4.
24 For the Witch's invasion of London, Lewis (like Nesbit) may also be drawing on the impact of an imperious statue of Venus brought to life in late Victorian society in F. Anstey's [Thomas Anstey Guthrie's] *The Tinted Venus, a Farcical Romance* (1885), esp. chs 9,14.
25 For a comparison of Lewis's and Milton's versions of creation, see Charles A. Huttar, 'Lewis's Narnia and the "Grand Design"', in Schakel (ed.), *The Longing for a Form*, 123-5.
26 Compare Glover, 179-80: '*The Magician's Nephew*' clearly shows the end drawing near as he [Lewis] gives us the beginning of the *Chronicles*.... In terms of theme, it was inevitable that having given thought to the genesis and redemption of Narnia from evil, Lewis would inevitably give the apocalypse.'
27 This is the recurrent theme of the analysis in Thomas Howard's *The Achievement of C. S. Lewis*.
28 Walter Hooper, 'Narnia: the Author, the Critics and the Tale', in Schakel (ed.), *The Longing for a Form*, 114, cites Christ telling the Disciples how they will know when the end of things is coming: 'If any man shall say unto you, Lo, here is Christ, or there; believe it not. For there shall arise false Christs, and false prophets, and shall shew great signs and wonders; insomuch that, if it were possible, they shall deceive the very elect' (St. Matthew 24,23-4: see also St Mark 13,21; St Luke 21,8).
29 See also Glover, 181-4, on Narnian moral decrepitude. Hooper, loc. cit., cites the biblical parallels to these Last Things in Matthew 24, Mark 13 and Luke 21: there will be wars, invasion and overthrow by foreign powers, engulfing by the ocean, the fall of the sun, moon and stars, and the coming of the Son of Man.

CHAPTER 8

Till We Have Faces (1956)

This book is quite singular in Lewis's work, though he had from the earliest stage in his career been intending to write a novel round the Cupid and Psyche myth. He thought it his best book, but it was as he put it 'a flop' on publication.[1] It is plain in style, lacking the evocation of *Sehnsucht* and the wondrous worlds or beings that are present in the earlier works. Yet it has a far more complex and less judging awareness of the fallibilities of people and the moral uncertainties of life than Lewis has admitted before: thinner in one sense, it is far 'thicker' in another.

It is possible that Lewis also took inspiration from Naomi Mitchison's epic novel, *The Corn King and the Spring Queen* (1931). Mitchison's novel is partly set in the 'barbarous' realm of Marob (Scythia) in the third century BC, and concerns a girl called Erif Der (Red Fire backwards) who can do magic such as making the corn grow or healing the sick – like Psyche in Lewis's story. She becomes joint ruler with the king her husband, and like Orual has dealings with much more 'civilised' peoples from Sparta. Through her Mitchison celebrates the powers and abilities of women that she felt were so ignored in her own day. Lewis's book also has a woman of this kind at its centre. (The number of female heroines in Lewis's work is surely a counter to his supposed male chauvinism.) Orual faces down her father and the priesthood of Glome, and defeats an enemy king in single combat; Erif Der defies and finally slays her father, ruining the sacred annual ritual that keeps the Marob land fertile. There is a learned Greek exile the Fox, who instructs Orual in *Till We Have Faces*, and a similar Hellene, Sphaeros, who teaches Erif Der and Tarrik her husband in *The Corn King and the Spring Queen*.

For all its singularity this book does complete a circle in Lewis's work. The God on the mountain in this story is another version of the God on the mountain in *The Pilgrim's Regress*. The central character here rejects that God just as John did. But the difference is that John travelled all over the world only to return to the mountain, where Orual, the heroine here, stays still: here the mountain, in a sense, comes to Orual. Here there is no journey outwards to discover more of the truth in the wider universe, but rather a journey in to the interior of the self, a shrinkage to a more exact and exacting point. In a sense *Till We Have Faces* marks the culmination of a process begun in Lewis's fiction with *That Hideous Strength* – not a journey outwards from a home, a planet, or even Hell, but a journey inwards to Earth, to a pocket universe reached through a wardrobe, and thence 'farther in' to an individual Psyche in one punctual spot.

And the story is a tale within a tale, a retelling of the Cupid and Psyche myth found in Apuleius's *The Golden Ass* (c.160-190 A.D.). Lewis sets us in the semi-barbaric kingdom of Glome, somewhere to the north of Greece in classical times. The King, Trom, has two daughters, Orual and Redival; his Queen dying, he takes another princess to wife and has by her a further daughter called Istra (Psyche). His second wife dies in giving birth. Orual, who is ugly and passionate, loves the beautiful Istra, but Redival is jealous and mocking of her. The children grow up together.

Bad fortune falls on Glome and the priest of the shapeless Goddess Ungit who is worshipped in that country tells the King that Ungit is angry and can only be satisfied when someone pure is chosen as 'the Accursed' to be given to the dark Brute that has been seen on the Grey Mountain near the city of Glome. Psyche has been discovered by priestly lot to be this "Accursed". Actually the priests are also jealous of her because the populace have given to her some of the worship that was Ungit's due. Despite Orual's efforts, Psyche is left chained on the mountain for the Brute to devour.

When Orual later sets out to bury Psyche's remains, she finds nothing at the spot, but instead is amazed to meet Psyche in a nearby valley. Psyche says she is married to a God who comes to her every night and forbids her to look on him. Orual eventually persuades her to disobey this divine command. When she does, Psyche is cast out into exile and the God, a shining being, comes to Orual to tell her, '"You also shall be Psyche."'

We are now more than halfway through the book. After this, Orual tries to put Psyche out of her life. Her father is dying, and she becomes Queen in fact if not yet in name. She establishes royal power over the soldiers of the priesthood, makes successful war on surrounding kingdoms that threaten Glome, liberates slaves, improves the economy, makes laws, advances learning and builds public works. One year when she is on a royal tour abroad, she comes across a temple at Essur dedicated to the worship of a Goddess called Istra. The priest there tells her a story of the Goddess that matches details of her meeting with Psyche, details Orual alone knew; yet the story also diverges, claiming that Istra's life with the god was destroyed through her sisters' jealousy. This is in fact the version of events we have from Apuleius.

Orual is outraged at this account, and decides that only the gods could be the source of it, because they want to cover their own wrongdoing. Not only have they taken Psyche from her, but they are putting about a false story of Psyche's ruin. She determines to write an account of her life that will justify her doings with Psyche, and also become a complaint against the gods. And at last, when she old and is free enough of duties, she writes the story we have been reading so far. It has been written as a long apology for her life and her dealings with Psyche. And it ends with a complaint that the gods first deceived Orual and then spread lies about her. They would not show her the god or the palace clearly, so that she could not tell if Psyche had been taken by a god or by the monster of the mountain, and therefore must tell Psyche to break the command and look on his face. And now the gods have spread their version of what happened, and it flies in the face of the truth as Orual saw it. She ends this, 'Part One' of her narrative by cursing the gods for their trickery of mortals and their lies (*Till We Have Faces*, 258-9). We are now almost within sight of the end of the book.

But Orual is driven some days later to write more. She is now dying, and two things have happened, during and since her writing. She has learnt that her sister Redival suffered dearly when Orual turned her affections away from her to Psyche and to the Fox (265). Then, when Orual's own beloved soldier Bardia dies and she goes to comfort his widow, she learns of this lady's selfless love over the years in giving Bardia the freedom to serve Orual as his Queen much more than herself as his wife. When she learns how Orual also loved Bardia in secret, the lady says, '"Yours is Queen's love, not commoners'. Perhaps you who spring from the gods love like the gods. Like the Shadowbrute. They say the loving and the devouring are all one, don't they?"' (275).

A few days after this Orual experiences a vision ('certainly vision and no dream') in which she is shown that she is herself the devouring Ungit. She tries to kill herself, only to be forbidden by the god who took Psyche. Then she sees herself as undergoing Psyche's various tasks; until at last she is taken before the gods to make her complaint. When she has done so, she finds that she needs no answer, for the complaint itself was her answer. Then it is the gods' turn to judge Orual. But first she meets Psyche, who has come from Persephone with beauty for her. Orual becomes Psyche, and the god, unseen still, says once again, "'You also are Psyche.'" At this the vision ends, and Orual dies shortly afterwards, but now in the knowledge of love, and of why there can be no answer from the gods.

A postscript added by another hand to her broken-off narrative asks the reader of the roll on which it is written to take it, if that is his direction, to Greece, as Orual would have wished. For Orual's closest friend apart from Psyche was a captured and intelligent Greek nicknamed 'the Fox', who died in her service without returning to his homeland; and she was drawn to his culture. Further, it was the only sophisticated culture she knew of. However, since the Fox's temper was both rational and sceptical, we wonder whether the manuscript went to the right audience. Maybe this is a way of telling us that the rational way of thinking will find itself inadequate to understand Orual's story, and so itself be changed, as pagan philosophy was superseded by Christian theology. On the other hand it may not at all. Late Greek culture's version of Orual's story becomes the myth of Cupid and Psyche as told by Apuleius, which is similar to the judgemental version of the priest of Essur that so angered Orual.

In *The Great Divorce* as in most of his fiction before this last book, Lewis dealt with polar separations between different forces. In *Till We Have Faces*, it can be said, his concern is with a Great Marriage. This is his first book to be centrally concerned with a relationship: some have said that this is the result of Lewis's love for and eventual marriage to Joy Davidman. *That Hideous Strength*, nearest in character to *Till We Have Faces*, has the married couple John and Jane Studdock at its heart, but for most of the book they are apart and are considered in isolation as different kinds of spiritual failures without much reference to one another. But the whole of *Till We Have Faces* could be said to describe the relationship between Orual and Psyche, with what is wrong in Orual's attitude, and with its eventual correction, so that the two can come together once more.

The book is also about man's relation to the gods. This actually starts as the gods' relation to man, in the sense that Orual demands of the gods how they could behave so unjustly: but as the book develops we see that the issue is in part at least to be reversed. More than this: identities are shown in the book to be related at deeper levels than are supposed. At first Orual breaks a relationship between god and man, that of Psyche and her divine husband. Told by the god that she will also be Psyche, Orual finds that she has taken Psyche's image at the end; and is shown that what she seemed to do for herself during the story were actually Psyche's tasks. During the narrative she has seen herself as partaking in the devouring nature of Ungit or even of the Shadow-Brute of the mountain. Networks of relationship are suggested by the imagery too, whereby Psyche is both herself and the soul, her story partakes in that of the fall of man, and the god is at once Cupid and Christ (without being reducible to either).

With all the complexity of *Till We Have Faces*, the narrative is not of the gripping character of many of Lewis's other stories, nor, as narrative, is it central. In *Perelandra* we know increasingly what Ransom must do, and we know how important it is that it be done. But in *Till We Have Faces* only the sense that the story is based on the Cupid and Psyche myth drives us forward at the level of 'doing'. When Psyche was taken by the Brute, in a sense nothing happened – at least at the vulgar and expected physical level. The issue concerning Psyche's sacrifice does not surface till we are well into the book and we are not taken to witness it (Orual is left behind). When Psyche is exiled, the 'Psyche-motive' at a most obvious level ceases, and Orual puts her aside while she gets on with the business of being a queen. Further, insofar as the book is laid out as an account of a life which will make a case against the gods: we are to attend throughout to the justification for the case, and increasingly, as the narrative proceeds, as much to the nature of the plaintiff as to that of those she accuses. We are not concerned with a sequence of action.

In short the book is about what the nature of a thing is – the gods' relations with man, Orual's love for Psyche – rather than with what it does or becomes. It is essentially introspective: no other of Lewis's novels is so preoccupied with examining its own past. Its concern is with 'seeing' – imagery of which pervades the story – by which Orual may come to understand what lay at the bottom of her love for Psyche. Nor, as story, is it a new one, but 'a myth retold'. Lewis chose to recreate a known myth, a tale that existed even before Orual, partly because this is a story that involves every man in his relations with the divine and with others. (The myths of Eden or of the Arthurian story that Lewis recreates in the space trilogy Lewis transforms by giving them new outcomes.) The introspective character of the book is perhaps imaged in the way that Orual's complaint against the gods achieves nothing, but becomes its own answer. It has its tail in its mouth.

There is a progressive narrowing of focus in *Till We Have Faces*, as the narrative turns in on Orual herself. She tells her story in the first person, unlike any other of Lewis's characters. After she has lost Psyche, she cuts herself off from the world with a veil over her face. At the end of the narrative, when her father comes to her in a vision, he makes her dig down through a room of the palace into a chamber beneath, and thence into a smaller chamber beneath that, at the bottom of which she becomes convinced that she is the devouring Ungit. This descent is an image for that progressive descent through the various layers of the self that constitutes the essential concern of the book.

Yet this story is full of people, more or less 'lovingly' described. Psyche, strangely beautiful, but with a beauty that seemed so natural while one was with her it only seemed exceptional in retrospect, could perhaps have been a prig, or somewhat remote: but she is portrayed in the book as Orual's young half-sister who delights in girlish games and has a belief at the bottom of her soul, which is allowed to stand at first as a young girl's fancy, that some day she will meet with a King-husband on the Grey Mountain and live in happiness. Yet while she is believable as an individual, there are deeper hints about her from the start, not least in her exceptional beauty, however ordinary her parentage; and while she is thoroughly natural as a girl, she is innocent and pure.

The people of Glome come for a time to regard Psyche with awe – largely because of her beauty – and believe that her touch will save them from disease or harm. On one occasion they all come together and demand Psyche's help against an attack of plague, and she is sent out from the palace dressed as a Queen 'walking slowly and gravely, like a child going to say a lesson, right in among all the foulness' (40). The balance between her spiritual stature and her 'everyday' self is finely caught. When she is on the mountain in the god's palace she still speaks as herself. She is less willing to give Orual the exclusive love she has had before, but that is only 'natural' since she now has a husband. She is quite unlike the 'coldly' dismissive girl met by her father in Heaven in the Middle English Poem *Pearl*. Even at the end, when Orual meets the redeemed Psyche and finds she is a goddess,

> She was the old Psyche still; a thousand times more her very self than she had been before the offering [her sacrifice to the 'Brute']. For all that had then but flashed out in a glance or a gesture, all that one meant most when one spoke her name, was now wholly present, not to be gathered up from hints nor in shreds, not some of it in one moment and some in another. Goddess? I had never seen a real woman before. (317)

This is something analogous to Dante's dual view of Beatrice.

Lewis had *said* such things before, that one became more truly oneself in Heaven, but somehow he had never quite dramatised it. The Lady in *Perelandra* is wonderfully created, but she does not have a 'local' personality. Rather, her person – young, feminine, innocent, accepting, physically beautiful – expresses the character of the whole planet of which she is Queen. It is not that she is an abstraction – quite the reverse – but that her peculiarities do not emerge from herself alone. And other characters in Lewis's work are often more or less 'representative' in the same way.

But if Psyche clearly combines individual personality with divinity, the other characters in the book, particularly Orual, do so less evidently. Orual for example – ugly, passionate, loving, demanding Orual – may seem only herself, eldest daughter of a king of a particular little semi-barbarous kingdom, and with her own special experiences, characteristics, longings and regrets. We have to remember her humanity as we consider Orual morally. However we have also to remember that throughout this book Orual is telling the story not only of her own life but of her approach to the gods. The one, so particular, detailed, rambling – a mere chronicle it seems – is actually underneath the story of a soul's fashioning by its divine makers.

Orual is the book's narrator, and alone among Lewis's works this is a book where we are asked to be aware of the narrator as a particular person whose views we need not accept.[2] There is as we have seen a measure of 'development' in the first-person narrator of *The Great Divorce*, but Ransom in the space-trilogy has usually to be taken at face value, and in any case is pointing out his own limitations himself, as when he attempts to shirk Maleldil's demand that he fight the Un-man. Ransom is self-knowing, but in Orual we have someone who is concealed from herself, and it is up to us to see for ourselves. Concealment is part of the imagery of the book – Ungit hidden in the temple, the god hidden from Psyche, Orual hiding herself from the world with her veil.

Beyond Psyche and Orual, the whole book is scattered with particular people. There is Orual's general, Bardia, simple, blunt, foursquare, courageous, loyal – he is beginning to sound like a cliché until we recall others of his characteristics, such as that he is lecherous and hen-pecked. Trom, Orual's father and King, is a gross old hypocrite, cruel to Orual and prepared without much ruth to sacrifice his own daughter Istra – yet one knows too how much he wanted a son as successor, and how frustrated he was to have begotten only daughters. Redival, Orual's sister, pretty, lecherous, treacherous, jealous, sneering, perhaps comes in for some of Lewis's dislike of female flirtatiousness, yet she is also a pathetically helpless figure, her lover Tarin castrated, she herself ignorant and excluding herself from the learning group of Orual, Psyche and their teacher the Fox.

Only the god does not have personality in this sense. Perhaps in one way that is odd, for in the myth the god was the very particular deity Cupid, child of a no less particular Venus. Venus was jealous because Psyche was being worshipped for her beauty in place of herself; she sent Cupid to punish Psyche but he fell in love with her instead; and, after her exile, Psyche was driven back to Venus and set four apparently impossible tasks before she gained Cupid once more. The myth might later be allegorised, but in its immediate form it was a story of human love and jealousy among the pantheon of the Greek gods. But in Lewis's account, there is no Venus with her personal motives; and Cupid's equivalent is a great golden figure of light that 'appears' once, briefly and terribly, to Orual on the mountain.

Lewis has distanced the gods in another way, by removing the certainty of their presence and their causality. For most of the story it seems that Orual, either as the friend of Psyche or as the Queen of Glome, is the driving force behind most of what happens. A god is presented, but she is not sure if he is real. Lewis is not shy of presenting us with supernatural agency elsewhere in his fiction: for example the children in *The Silver Chair* are sent to Narnia by Aslan to set Prince Rilian free, Ransom is sent back by Maleldil to Perelandra to help the Lady of the planet keep her innocence. But in *Till We Have Faces* Lewis introduces other motives, blurring the picture, removing such clear-cut certainties. At a human level Psyche is given to the god of the mountain because in being treated as a miracle worker, a healer, she has received the kind of worship that the Priest feels should have been accorded to Ungit; and also because she is a failed miracle worker, reviled by the populace as "The Accursed", after her touch has failed to stop the plague. And her 'tasks' – at least the first one – are subsumed in the doings of Orual, whose sufferings during the narrative are seen as her carrying the burden of Psyche's tasks, and whose writings are seen as an attempt to perform the first task, the separating of the myriad grains (here of truth) into their proper kinds and order (266-7).

And this is part of the character of *Till We Have Faces*: nothing is clear-cut or definite, even the very statement that it is not. Looked at one way, an event is 'supernatural'; but like the image in a trick mirror, it can shift back to something else, the 'natural'. Looked at one way, Orual is a forgivable person; looked at another, she is a spiritual vampire. These opposed views are neither exclusive nor complementary: they simply exist together, side by side, in suspension. In others of Lewis's books the landscape or 'events' may be outside or inside the self, but we usually know which – Perelandra has objective reality beyond Ransom, while the landscape of *The Pilgrim's Regress* or 'The Shoddy Lands' is the inside of someone's spirit. But here we do not know which it is. We are forced as it were to go without identity, without a 'face' ourselves, throughout the novel. It would be quite possible to see the whole of Orual's experience – and after all, it is told through the medium or her organising mind – as a picture of the state of her spirit: her rejection of Psyche, a rejection of her soul, her ugliness expressing her own evil, her rejection of the gods reducible to a rejection of herself. That is true, but it is not allowed to be the only truth. The gods are real, for all her saying, and so is Psyche.

Even the landscape of the book has a strange mixture about it of both the elemental and the vague. We deal with basic things, the palace, the mountain, the temple, the throne-room, but they shift and waver before the eye. In Lewis's other fantasy he would deepen and solidify our vision with descriptive details 'irrelevant' to the narrative. When for example, Ransom in *Perelandra* fights the Un-man, the setting of the fight is continually put before us – the clearing in which they begin, with the Un-man found tearing a bird to pieces and then running howling at Ransom with its arms hooked and its great nails ready to slash and tear; then, during their chase over the island, the Lady asleep and the Un-man trying to claw her, the wallaby-like creatures asleep in rows, the dragon curled about a tree, the crashing of the pursuit.

But the fight in *Till We Have Faces* between Orual and Argan, an invading prince, is far more sketchy so far as the setting goes. We are told that it takes place in a field by the river, and no more. Later it is mentioned that 'There was a white sun in a grey sky that day, and a biting wind' (227). We learn that a bull has to be sacrificed before the fight, but we do not see this, only hear Orual's reflection that the gods are given a hand in everything. Argan's character is to be suggested through his appearance, yet his appearance is left somehow uncertain, 'He was a man with straw-coloured hair and beard, thin, yet somehow bloated, with pouting lips; a very unpleasing person' (226). These details are quite specific, but they do not give us a strong impression of the man, because they concern his unattractiveness to Orual personally rather than to all people. Further, the emphasis is less on him than on Orual's reaction to him. We may get some faint impression of him from this, but the items appear rather as a list of separate features than a unified portrait. Certainty is further removed as we are told, in a way that is typical of the novel, that he was both thin and bloated. As for his 'unpleasing' nature, we may not by now be willing to take that as a portrait of Argan so much as of Orual's own dislike of ugliness.

The fight itself could also have had individuality, as between an unpractised swordswoman and a man, but instead we hear only that it was pretty much as with all Orual's practice bouts with Bardia. First Argan was lazy, thinking her easy prey; then she grazed his knuckles and they got down to serious matters; then – a detail that sticks out – there is a sudden moment when Orual sees Argan's face register the beginning of belief that he will die; then Orual misses one chance when Argan makes a mistake (not described) but on the next cuts him deeply on the inner leg so that he will bleed to death, and jumps back so that in his fall he should not take her with him. That is all: a list of functional details, but not a strong sense of an experience lived through. Perhaps it is consonant with Orual's reserved nature: she hides her face, and as Queen her sex, from the world, and even Bardia and the Fox are not told quite what happened with Psyche; indeed concealment of herself from not only her reader but herself is what she practices throughout the story. We are left with the dual impression that a setting or an act has been stripped to its barest, most elemental essentials, and yet that it is also curiously ghostly and uncertain.

How far should the point be taken? Orual lives in inaccuracy. She blames the gods when she should look into herself. Her complaint turns into something else, its own answer. Her feelings themselves in her complaint are in part misdirected and insubstantial: Psyche is to some extent an externalisation of what she feels (wrongly as it appears) she lacks in herself; her grief at the loss of Psyche is in this sense not grief over Psyche herself but over a renewed sensation of what she feels is her Psyche-less nature. And at the end Orual learns that her grief was always unreal in another sense, for as the god promised her, "'You also shall be Psyche'": she is the thing she thought she had lost.

Perhaps in this respect we can find the style of *Till We Have Faces* functional: it expresses an inaccuracy of soul on the part of Orual its narrator. When she finds the temple to Istra on her travels and hears the story of how Psyche's sisters were jealous of her and how they saw the palace of the gods plainly, and not as one vague hint, Orual is furious at what she sees as a perversion of the truth by the gods, done in order to mock and spurn her.

> It was as if the gods themselves had first laughed, and then spat, in my face. So this was the shape the story had taken. You may say, the shape the gods had given it. For it must be they who had put it into the old fool's mind or into the mind of some other dreamer from whom he'd learnt it. How could any mortal have known of that palace at all? That much of the truth they had dropped into someone's mind, in a dream, or an oracle, or however they do such things. That much; and wiped clean the very meaning, the pith, the central knot, of the whole tale. Do I not do well to write a book against them, telling what they have kept hidden? Never, sitting on my judgment seat, had I caught a false witness in a more cunning half-truth. For if the true story had been like their story, no riddle would have been set me; there would have been no guessing and no guessing wrong. More than that; it's a story belonging to a different world, a world in which the gods show themselves clearly and don't torment men with glimpses, nor unveil to one what they hide from another, nor ask you to believe what contradicts your eyes and ears and nose and tongue and fingers. In such a world (is there such? it's not ours for certain) I would have walked aright. The gods themselves would have been able to find no fault in me. And now to tell my story as if I had had the very sight they had denied me.... Is it not as if you told a cripple's story and never said he was lame, or told how a man betrayed a secret but never said it was after twenty hours of torture? And I saw all in a moment how the false story would grow and spread and be told all over the earth; and I wondered how many of the other sacred stories are just such twisted falsities as this. (252-3)

This is a very revealing passage. We may wonder what in the priest's story could be equated with the gods' laughing, in so far as it is in contrast to their spitting. When Orual says, 'So this was the shape the story had taken,' she begs the question of the shape of her own story as presented in this book – indeed reduces her whole experience to story (later in the passage she speaks of the 'true story'). Then she alters the statement to one of a shape given not by narrative evolution but by the gods. To ask how any mortal should have known of the palace at all is to forget that Psyche knew of it long before she went there (31, 41, 83). The palace is, in a sense, man's intuition of Heaven and a form of it could have arisen in any man's soul as an objectification of desire.

Orual's imprecision is conveyed in the vagueness of 'That much of the truth they had dropped into someone's mind, in a dream, or an oracle, or however they do such things'; or again in the repetition of 'the very meaning, the pith, the central knot, of the whole tale'. And *was* it the central knot? Was it the gods' refusal of a clear sight of the palace that led Orual to insist that Psyche discover the appearance of her husband? Was she really worried that Psyche had married something horrible or a beggar? Was it not rather that she disliked the idea of Psyche marrying anyone else at all? And surely it could have been a case not so much of the gods withholding a clear view of the palace, as of Orual refusing to look at it, to allow its existence? So long as she will not admit at least the possibility of these things, for so long she will be inaccurate, and use inaccurate and blurred language. She will not allow that she rather than the gods could be guilty. And therefore anything that suggests her responsibility is met with the paranoia that shrilly blames others.

That 'Do I not do well...?' of Orual's again begs the question, sounds like special pleading. Who is really the false witness caught in a cunning half-truth? To say that no riddle would have been set her if the true story had been like the gods' story is confusingly to separate act from act: the riddle was in the experience of the palace, it is not something subsequent to the story. Confusing too is that 'no guessing and no guessing wrong': it seems tautologous, yet Orual is actually trying to have it both ways, to say that the gods make it difficult for us to decide, and that they make it inevitable that we decide wrong.

The next sentence beginning 'More than that...' does not really add much more to Orual's case. Again it is repetitive, 'show themselves clearly and don't torment men with glimpses', or in the curiously specific lists of eyes, ears, nose, tongues and fingers when she could simply have said 'your senses'. And yet in another way it does add something, for it shows that Orual's complaint is futile. If the gods are constantly open only in some other world, which in the next sentence she goes on to say is 'not ours, for certain', then what is the point of her complaint? What can it achieve except a release of spleen against the inevitable?

She cannot expect the gods to change the ground rules of the world for her sake. In attacking the gods she is really exposing her own guilt.

And so it goes on. What does Orual mean when she says that 'In such a world...I would have walked aright. The gods themselves would have been able to find no fault in me'? – her whole concern till now has been with finding fault with the gods, not with any fault they might find in her. Or has it? The two analogies for the 'gods' story' that follow are confusing enough in being two analogies where one would have sufficed: but again she senses that she has not grasped the situation through them. The word order of telling 'a cripple's story' suggests at first that the crippled condition would be already known; but then she says it is a story that leaves out this fact. And using the analogy of the cripple suggests that the defect is in the see-er rather than in the creators of what is seen: that is why she shifts to the idea of someone else doing the wrong in the second analogy. Nor are the analogies morally compatible: one does not blame a cripple for his condition as one might a man who betrays a secret or someone who refuses a vision. Orual returns to repeat the argument of this passage later (258).

It is as if the thing can never be said clearly and Orual has to go on repeating it, just as at the end, when she utters her complaint before the court of the gods, she realises when she is silenced, 'that I had been reading it over and over; perhaps a dozen times' (303). The curious thing is that all this is from a woman whose one objective is to expose the true nature of the gods, remove their concealment. She objects to their refusal to "show themselves openly and tell us what they would have us do", and asks, 'Why must holy places be dark places?' (258-9). Yet she is the woman who does not show herself openly to herself, who lives in vague hints and confusing misstatements and evasions, who goes about with her face covered by a veil. The clarity she seeks from the gods she really needs – and seeks – from herself.

At the end of the story, when, re-united with Psyche, she has reached the self-knowledge she has so long lacked, Orual's style gains a certainty and direction it has not before possessed. Told that '"The god comes to judge Orual,"' she says,

> If Psyche had not held me by the hand I should have sunk down. She had brought me now to the very edge of the pool. The air was growing brighter and brighter about us; as if something had set it on fire. Each breath I drew let into me new terror, joy, overpowering sweetness. I was pierced through and through with the arrows of it. I was being unmade. I was no one. But that's little

> to say; rather, Psyche herself was, in a manner, no one. I loved her as I would once have thought it impossible to love; would have died any death for her. And yet, it was not, not now, she that really counted. Or if she counted (and oh, gloriously she did) it was for another's sake. The earth and stars and sun, all that was or will be, existed for his sake. And he was coming. The most dreadful, the most beautiful, the only dread and beauty there is, was coming. The pillars on the far side of the pool flushed with his approach. I cast down my eyes. (318-19)

Now we are dealing not with inaccuracy but with mystery: now we are not going away from that which could be said, but moving towards that which cannot; now the struggle is for precision. The air felt as though it had been set on fire: the experience is both physical and metaphysical – joy and terror come in with each breath. And that list, 'new terror, joy, overpowering sweetness', captures the shock of the opposites, whereby terror and sweetness come together; just as, in another way, Orual and Psyche are to be one at the end of the passage. It is also a developing process, in a sense: the terror is the first experience, then it turns suddenly to joy, then the terror comes forward again to make a synthesis or bliss and pain in 'overpowering sweetness'. The air being on fire reminds us of the elements. Orual is standing by water, ready to sink to the 'earth' later mentioned in the passage: here in a sense all is being reduced to its primary constituents so that it may be refashioned and redeemed – 'I was being unmade.'

Pierced by arrows of sweetness, Orual is Sebastian, and Mary, and Christ Himself: she is participating in, reliving their experience. 'I was no one' has dual meaning: both that she was unmade and, morally, that self or 'I' no longer mattered. And then when she shifts it to saying that 'rather, Psyche herself.... was no one,' we see that she is again anticipating the sense that she is herself Psyche. Now the logic of emotion makes her see more exactly rather than try to obfuscate: first Psyche was no one, then she loves her more than ever she could have thought possible; then again it is not Psyche that counts, or if it is, it is she for another's sake. Again we have moved to a synthesis through paradox: Psyche both is, and is not, important, and is loved the less for herself the more real she is. Each sentence marks another step into awareness by Orual.

Yet if this passage is radically different in orientation, it is still bare of imagery and not strongly visualised. Compare it, for example, with Ransom's experience of meeting the angels of Mars and Venus in the high place of Perelandra. We have strong image of that scene, however much we know that the angels are beyond imagery and the Lord and Lady's innocent faces beyond any categorisation. We see the red flowers, the pool with the white 'coffin' by it, the assemblance of persons and beasts, the great golden sky overhead. But the focus in *Till We Have Faces* is not on the gods or even on Psyche, but on Orual and her seeings: we are concerned only with her experience, her grasping of the truth. When the moment comes, 'a great voice' says again, '"You also are Psyche,"' but no god appears, and Orual is returned to the palace gardens of Glome. This does not mean that the gods are subjective here: rather we can only understand how factual they are when we have come to believe them.

The book is concerned first and foremost with the movements of a soul, a Psyche: we have to spend our lives like Orual, in a world of hints and riddles. The focus is not so much on what happens to Orual in the outer world – that for a time, is the way she wants it – but on what she herself makes of her experience. Here in his last book Lewis turns to something like the ordinary man's experience of life – he has deliberately de-Christianised the god and made Orual a 'natural' woman, a pagan – so that he can present the basics of human experience without benefit of clear supernatural intervention. No angels here, no Aslan, no trips from Hell to Heaven, no devils leering over the frailties of a sinner, only a person of intellectual and spiritual ignorance forced finally to confront the reality of herself. The gods stand back – they do not exist the less, rather the more, for that. They are like psychiatrists (Psyche-atrists), steadily refusing answers until the patient is forced to look for them for herself, and then have a self to address: 'I saw well why the gods do not speak to us openly, nor let us answer. Till that word can be dug out of us, why should they hear the babble that we think we mean? How can they meet us face to face till we have faces?' (305).

In this last fiction Lewis goes back to something like the idiom of his first, *The Pilgrim's Regress* when he had just become a Christian: there too the central character moves through a world of confusing hints and of self-betrayals, there too the interest is in the true nature of something, the source of the desire and joy that John feels, rather than in a series of actions. But *The Pilgrims's Regress* is still different from *Till We Have Faces* in its concern with a stimulus from outside the self. Its central portrayal is of man's relations with a confusing world rather than with the confusions of the self.

If *Till We Have Faces* portrays the imprecisions of long-unacknowledged guilt, it also insists that uncertainty is of the very character of reality, and that if we look for simple, clear or vivid solutions to experience, they are not to be had. This is partly where the sheer complexity of the book – narrative and structural – is functional. And that is, finally, why the style is indefinite. To ignorance, reality is confused and obscure; to understanding, it is plastic, elusive, multi-faceted. So far as identity is concerned, the book's leitmotif is 'Is, and is not'. When Orual describes how the priest of Ungit enacts the birth of the new year by shutting himself in the temple on the last day of the old and 'fighting' his way out with a wooden sword on the first day of the new, she says, 'But of course, like all these sacred matters, it is and it is not' (279).

Perhaps the central area where this is seen is in the treatment of Orual herself. Most commentators on the book – and there have been some able ones of late – concentrate on her culpability.[3] And it is true that she is culpable. Her initial love for Psyche had real purity, but she could not tolerate Psyche's being taken away from her. When she heard Psyche's account of her bliss, and had her own partial vision of it, and yet still acted to make Psyche disobey the gods, Orual was not doing this out of care for her so much as out of the desire to smash any love that was not for herself. Psychologically we might say that Orual was suffering from a terrible insecurity brought on by her ugliness and her father's rejection of her, but the sin is not the less for that. We both forgive and judge.

But it is as well to remember that this judgment is not so easily reached as this might suggest. Not the least difference between *Till We Have Faces* and the myth as presented in Apuleius is that in the myth Orual and Redival are alike visitors to Psyche, and destroy her happiness through jealousy of it, while in *Till We Have Faces* Orual goes to Psyche out of love (Redival, who envies her, stays behind), and ruins her through what at first could seem mistaken love too. Now there are two ways to read this. We say that our sense of Orual as loving Psyche is gradually stripped away as we come to realise its true nature; or we say that somehow our original impression remains, despite the subsequent revelations. The one is, if one likes, a 'dynamic', the other a 'static' view. The book seems in fact to insist on both, however irreconcilable they may seem. Orual loved Psyche for herself in both senses.

It is also made harder for us to criticise Orual by our being made to see everything through her eyes, and thus understand how she feels as she does. Moreover, in comparison to Redival, Orual comes over as the loving sister. It is she who sets out on the long journey to the Grey Mountain to collect and bury, as she supposes, Psyche's bones. And she really loves Psyche, at least at the beginning: 'She made beauty all round her. When she trod on mud, the mud was beautiful; when she ran in the rain, the rain was silver' (30). It is a long time before we are prepared to call Orual's inability to see Psyche's palace spiritual blindness. For the time it seems as though the gods did, as she maintains, hide it from her; and that when, once, it was briefly seen by her through twilight mist, it was to torment her mind. In a pagan context we have no reason to suppose that the gods will behave "morally", like the Christian God – we only discover that this god operates on the same basic lines much later in the narrative.

It can be argued that this simply shifts the ground of the indictment. For if we sympathise with Orual, then we too are guilty with her. And in a way that too is the purpose of the book, and why it is written as it is – to work as a trial of us as much as of Orual. In this book Lewis deals with the native evasiveness of the soul – no simple or obvious crime, only the one done for what we think is the 'best' of reasons. He wants to put us very close to our self-deluding selves.[4] And he does it in a pagan context because if we smelt the clergy about we might be alerted and become morally respectful as we are not in our relaxed condition – we would switch on the 'Christian programme' of response.

But if this is true too, it is again not the sole truth. Orual is saved at the end of the story largely through the purity in her love for Psyche. Her perversion of love into selfish need made her suffer, the suffering embittered her, made her turn from herself, until a shock from outside in the form of the 'twisted' story of Istra brought her to utter her final complaint against the gods and thus obtain her answer and peace. Of course she is also saved through the divine mercy: when Orual asks, "'Are the gods not just?'" the Fox replies, "'Oh no, child. What would become of us if they were?'" (308). But Orual's love, for all that it was, also saved her. It is wrong simply to condemn her. Here Lewis refuses all simplifications, all absolute polarities of good and bad. In one sense it is the truth that Orual was afraid for Psyche, thinking that in ignorance she was the prey of the Shadowbrute as Bardia said, or else the deluded victim, as the Fox believed, of one of the numerous thieves and vagrants around the Mountain. Neither is a welcome truth to Orual. She does not receive either as an image of her own hidden desires: rather she says, 'His [Bardia's] thought was not new to me; it was only the most horrible of the guesses which had been jostling and wrangling in my head' (145); and

> I felt as, I suppose, a tortured prisoner feels when they dash water in his face to rouse him from his faint, and the truth, worse than all his fantasies, becomes clear and hard and unmistakable again around him. It now seemed to me that all my other guesses had been only self-pleasing dreams spun out of my wishes, but now I was awake. There never had been any riddle: the worst was the truth, and truth as plain as the nose on a man's face. Only terror would have blinded me to it for so long. (146)

Here she believes Bardia's view: later however she is as ready to believe the Fox's more mundane answer. She wonders at this, but explains it as the result of the two threads in her nature, the superstitious beliefs of Glome and the rational wisdom of Greece: one of the explanations must be false but she cannot discriminate which, and must hold to both for the time (160). Who is to say that this is *only* another rationalisation – that she does not believe either explanation, but is using them as means of justifying her jealousy of Psyche's happiness without her? That also is part of the truth, but it is a truth which, like both opposed accounts of what has removed Psyche, has to be heard together with its opposite. Of course there is the fact that Orual has seen Psyche happy on the Mountain, and therefore could leave her alone to her bliss, and Orual's heart tells her this. But there is also an answer to that: 'My heart did not conquer me. I perceived now that there is a love deeper than theirs who seek only the happiness of their beloved. Would a father see his daughter happy as a whore? Would a woman see her lover happy as a coward?' (147). Again true and not true: again both an answer, and a rationalisation of a deeper and darker refusal.

In this same area of 'truth' it is the case that Orual was in a sense given insufficient evidence to go on by the gods – a "mere" dubious glimpse of the palace in the grey of twilight. How could she have known that Psyche was indeed well cared for? Or again, is the story of her motivation of jealousy given by the priest of Essur the truth? Orual does not seem to recognise it at any rate: 'Jealous of Psyche? I sickened not only at the vileness of the lie but at its flatness' (254). Why should the other story be any more true than her own? – for again, both are stories.

And then there is the area of truth that is reductive and analytic, which says that all of Orual's explanations are attempts to hide from the reality of her hideous nature. On this level she is the devouring side of Ungit. This is the level where she can hate Psyche for leaving her, hate the god for taking her, hate any love offered to her which is less than a total and exclusive. '"We have been free loving friends." (Why must she say bare *friends*?)'(77); '"Love you? Why, Maia, what have I ever had to love save you and our grandfather the Fox?" (but I did not want her to bring even the Fox in now)' (81); 'And now she was saying *he* every moment, no other name but he – the way young wives talk. Something began to grow colder and harder inside me. And this also is like what I've known in wars; when that which was only *they* or *the enemy* all at once becomes the man, two feet away, who means to kill you' (131). This is the Orual who portrays herself with Psyche as a mother looking after a wayward child, and uses that to justify her destroying Psyche's happy 'play' on the Mountain (161). This too is the Orual whose complaint when it is at last read to the gods appears, finally stripped of all justification and evasion, as a hideous gnawing of self. What begins as an attack on the gods for deceiving her, and for their thefts of the things men love most, ends as the absurd '"You'll say I was jealous. Jealous of Psyche? Not while she was mine"' (302). Then she becomes plainer: '"What should I care for some horrible, new happiness which I hadn't given her and which separated her from me? Do you think I wanted her to be happy, that way? It would have been better if I'd see the Brute tear her in pieces before my eyes."' The bedrock here is: '"Did you ever remember whose the girl was? She was mine. *Mine*; do you not know what the word means? Mine! You're thieves, seducers"' (303). At this level Orual has reduced Psyche to a mere thing, her love has been shrivelled to a bare need to be needed, to glut herself with another. At this point she has become the devouring Shadowbrute which, it was believed, would eat Psyche on the Mountain. This is the totally damnatory view of Orual.

So much for that level of truth, but there is still another: yet all these layers are mixed up with one another like the mixed seeds of Psyche's task, and while they can be put in separate piles, the piles belong together. Just as Orual digs down from chamber to chamber in the vision in the palace of Glome, so there is another stage, one no more and no less true than the others. For beyond the reduction of her 'superficially' good impulses to bad ones, there is a level at which all the bad turns once more to good. When she is able to find voice for the evil that is in her heart, she is able to admit the good. Her complaint is her answer, and her cry of hatred a prelude to renewal of true love for Psyche.

One other layer in our experience of Orual's moral nature is to be found in what can be called the transformation of the past. We have seen so far the area in which the good and the evil lie side by side; and that in which apparent good is revealed to be a mask for evil, and that in turn becomes a way to good. But there is also a process by which 'good' and 'evil' are made retrospective. An act carried out in relative innocence in one moment, from another perspective becomes a guilty one. An instance is the tale of the priest of Essur, which describes Psyche's sisters as having seen the palace in which she lived, and yet, out of jealousy, having ruined her bliss. This later version turns the view of Orual's past dealings with Psyche from just to unjust. This is the main thrust of Orual's complaint against the gods, that they have falsified her actions, that originally they gave her only a faint hint of the palace and forced her to guess, and guess wrongly about Psyche's life on the Mountain.

When we were given Orual's original account of this we had no reason to doubt it. She had drunk at the river in the gods' secret valley to clear her mind, yet wondered whether a stream in the gods' country might in fact create the reverse of mental clarity. And it was twilight. Suddenly, looking into the mist across the water, she saw the palace:

> There stood the palace; grey, as all things were grey in that hour and place, but solid and motionless, wall within wall, pillar and arch and architrave, acres of it, a labyrinthian beauty. As she [Psyche] had said, it was like no house ever seen in our land or age. Pinnacles and buttresses leapt up – no memories of mine, you would think, could help me to imagine them – unbelievably tall and slender, pointed and prickly as if stone were shooting out into branch and flower. No light showed from any window. It was a house asleep. (141)

No imagination this: for this is a medieval castle, a building in the far future. Yet as Orual prepares to go across the river to make her apology to Psyche and to the god for disbelieving them, all at once 'the whole thing vanished', and Orual is left with the riddle: is the place real or a trick of the gods? Nothing in the account makes us disbelieve what Orual is saying, particularly because as she says she could not have imagined a palace of this construction. Because the place is so objective we have no grounds here for feeling that Orual refuses the vision rather than that it is withdrawn.[5] It seems as she says that the gods have both given and taken away. Yet later the version in the story of the priest of Essur says that the wicked sisters saw the palace and that '"They wanted to destroy her [Psyche] *because* they had seen her palace....because they were jealous. Her husband and her house were so much finer than theirs' (253). And still later we find Orual in her complaint to the gods, admitting to this, "'You will say the real gods are not at all like Ungit, and that I was shown a real god and the house of a real god and ought to know it. Hypocrites! I do know it'" (301).

What are we to make of this? Why has she changed her mind? Well, the complaint to the gods is not the one Orual wanted to utter. When she is before them she finds that her prepared indictment, her book, has gone and that she is left with a few rags of paper savagely scrawled over. Though she refuses to read it and demands back her book, she finds herself reading the scraps nevertheless. Is the complaint she reads the true one, stripped of all covering to a mere savage shout of rage and self-pity? If it is, then she has been cheating us during her narrative – or rather us along with herself. We know that she held back all mention of the palace from Bardia and the Fox, indeed struggled to give a favorable account of her doings to the Fox that he saw through but refrained out of compassion from criticising. Perhaps she has done the same to us.

Yet we need not simply accept this evolutionary view, whereby the past is only an immature form of the present. It is equally possible that the experience was as she described it. It is in the same way possible to argue that the present is an inaccurate rendering of the past. Is not self-indictment as much an over-simplification as self-justification? Certainly the gods seem to think so, on the basis of making Orual in the depths of her hatred one with Psyche. And when the Fox accused himself of having known that the gods were real and of having lied and fed Orual on words and maxims rather than the living truth, we know too that his disbelief in the gods was also not evasion but as far as he saw it honest rationality, and we are inclined, in part inaccurately, to agree with Orual: 'I wanted to cry out that was false, that he had fed me not on words but on love, that he had given, if not to the gods, yet to me, all that was costliest. But I had not time' (306). Everything is both true and not true.

And everything is continually subject to alteration without notice. We begin the book with Orual's statement that the whole is to be her indictment of divine justice: 'I will accuse the gods; especially the god who lives on the grey Mountain' (11). The book continues on these lines for five-sixths of its length and concludes, 'I say, therefore, that there is no creature (toad, scorpion, or serpent) so noxious to man as the gods. Let them answer my charge if they can....But.... they have no answer' (259). But then, in Part II, she adds more, which reverses this purpose. She has had a visionary experience that has denied all that has gone before. Yet what went before was part of the changing, so that it must stand. But our immediate experience of the book is that it has gone into reverse. We thought the whole thing constituted an attack on the gods and now it is turned round as a defence of them. Of course, in retrospect, it is possible to see how the two are in fact fused, the natural merging into the supernatural, not conflicting with it as in Orual's first encounter with Psyche on the Mountain when she felt the two worlds grating against one another 'like the two bits of a broken bone' (129). But the most direct impression is that she is rewriting the past. And that, we are told, is what only the gods can do for us: '"This age of ours will one day be the distant past. And the Divine Nature can change the past. Nothing is yet in its true form"' (316; compare 182).

This story is a myth which, as Lewis said, is an image, not the very real; and it is 'a myth re-told'. Every statement is true and untrue. It is not that stories are inherently unreliable: indeed Orual says that her writing enables her to see truths which might otherwise have remained concealed from her, and that her tyrannic memory and the need to speak *truth* in complaining to the gods forced her to be accurate (263). Rather, what we are dealing with here is the fact that truth and reality are plastic: what is true in one place is not in another. Of course it is also the case that Orual evolves from evasion to direct statement, from half-truths to real ones, but that is not the point here. Here even in analysis the past becomes active in the present, 'What began the change was the very writing itself' (263). Out of the attempt to lay a past reality to rest through writing, a new reality emerged and would have no rest. What seemed a mere record became a transforming act. The gods themselves are in constant metamorphosis, '"We're all limbs and part of one Whole. Hence, of each other. Men, and gods, flow in and out and mingle"' (311-2; see also 292).[6]

Truth itself is continually mobile and changing. Orual is and is not guilty. Orual's evil turns to good and she to Psyche. Orual's story is true; yet it is also an evasive falsehood. Orual's story shifts to that of the gods and thence to any version of the story, including the reader's interpretation of it. This multiplicity of truth is not anarchy or confusion: it is part of the variety of divine fact. For truth is no single thing, nor is it ever finished: rather it becomes more and more itself as it gathers more identities; '"Nothing is yet in its true form."' The book ends unfinished in mid-sentence as Orual falls dead over her manuscript; and yet at the same time it is finished. Reality, which is ultimately divine reality, is not to be caught by definitions and definite statements: 'I ended my first book with the words *No answer*. I know

now, Lord, why you utter no answer. You are yourself the answer. Before your face questions die away' (319).

So it is that one identity slides into another throughout the narrative, and one assumption shifts to different ones. Orual, who we think solid and real enough – it is part of Lewis's skill in this book that he makes his characters at once very natural and individual, and yet at the same time thin-walled or even abstract – Orual is shown also to be Psyche (who is also the soul), and her story, which seemed to be separate from Psyche's after her exile, is shown actually to have absorbed Psyche's exiled experience. Orual wanted to regain Psyche: the god grants her request in a way she could not have imagined. This Orual is one who sought to separate herself from life. She hid behind her veil; she tried to shut away her past when she locked up Psyche's house and became Queen (192, 234, 235); and she turned herself from the gods in her detestation of their interference in human affairs. Yet in her very isolation from the gods Orual was being operated on by them continually.

In a sense, perhaps, Lewis has moved away from his former voluntarist view of evil and Hell to something nearer the universalist view of his mentor George MacDonald: we cannot, finally, divide ourselves from the divine nature. Indeed in one way, so to try to separate ourselves is sometimes to begin the process of throwing ourselves on the divine mercy. Yet the individual self remains real enough too. Orual 'became' Psyche in her exile, but Psyche herself also had to perform tasks the pain of which Orual bore (309-11). Throughout it is always 'is, and is not'. In the story of the priest of Essur, both sisters went to see Psyche in the palace; in Orual's story only she did: but perhaps in a sense Orual took some of Redival's nature with her when she went – some jealousy, cruelty, scorn, that made her choose as she did. Why else three *sisters*?

Again, nature and supernature slip in and out of one another. Is the entire story largely a delusion on Orual's part? Is her experience of the gods at the end a creation of her own dying mind? Suppose we said that at the end she is in fact putting a supernatural gloss on a process she followed naturally. We could then say that in her writing her account of her feelings about Psyche she has 'got it off her chest', and can then perceive her own errors and learn about herself. After all, the gods 'do' nothing. Orual complains, and finds her complaint its own answer. The moral level of reading is justified because there is a 'psycho-logic' in Orual's growth. But at the same time it is also a spiritual journey, one which could only be made through the intercession of a god.

And in some ways the things that we look at as most natural are supernatural, and vice versa. We may think that there is hardly any god at all in the story, except in that brief appearance on the mountain to Orual, but in a way the god is most present in those seemingly secular actions of running a kingdom or writing a book. For these common duties turn out to have been the carrying of another's burden, through the mercy of a god for whom 'the earth and stars and sun, all that was or will be, existed' (318). In a sense, when the god is most hidden, he is most revealed: when most shut out he comes in to act on Orual.

At other times the supernatural seems to be present in the world, and then abruptly not. When Psyche is used to give the healing touch to people in Glome, it seems to have 'worked' for a time, but then her hands do not appear to heal, and she is even accused of causing disease and evil, and is called 'the Accursed'. Who is to say whether her 'healing' was real, and whether the god was present or not? When the land is afflicted by drought and plague and threatened by foreign powers, the priest of Ungit says that Ungit is angry and that she must be appeased with a sacrifice to the Brute on the mountain; and indeed, when Psyche, the chosen victim, has been left to die, the plague and drought go, and the King's enemies fall before him. Yet in a short time some of these threats return. Who is to say or not say that the offering of Psyche brought about a miracle?

Then there is the identity of the god himself. He is not merely 'pagan', he is one with the nature of Christ without being lost in any simple identification – golden with life as Pythian Apollo, yet in no way led by the whims of a Greek god – a being who sums the essential supernatural fabric and law of being. To put it another way, 'Christianity' is, like much of what happens in the story, a changing of the past, for Christ takes this god into Himself. At the moment when the god is most richly himself, he flows into another form.

So too with this book. The long 'complaint' section seems to stand alone, capped off and reversed by the subsequent vision, which leaves Orual to wish she could have re-written the whole: yet the complaint is actually part of, indeed another form of, revision and answer, so that the whole makes up a unit that Orual would not see, still wanting to make all things evidently consistent with one another. And there are the biblical inter-relationships. The movement from complaint to vision is not only like, it participates in, the same movement that constitutes the shift from the natural law of the Old Testament to the grace of the New. It is part of that great turning of a historical and spiritual cycle.

Orual's persuasion of Psyche to disobey the god is not just *like*, it is a version of, the temptation and fall of man.

Is and is not: the chains that Orual hears squeaking at night outside her bed chamber sound not only like, in a sense they are, Psyche weeping, and she tries to shut them out (238, 244). Orual's story is and is not the search to separate the grains in the Cupid and Psyche myth (266-7). In a sense she herself has taken on Psyche's tasks, and has been seeking fleece and water and beauty all her life. Is and is not: the whole story both participates in and re-works the myth as Apuleius has it. And it suggests its own contingency in speaking of other versions, or of this version as mere story. Words and images themselves both conceal and reveal, both act as masks to hide the face of something and yet the more fully display it through those masks. The priest of Ungit says that the Brute has been seen by a shepherd on the mountain as a great dark shape, with the first lion to enter Glome close behind it. When the Fox tells him that his Brute is merely a shadow cast by the lion, the priest replies, "'That is the wisdom of the Greeks...And if the Brute was a shadow... what then? Many say it *is* a shadow'" (56). Words lie: Orual sees how the common talk has already falsified her deeds and mixed them with those of another queen, so that 'a fine patchwork of wonders and impossibilities [has been] made out of both' (235). She rejects her book as an assemblage of falsifying words: and yet the writing of it has been her way to the truth.

The book is called *Till We Have Faces*: yet curiously the formlessness of the goddess Ungit is more spiritually satisfying to her worshippers than the beautiful and definite statue of her as Aphrodite which is imported to Glome from Greece and placed beside the old image. It is the faceless Ungit, blood-besmeared, that the people of Glome still prefer (281-3), because it will take what form they choose. To fix on one appearance is in a sense to have no appearance: indeed, to 'fix' life generally is to forfeit self. Orual will not let Psyche go, will not accept the reality of Psyche's love for the god, will not allow identity to another person. We see her swallow the Fox and Bardia in her purposes, not seeing their needs for homeland, or wife, or peace (274-7, 307).

Because Orual cannot allow their selfhood to others, she loses her own: alone with herself she is "with a nothingness" (245). Her veil before her ugly face is not just her disguise but is a symbol of her refusal of identity. The ironic conclusion of all this is the point when she goes about with her face exposed and is not recognised. Her whole story is an attempt to justify and fix herself, and a struggle to define the indefinite character of life. It is only when she gives her self away that she gains it: and the self that she gains is no fixed thing but has many faces, not excluding Psyche and Ungit. At that point the self is another kind of 'nothing', not an empty void on its own, but a thing without boundaries, merged in the natures of all others:

> I was being unmade. I was no one. But that's little to say; rather, Psyche herself was, in a manner, no one. I loved her as I would once have thought it impossible to love; would have died any death for her. And yet, it was not, not now, she that really counted. Or if she counted (and oh, gloriously she did) it was for another's sake. The earth and stars and sun, all that was or will be, existed for his sake. (318)

The god does not appear here, and only 'indefinitely' elsewhere because he has all identities and no single one. The priest of Ungit says "'I know that they [the gods] dazzle our eyes and flow in and out of one another like eddies on a river, and nothing that is said clearly can be said truly about them. Holy places are dark places. It is life and strength, not knowledge and words, that we get in them'" (58). Again, true and not true.

Till We Have Faces is in a way a fine achievement. But it has never been a popular book, perhaps because of its 'facelessness' of style, its refusal of narrative excitement and wonder, and above all its exhaustive analysis of the spirit. Certainly it is not a book that we would readily recognise as being by Lewis: it is as though he himself had shifted to a quite new identity in writing it. Its strength lies in part in its refusal of literariness, its rejection of easy moral judgments, its truth to life. Never before had Lewis created characters of such realism while making them parts of so subtle a moral and metaphysical pattern. Here in action is something of the dance of contraries he described at the end of *Perelandra*.

In this book Lewis implicates the reader more perhaps than in any other. Looking through Orual's eyes, we learn to sympathise with her and her judgments, only to realise, as the story seems to 'reverse' itself in that final version, that we have missed a greater or lesser part of her evil; and, to the extent that we have, we participate in her wrongdoing. The sharing of identity that occurs at the end of the book radiates outwards to take us in too. No 'smuggling in' by Lewis of Christian doctrine under fairytale guise here: only someone whose faith is now so fused with his everyday life that whatever he writes will be drawn into it naturally, and his readers with it.

There are ways in which this book may remind us of the novels of Henry James, particularly *The Sacred Fount* or *The Golden Bowl*. For in those books we learn to distrust the narrator, but are never able to be certain how far he or she is wrong. The truth is left indeterminate. In *The Sacred Fount* the theory of the mutual parasitism the narrator thinks he detects between a husband and wife is defeated by a more powerfully put alternative view by one of the suspects, and he is driven to conclude, 'What I too fatally lacked was her tone.' In *Till We Have Faces* we are left uncertain between Orual's view of events and that of the priest of Essur. And like the narrator of *The Sacred Fount*, Orual can in part be viewed as a spiritual vampire. But the contrast with James is that in *Till We Have Faces*, both views, of Orual innocent and of Orual guilty, are simultaneously true. Where James leaves us with a hideous indeterminacy, Lewis leaves us with a paradox. This is because his vision is *sub specie deorum*, for paradox is the language of heaven. Paradoxes have recently been made the essence of the 'postmodernist' novel, in which reality and truth are treated as a multiverse of mutually contradictory visions. But Lewis is not playing with reality like these novels. He is living it, through Orual, who is living in the idiom of the gods when she most opposes them. Her complaint is her answer, she is Psyche, myths can alter facts, Christ is present in a pagan world where one person and one god can substitute for another: for divine reality is most truly plastic, and 'nothing is yet in its true form.'

Endnotes

1. Letter of 20 Apr. 1959, to Joan Lancaster, quoted in Glover, *C. S. Lewis*, 189. See also Charles Wrong, 'A Chance Meeting' in James T. Como (ed.), *C. S. Lewis at the Breakfast Table and Other Reminiscences*, 109.

2. Peter Schakel, *Reason and Imagination in C. S. Lewis: a Study of 'Till We Have Faces'*, traces a growing stress on subjectivity of vision throughout Lewis's literary career, especially marked after his autobiography *Surprised by Joy* (1955).

3. Kilby, *The Christian World of C. S. Lewis*, 51-2, 58-64; Kilby, '*Till We Have Faces*: An Interpretation' (1972), repr. in Schakel (ed.), *The Longing for a Form*, 171-81; Urang, *Shadows of Heaven*, 42-7; Walsh, *The Literary Legacy of C. S. Lewis*, 78-81; Schakel, *Reason and Imagination in C. S. Lewis*, 6-86; Doris Meyers, *C. S. Lewis in Context*, 206-09.

4. Compare Paul L. Holmer, *C. S. Lewis: the Shape of his Faith and Thought*, 21, 39-41, who sees Lewis's work as drawing in that reader, and says of *Till We Have Faces* that 'it says things that are unfamiliar and which indict the reader when understanding dawns' (39).

5. Steve Van Der Weele, 'From Mt. Olympus to Glome: C. S. Lewis's Dislocation of Apuleius's "Cupid and Psyche" in *Till We Have Faces*', in Schakel (ed.), *The Longing for a Form*, 190, says, 'though there may be some legitimate doubt about the reality of the vision, the truth of the matter is that she doesn't want to see it, and the castle vanishes. She chooses to deny its reality'. (This is a common view taken by critics who see Orual only as guilty of selfish love.) No basis is offered for the certainty of this statement: this is not to deny that it is later given some truth, but that cannot be used to obliterate the other possible views here. Equally questionable is Van Der Weele's statement of Orual's 'refusal to act appropriately – crossing the river and asking Psyche for forgiveness' (188): in the novel we are told that she intends to do just that and is addressing herself to the river when the vision disappears (142).

6. Several commentators link this to the concept of a great web of divine co-inherence and exchange within creation that forms the basis of the theology of Charles Williams, close friend of Lewis – see e.g. Schakel, 82; Joe R. Christopher, 'Archetypal Patterns in *Till We Have Faces*' in Schakel (ed.), *The Longing for a Form*, 206-10.

Chapter 9

Conclusion

If we look back over what we have seen in all these works by C.S. Lewis, the first thing that strikes us is the diversity, both of the works themselves and of the kinds of interpretation they ask. Even within the Narnia books, apart from Narnia itself and the presence of Aslan, one might not be sure that the same man wrote *The Horse and His Boy* as wrote *The Lion, the Witch and the Wardrobe*, or *The Silver Chair* as wrote *The Magician's Nephew*. *The Pilgrim's Regress*, Lewis's only direct allegory, seems also rather an isolated work, and in fact he bids us reject it as too idiosyncratic.[1] *That Hideous Strength*, while it partakes in the cosmic history of the earlier two space novels, and still has Ransom (if in a more reserved role), seems quite starkly different from the others. *The Great Divorce* is a new adventure in genre; *Till We Have Faces* is a totally new start in literary idiom and vision.

Of course there are common features in all the books. All are more or less Christian, and involve a journey out of the self towards the 'other'; most concern joy and our various misinterpretations or refusals of it; all have the same vision of evil as constriction (from the bracelet on Eustace's dragon arm in *The Voyage of the 'Dawn Treader'* to the tiny Hell in *The Great Divorce*), and Heaven as solidity, 'joy' and dance. And there are recurrent ideas in the apologetics and literary criticism; and it is quite possible to show the central principles of Lewis's thought. But he loved variety for itself, and he shows it throughout his fiction. His short stories, too, range from 'The Shoddy Lands', describing the dreary interior landscape of a certain woman's mind, to 'After Ten Years', which portrays Menelaus's feelings about Helen after the fall of Troy, and to a terrifying vision of the future in 'The Dark Tower'.[2]

Lewis writes about 'other' worlds partly to make each 'other' in relation to the one prior to it. After Malacandra, Perelandra; after the precincts of Heaven, Narnia; after Narnia, Glome. It is in a way an imitation of the creative idiom of Maleldil that the Oyéresu describe in *Perelandra*:

> 'Never did He make two things the same; never did He utter one word twice. After earths, not better earths but beasts; after beasts, not better beasts but spirits. After a falling, not a recovery but a new creation. Out of the new creation, not a third, but the mode of change itself is changed for ever.' (*Perelandra*, 198)

All his life Lewis loved the 'new', not for the mere sake of novelty but for the sake of the freshness that came through it, often a freshness of re-discovery of the old. He valued George MacDonald's mythic work because it 'shocks us more fully awake than we are for most of our lives'.[3] All his literary criticism is devoted to taking the reader out of self to become part of the different works, from a dragon-hunter with Beowulf to an angel with Milton or a man who has met a ghost with *Hamlet*; equally he asks that we learn to see the universe in the many different ways in which it has been viewed by minds in the past.

Lewis's own work is inherently revolutionary. He inverts Bunyan's *The Pilgrim's Progress* with his *The Pilgrim's Regress*. He directs serious critical attention to science fiction and to children's literature. He transposes the science fiction of H.G. Wells into a genre of religious power. He makes a children's book able to carry the deepest truths of the Gospels without strain. He demands of his academic peers that they attend to works and authors they have unjustly neglected. He insists that we become continually aware of how our view of the world is but a tiny shuttered thing, how we need to see Earth in the cosmic context we ignore, or how we might look to a Martian or a devil. And the whole of his Christian life is founded on a totally new approach to God by way of a 'dialectic of desire', by tracing the powerful emotions awakened by certain images to what was for him their divine source. As for his apologetics, there was nothing for Lewis so dead as some doctrine he had just defended.[4] And throughout his work his style shows him a master of the revitalising analogy that joins the ineffable and the commonplace.[5] His 'nature' – and for him nature is only one among many other possible natures[6] – eludes all our categorisations and is constantly subject to what seem to us alterations without notice:

I do not say that the normalities of Nature are unreal. The living fountain of divine energy, solidified for purposes of this spatio-temporal Nature into bodies moving in space and time, and thence, by our abstract thought, turned into mathematical formulae, does in fact, for us, commonly fall into such and such patterns. In finding out these patterns we are therefore gaining real, and often useful, knowledge. But to think that a disturbance of them would constitute a breach of the living rule and organic unity whereby God, from His own point of view, works, is a mistake. If miracles do occur then we may be sure that *not* to have wrought them would be the real inconsistency.[7]

That last point is a typical Lewis inversion of old habits of seeing.

A central 'spiritual' theme in Lewis's work is the need to come out of the self towards Reality. The narrow categories by which people define themselves and the world are to be broken down, whether in our view of nature as described in *Miracles,* or in the ill-examined 'progressivism' of Mark Studdock in *That Hideous Strength.* John in *The Pilgrim's Regress* is continually being shaken from his misinterpretations of the source of his desire. In *Out of the Silent Planet* Ransom has to emerge from himself and his fears, to communicate with the alien and meet the 'other'; in *Perelandra* he has to understand how limited was his own previous view of himself. In *That Hideous Strength* Mark Studdock and his wife are brought to see how shallowly they have understood an 'ordinary' world that proves to be surrounded by angels and devils. The damned in *The Great Divorce,* most of them refuse to leave their selves, refuse the shining reality all about them. The shut-in self is a theme in *The Voyage of the 'Dawn Treader'* with Eustace made a dragon, in *The Silver Chair* with Rilian's enchantment in the Underland, with Jadis and Uncle Andrew, both unable to grasp the joy of the creation of Narnia in *The Magician's Nephew,* and with the self-blinding dwarves in *The Last Battle.* In *Till We Have Faces,* Orual is for long deluded that she has done right, but from one point of view at least she is a murderess, and her evasions are demolished.

That is why one of the recurrent techniques of Lewis's fiction is 'rug-pulling'. The mountain John seemed to be going away from in *The Pilgrim's Regress* he was actually approaching; and his journey as a Christian involves not going on but 'back' through the landscape he has just traversed. Ransom's notions regarding Malacandra are continually being revised during *Out of the Silent Planet.* In *Perelandra* the prohibited Fixed Land partly symbolises the fixed mind, in contrast to the floating islands: both Ransom and the Lady have their preconceptions reversed throughout. In *The Great Divorce* Hell is a place not of melodramatic torments or grandly evil souls, but of spiritual seediness inhabited by boring ghosts; and any notion we may have had of Heaven as a vague place is cancelled by its extreme solidity. The rules of magic in *The Lion, the Witch and the Wardrobe* are first sprung on us and then overthrown in a quite unexpected manner by Aslan. The order of the Narnia books is 'dislocated'. Narnia is created in *The Magician's Nephew* long after we have taken its existence for granted; and then destroyed and re-created in higher form 'immediately afterwards' in *The Last Battle*. In *Till We Have Faces* the actions of Orual are subject to continual re-interpretation; and her rejection of the gods becomes their way of bringing her to them. Always truth is shown to lie both nearer to and further from us than we could have thought.

There is another reason for the variety of the worlds of Lewis's fiction, one connected with his notion of *Sehnsucht* or desire itself. In the *Voyage of the 'Dawn Treader'* the travellers to the uttermost East must keep continually moving: each stage in the latter part of their journey – Ramandu's island, the sea of sweet water and mer-people, the great expanse of water lilies – is a harbinger of the joys to come; yet for the children those joys are not to be kept, for they are sent back to their own world, and Reepicheep's attainment of bliss is lost to view. It is always a case of 'Farther up and farther in'; and so far as images go, Charles Williams's phrase 'This also is Thou: neither is this Thou,' also applies. When the children arrive in Aslan's country, the romantic images of longing give way to 'plain' scriptural realities, as they are met by a lamb offering them, as in St John 21, a breakfast of roasting fish. As Lewis said,

> the scriptural imagery has authority. It comes to us from writers who were closer to God than we, and it has stood the test of Christian experience down the centuries. The natural appeal of this authoritative imagery is to me, at first, very small. At first sight it chills, rather than awakes, my desire. And this is just what I ought to expect. If Christianity could tell me no more of the far-off land than my own temperament led me to surmise already, then Christianity would be no higher than myself. If it has more to give me, I must expect it to be less immediately attractive than 'my own stuff'.[8]

Each of Lewis's books starts from 'his own stuff', from subjective and more romantic images: in the Narnia books he said he deliberately avoided the 'Sunday school' associations of anything more directly biblical, to steal past our inbuilt resistance to such imagery and teach us unawares. Through each of Narnia, Malacandra and Perelandra, Lewis presents one image of the desirable, and in all his books he writes about a quest for the image of desire or, in *Till We Have Faces*, a stubborn refusal of it when it is presented. But the image must change from book to book, because it is always inadequate:

> The books or the music in which we though the beauty was located will betray us if we trust to them; it was not *in* them, it only came *through* them, and what came through them was longing. These things – the beauty, the memory of our own past – are good images of what we really desire; but if they are mistaken for the thing itself they turn into dumb idols, breaking the hearts of their worshippers. For they are not the thing itself; they are only the scent of a flower we have not found, the echo of a tune we have not heard, news from a country we have never yet visited.[9]

The dialectic of this desire in Lewis's work is also that the existence of the desire is a measure of the distance of its source, as is our sense of the 'other': once we reach its object, the desire will cease and a different joy begin. Our longings both join us to and show our separation from God.

More generally, the interplay of opposites, which continually produces spiritual mobility and exposure to the new, is part of the fabric of Lewis's work. Stories are at once sequential and nets for catching something that is not sequential at all. There are narratives, but they are continually interrupted by discourse, speculation, contemplation or even reversal of direction or sequence. Lewis believed that we must grow, develop and evolve spiritually: but in a sense he also believed that in eternity such growth is already accomplished: that is the vision his fictional self is given in *The Great Divorce*. He attacked 'the fatal serialism of the modern imagination – the image of infinite unilinear progression which so haunts our minds.... There are progressions in which the last step is *sui generis* – incommensurable with the others – and in which to go the whole way is to undo all the labour of your previous journey.'[10] Equally, the pattern of his narratives is often one in which the schemes of the evil serve only to further the cause of good. Weston takes Ransom to Malacandra, the doings of the N.I.C.E bring down Deep Heaven upon their heads, the Witch's killing of Aslan only gives him greater life, Orual's elaboration of her case against the gods becomes its own answer. This of course is a pattern fundamental of Christian narrative, that out of evil will come some greater good.

Lewis's stories thus stay still as well as go forward. The 'staying still' can be seen in their circularity of form. John in *The Pilgrim's Regress* journeys west till he finds himself back close to where he started. Many of the books end where they began, with Ransom back on Earth or the children returned home from Narnia. The last two of the Narnia books portray the creation and then the destruction of Narnia, telescoped together almost to show that history and length are as nothing. In *Till We Have Faces* Orual finds that her complaint is its own answer. And Lewis's work as a whole describes a circle in that the journey in the last book, *Till We Have Faces*, both parallels and contrasts with the journey in the first, *The Pilgrim's Regress*.

Circularity is also seen in the way that Lewis's stories often involve a restoration of the status quo. In the 'space trilogy' change is threatened and Ransom acts to keep things as they are. He protects the innocence of the Land on Perelandra and helps to keep the devils from gaining a foothold on Earth. In *The Lion, the Witch and the Wardrobe* Narnia is returned to its true self; in *Prince Caspian* and *The Silver Chair* a usurped or kidnapped heir is restored to the throne; in *The Horse and His Boy* a long-lost prince recovers his identity.

But each book also involves a more 'linear' journey out of self, and from darkness to light. Though John in *The Pilgrim's Regress* ends where he began, his journey has been a necessary one involving a transformation of his spirit. While the Lady of *Perelandra* remains innocent, her innocence has changed with her new knowledge of her free will. In *That Hideous Strength* Mark and Jane Studdock's marriage is transformed. *The Voyage of the 'Dawn Treader'* describes a journey to the Uttermost East that is also a journey of the spirit. *The Lion, the Witch and the Wardrobe* shows us Narnia being changed from winter to spring. *The Magician's Nephew* portrays the creation of Narnia as a new world. In *The Last Battle* Narnia is ended, and the story opens into heaven. *Till We Have Faces* describes the gradual purification of Orual's love for Psyche. There is however one book where scarcely any change occurs, and that is *The Great Divorce*, where the unaltered Ghosts return to Hell: this is the antitype.

Those who journey out of the self become able to meet the not-self, the 'other'. John's spiritual journey leads him to the Landlord. Ransom meets Oyarsa on Malacandra when he has come so far out of his original fears of the planet's inhabitants as to be almost a Malacandrian himself. Aslan is hidden from the children in *Prince Caspian* until they drop their self-will, as the god (in one way) is hidden from Orual in *Till*

❧ Conclusion ❦

We Have Faces. Encounter with the 'other', whether through *Sehnsucht* or more direct contact like that of Ransom, is one of the leitmotifs of Lewis's work, and puts its character close to the mystical.

There is another dialectic operative in Lewis's work, between things 'accidental' and things 'designed'. Every move in John's search for his Island was, unknown to him, part of a pattern of spiritual development leading him to God. Ransom's apparently accidental involvement with the powers of Deep Heaven, even his name, is part of an action both designed and already in a sense complete. The choices of the ghosts in *The Great Divorce* are being made 'now' and yet are long since determined. The random-seeming sequence of the Narnia books, oddities such as a lamp-post in a snowy waste, and all the different protagonists involved, become clear in a larger design. Orual's complaint against the gods falls in to a larger complaint by them against her. Many of the stories have a mythic dimension - the Fall and Christ stories behind the space trilogy and *The Lion, the Witch and the Wardrobe*, the journey to the Promised Land in the *The Horse and His Boy*, the Cupid and Psyche myth behind *Till we Have Faces*. Always reality is more elusive, more mobile, and yet more close to us than we might have supposed. And that is why the image of the Great Dance, that medium of Reality in which all lesser realities have their place, is the one to which these novels belong.

As far as we as literary critics are concerned the themes of deeper realities and patterns than one might have imagined or of the apparently accidental and the designed apply also to our experience in interpretation of Lewis's books. What often seemed 'mere' stories have shown themselves to be patterned in ways we could not have supposed, with formal structures far beyond those of simply linear narrative or fictional apologetics. In this way this book has been a kind of journey outwards too; and Lewis's fiction has shown as much complexity in its way as his worlds do to those who travel them.

But we should not, while they enrich, make the mistake of seeing the patterns as more 'real' than their constituent elements. The 'otherness' of Lewis's fiction is not simply to be found in its depths, but on the surface, in the immediate object as much as in that object as a participant with others in a larger structure. For Lewis it is part of the truth that all things are at the 'centre', even the meanest grain of dust (*Perelandra*, 200): and reality is in character supremely concrete and individual.[11] The stories and each thing in them matter supremely in themselves (even while they also do not), and all begin with images: in a sense all Narnia exists for that first crunch of snow beneath Lucy's feet as she goes through the wardrobe, but no more than for any other action. Oyéresu, Orual, Malacandra, Dwarves, Dufflepuds, *hrossa*, bubble-trees, these things are to be savoured, as it were, for their 'quiddity', the sheer solidity of their separate being, before those beings will join themselves in the patterns we have found. Rightly apprehended, the patterns and the elements of which they are made share natures without being less themselves; just as, at a higher level, myth and fact become one.[12] Beyond that, in the Great Dance of being Ransom sees on Perelandra, every element participates in a larger and larger living design that is in its way an image of the totality of Lewis's ever-changing works.

> 'In the plan of the Great Dance plans without number interlock, and each movement becomes in its season the breaking into flower of the whole design to which all else had been directed. Thus each is equally at the centre and none are there by being equals, but some by given place and some by receiving it, the small things by their smallness and the great by their greatness, and all the patterns linked and looped together by the union of a kneeling with a sceptred love.'[13]

ENDNOTES

1. Letter of 19 Jan 1953 to Mrs Edward A. Allen, in W. H. Lewis (ed.), *Letters of C. S. Lewis*, 248-9.
2. Published respectively in 1956, 1966 and 1977, and repr. in Lewis, *The Dark Tower and Other Stories*.
3. Lewis, *George MacDonald: an Anthology*, 17.
4. See Green and Hooper, *C. S. Lewis*, 230. Compare Lewis, 'The Apologist's Evening Prayer' in Walter Hooper (ed.), *Poems*, 139.
5. Dabney A. Hart writes well on this in her *Through the Open Door: a New Look at C. S. Lewis*, ch. VI.
6. Lewis, *Miracles*, 69-70.
7. Ibid, 101.
8. Lewis, 'The Weight of Glory', *Transposition and Other Addresses*, 25-6. See also Lewis, 'No Beauty We Could Desire', in *Poems*, 124; and the conversation of the Bishop and the faerie-crazed queen in 'The Queen of Drum' (c.1933-34) in Lewis, *Narrative Poems*, ed. Walter Hooper, 152-3.
9. 'The Weight of Glory', 24. Compare the story in Lewis, *Surprised by Joy: the Shape of My Early Life*, passim.
10. Lewis, *The Abolition of Man*, 54-5.
11. Lewis, *Miracles*, 90.
12. Lewis 'Myth Became Fact' (1944), repr. in Lewis, *God in the Dock: Essays on Theology*, ed. Walter Hooper: 'In the enjoyment of a great myth we come nearest to experiencing as a concrete what can otherwise be understood only as an abstraction' (42). Compare Clyde Kilby, 'The Creative Logician Speaking', in Carolyn Keefe (ed.), *C. S. Lewis: Speaker and Teacher*, 43: 'Lewis loved the truth but never, if it could be helped, in abstraction. He always preferred the poetic over the prosaic even when he was writing prose. His stories, he said, always began with a picture, not, as one would suppose from remembering his Christian interests, with ideas or "truths"'.
13. *Perelandra*, 201; see also 202-3.

Bibliography

WORKS BY C.S. LEWIS

The Abolition of Man, or Reflections on Education with Special Reference to the Teaching of English in the Upper Forms of Schools, Riddell Memorial Lectures, Fifteenth Series (London: Oxford University Press, 1943).

Beyond Personality: the Christian Idea of God (London: Geoffrey Bles, 1944).

The Dark Tower and Other Stories, ed. Walter Hooper (London: Collins, Fount Paperbacks, 1983).

Dymer (1926), repr. in *Narrative Poems*.

(Ed. and introd.) *George MacDonald: an Anthology* (London: Geoffrey Bles, 1946).

The Great Divorce: a Dream (London: Geoffrey Bles, 1945).

The Horse and His Boy (London: Puffin Books, 1965).

'The Inner Ring' (1944), repr. in *Transposition and Other Addresses*.

'It All Began with a Picture...' (1960), repr. in *Of Other Worlds*.

The Last Battle (London: Puffin Books, 1964).

'Learning in War-Time' (1939), repr. in *Transposition and Other Addresses*.

Letters of C. S. Lewis, ed. W. H. Lewis (London: Geoffrey Bles, 1966).

Letters to Malcolm: Chiefly on Prayer (London: Geoffrey Bles, 1964).

The Lion, the Witch and the Wardrobe (London: Puffin Books, 1959).

The Magician's Nephew (London: Puffin Books, 1963).

Miracles: a Preliminary Study (London: Collins, Fontana Books, 1960).

'Myth Became Fact' (1944), repr. in *God in the Dock: Essays on Theology*, ed. Walter Hooper (London: Collins, Fount Paperbacks, 1979).

'The Nameless Isle' (1930), repr. in *Narrative Poems*.

Narrative Poems, ed. Walter Hooper (London: Geoffrey Bles, 1969).

Of Other Worlds: Essays and Stories, ed. Walter Hooper (London: Geoffrey Bles, 1966).

'On Science Fiction' (1955), repr. in *Of Other Worlds*.

'On Stories' (1947), repr. in *Of Other Worlds*.

'On Three Ways of Writing for Children' (1952), repr. in *Of Other Worlds*.

Out of the Silent Planet (London: Pan Books, 1963).

Perelandra, or Voyage to Venus (London: Pan Books, 1960).

The Pilgrim's Regress: an Allegorical Apology for Christianity, Reason and Romanticism, 3rd edn (London: Geoffrey Bles, 1943).

Poems, ed. Walter Hooper (London: Geoffrey Bles, 1964).

Prince Caspian (London: Puffin Books, 1962).

The Problem of Pain (London: Collins, Fontana Books, 1957).

'The Queen of Drum' (c. 1933-34), repr. in *Narrative Poems*.

'A Reply to Professor Haldane', in *Of Other Worlds*.

The Screwtape Letters (London: Collins, Fontana Books, 1955).

'Screwtape Proposes a Toast' (1959), repr. in *Screwtape Proposes a Toast and Other Pieces* (London: Collins, Fontana Books, 1965).

The Silver Chair (London: Puffin Books, 1965).

'Sometimes Fairy Stories May Say Best What's To Be Said' (1956), repr. in *Of Other Worlds: Essays and Stories*.

Surprised by Joy: the Shape of My Early Life (London: Geoffrey Bles, 1955).

That Hideous Strength: a Modern Fairy-Tale for Grown-Ups (London: Pan Books, 1983).

Till We Have Faces: a Myth Retold (London: Geoffrey Bles, 1956).

Transposition and Other Addresses (London: Geoffrey Bles, 1949).

'Unreal Estates' (1964), repr. in *Of Other Worlds*.

The Voyage of the 'Dawn Treader' (London: Puffin Books, 1965).

'The Weight of Glory' (1941), repr. in *Transposition and Other Addresses*.

SECONDARY WORKS

Adey, Lionel, *C. S. Lewis: Writer, Dreamer, and Mentor* (Grand Rapids, MI: Eerdmans, 1998).

Callaghan, Patrick J., 'The Two Gardens in C. S. Lewis's *That Hideous Strength*', in Clareson, Thomas D. (ed.), *SF: the Other Side of Realism* (Bowling Green University Popular Press, 1971).

Carnell, Corbin Scott, *Bright Shadow of Reality: C. S. Lewis and the Feeling Intellect* (Grand Rapids, Michigan: Eerdmans, 1974).

Christopher, Joe R., 'Archetypal Patterns in *Till We Have Faces*', in Schakel (ed.), *The Longing for a Form*.

Como, James. T. (ed.), *C. S. Lewis at the Breakfast Table and Other Reminiscences* (London: Collins, 1980).

Cox, John D., 'Epistemological Release in *The Silver Chair*', in Schakel (ed.), *The Longing for a Form*.

Gibb, Jocelyn (ed.), *Light on C. S. Lewis* (London: Geoffrey Bles, 1965).

Glover, Donald E., *C. S. Lewis: the Art of Enchantment* (Ohio University Press, 1981).

Green, Roger Lancelyn, and Hooper, Walter, *C. S. Lewis: a Biography* (London: Collins, 1974).

Hannay, Margaret Patterson, *C. S. Lewis* (New York: Ungar, 1981).

Hart, Dabney Adams, *Through the Open Door: a New Look at C. S. Lewis* (University of Alabama Press, 1984).

Holmer, Paul, L., *C. S. Lewis: the Shape of his Faith and Thought* (London: Sheldon Press, 1977).

Hooper, Walter, see under Green.

Hooper, Walter, 'Narnia: the Author, the Critics and the Tale', in Schakel (ed.), *The Longing for a Form*.

Howard, Thomas, *The Achievement of C. S. Lewis: a Reading of his Fiction* (Wheaton, Illinois: Harold Shaw Publishers, 1980).

Huttar, Charles A., 'C. S. Lewis's Narnia and the "Grand Design",' in Schakel (ed.), *The Longing for a Form*.

Kilby, Clyde S., *The Christian World of C. S. Lewis* (Abingdon, England: Marcham Manor Press, 1965).

------, '*Till We Have Faces*: an Interpretation' (1972), repr. in Schakel (ed.), *The Longing for a Form*.

Lindskoog, Kathryn, *The Lion of Judah in Never-Never Land: God, Man and Nature in C. S. Lewis's Narnia Tales* (Grand Rapids, Michigan: Eerdmans, 1973).

Manlove, C. N., *Modern Fantasy: Five Studies* (Cambridge University Press, 1975).

Meilaender, Gilbert, *The Taste for the Other: the Social and Ethical Thought of C. S. Lewis* (Grand Rapids, Michigan: Eerdmans, 1978).

Murphy, Brian, *C. S. Lewis* (Mercer Island, Washington: Starmont House, 1983).

Myers, Doris T., *C.S. Lewis in Context* (Kent, OH: Kent State University Press, 1994).

Oury, Scott, '"The Thing Itself": C. S. Lewis and the Value of Something Other', in Schakel (ed.), *The Longing for a Form*.

Prickett, Stephen, *Victorian Fantasy* (Brighton: Harvester Press, 1979).

Purtill, Richard, *Lord of the Elves and Eldils: Fantasy and Philosophy in C. S. Lewis and J. R. R. Tolkien* (Grand Rapids, Michigan: Zondervan Publishing, 1974).

------, '*That Hideous Strength:* a Double Story', in Schakel (ed.), *The Longing for a Form*.

Schakel, Peter J. (ed.), *The Longing for a Form: Essays on the Fiction of C. S. Lewis* (Kent State University Press, 1977).

------, *Reading with the Heart: the Way into Narnia* (Grand Rapids, Michigan: Eerdmans, 1979).

------, *Reason and Imagination in C. S. Lewis: a Study of 'Till We Have Faces'* (Grand Rapids, Michigan: Eerdmans, 1984).

Shumaker, Wayne, 'The Cosmic Trilogy of C. S. Lewis' (1955), repr. in Schakel (ed.), *The Longing for a Form*.

Urang, Gunnar, *Shadows of Heaven: Religion and Fantasy in the Fiction of C. S. Lewis, Charles Williams, and J. R. R. Tolkien* (London: SCM Press, 1971).

Van Der Weele, Steve J., 'From Mt. Olympus to Glome: C. S. Lewis's Dislocation of Apuleius's "Cupid and Psyche"', in *Till We Have Faces*' in Schakel (ed.), *The Longing for a Form*.

Walsh, Chad, 'The Reeducation of the Fearful Pilgrim', in Schakel (ed.), *The Longing for a Form*.

-----, *The Literary Legacy of C. S. Lewis* (London: Sheldon Press, 1979).

Ward, Michael, *Planet Narnia: The Seven Heavens in the Imagination of C.S. Lewis* (Oxford: Oxford University Press, 2008).

White, William Luther, *The Image of Man in C. S. Lewis* (London: Hodder & Stoughton, 1970).

Wrong, Charles, 'A Chance Meeting', in James T. Como, ed., *C.S. Lewis at the Breakfast Table*.

Zogby, Edward G., S. J., 'Triadic Patterns in Lewis's Life and Thought', in Schakel (ed.), *The Longing for a Form*.

Index

A
Abbott, E.A.,
   Flatland, 7, 55
Adey, Lionel, 1, 7
Aldiss Brian, 6;
   Cryptozoic!, 7
Amis, Kingsley, 6
Andersen, Hans Christian, 130
Anstey, F. (Thomas Anstey
   Guthrie),
   The Tinted Venus, 192 n.24
Apuleius, *The Golden Ass*,
   194, 195, 196, 208, 217

B
Barfield, Owen, 2, 3
Barnes, E.W., Bishop of
   Birmingham,
   The Rise of Christianity, 120 n.5
Beowulf, 222
Bible, the, 130-1, 135, 152, 154, 169,
   191 n.9, 192 ns 28, 29, 216, 224;
   quoted, 152
Blake, William, 'Eternity', cited, 60
Blyton, Enid, 121, 124;
   Five Go Adventuring Again, 124;
   Five on Kirrin Island Again, 124;
   Five on a Treasure Island, 124
Bunyan, John,
   Grace Abounding, 13;
   The Pilgrim's Progress, 13, 14, 30,
   222

C
Callaghan, Patrick, 99 n.11
Carnell, Corbin Scott, 76 n.11, 99
   n.8, 99 n.4, 130
Christopher, Joe R. 220 n.6
Coleridge, S.T.,
   The Ancient Mariner, 15;
   Christabel, 159

Corkran, Alice,
   Down the Snow Stairs, 101-02
Cox, John D., 192 ns 16, 17, 18

D
Dante Alighieri,
   Commedia, 199;
   Inferno, 104
Davidman, Joy, 197
De La Mare, Walter, 121
Dunsany, Lord, 156

E
Eliot, George,
   Middlemarch, 86
Eliot, T.S., quoted, 41;
   'Prufrock', 104;
   The Waste Land, 104

F
fairy tale, the, 175
Fitzgerald, Edward,
   The Rubaiyat, 167
Flecker, James Elroy,
   Hassan, 167
Forster, E.M.,
   'The Celestial Omnibus', 103
Freud, Sigmund, 21

G
Glover, Donald E., 27 n.3, 76 n.7,
   99 n.11, 191 ns 13,14, 192 ns 20,
   26, 29
Grahame, Kenneth, 130
Green, R.L.,
   The Wood That Time Forgot, 191
   n.7;
   (with Walter Hooper), *C.S.
   Lewis: A Biography*, 76 ns 1, 2,
   120 n.2, 191 n.7, 192 n.19, 229
   n.4

H

Hannay, Margaret, 99 n.4
Hart, Dabney A., 47 n.5, 229 n.5
Holmer, Paul L., 220 n.4
Homer,
 Odyssey, 149
Hooper, Walter, 192 ns 28, 29
Howard, Thomas, 47 ns 2, 6, 99 n.10, 190 n.27
Huttar, Charles A., 192 n.25
Huxley, Aldous,
 Brave New World, 99 n.8

J

'Jack the Giant Killer', 8
James, Henry,
 The Golden Bowl, 219;
 The Sacred Fount, 219
Johnson, Dr Samuel, 45
Joyce, James,
 A Portrait of the Artist, 16

K

Kilby, Clyde S., 1, 27 n.3, 220 n.3, 229 n.2
Kilns, The, 121-2, 192 n.19
Kingsley, Charles,
 The Water-Babies, 191 n.5
Kipling, Rudyard, 121

L

Law, William, 15
Lawrence, D.H.,
 Women in Love, 86
Lewis, C.S.,
 as apologist, 2-3, 102, 124-5;
 as children's writer, 16-17, 121-5;
 composition, mode of, 5-8;
 his conversion, 3;
 images as inspiration, 5-6, 8-10;
 early intellectual history fictionalized, 13-27;
 on fairy tales, 6, 122-3; ;
 fantasy his genre, 3-5
 on the 'inner ring', 87;
 originality, need for, 4-5, 102, 128, 222-5;
 and the 'other', 53-4, 69, 71, 226-8;
 on science, 41, 80, 83;
 and *Sehnsucht*, 8-10, 11 n.13, 14, 15, 49, 54, 61-2, 71, 76 n.11, 156, 193, 224, 227;
 on the *Tao*, 91;
 The Abolition of Man, 99 ns 6, 9, 225, 229 n.10;
 'The Adam at Night', 76 n.15;
 'After Ten Years', 221;
 Animal Land, 122;
 'The Apologist's Evening Prayer', 229 n.4;
 Beyond Personality, 110;
 Boxen, 122;
 The Chronicles of Narnia, 6, 7, 9, 53,121-92, 164-65, 226, 227;
 'The Dark Tower', 221;
 Dymer, 120 n.3;
 (ed.) George *MacDonald: An Anthology*, 222;
 The Great Divorce, 4, 9, 81, 101-20, 122, 125, 187, 196, 199, 221, 223-7 *passim*;
 The Horse and His Boy, 126, 166-73, 221, 222, 227;
 'The Inner Ring', 99 n.7;
 'It All Began with a Picture', 5;
 The Last Battle, 127, 131, 135, 175, 184-90, 191 n.10, 223, 224, 226;
 'Learning in War-Time', 99 n.5;
 Letters of C.S. Lewis, 76 n.7, 220 n.1, 229 n.1;
 Letters to Malcolm,72, 76 n.14;

The Lion, the Witch and the Wardrobe, 4, 6, 7, 121, 124-7 *passim*, 129-39, 140-1, 143-4, 148, 152, 167, 182, 183, 221, 224-8 *passim*;
The Magician's Nephew, 126, 174-83, 184, 190, 191 n.8, 221, 223, 224, 226;
Miracles, 3, 11, 101, 120 n.5, 125, 222, 223, 229 ns 6, 7, 229 n.11;
'Myth Became Fact', 229 n.12;
'The Nameless Isle', 149;
'No Beauty We Could Desire', 229 n.8;
'On Science Fiction', 53;
'On Stories', 8, 49, 53, 191 n.15;
'On Three Ways of Writing for Children', 5;
Out of the Silent Planet, 6, 7, 9, 29-47, 49-56 *passim*, 60, 77, 78, 79, 80, 85, 86, 95, 97, 105, 109, 125, 179, 223, 225;
Perelandra, 6, 9, 38, 44, 46, 47 n.9, 49-76, 85, 86, 94, 95, 97, 122, 123, 125, 127, 156, 178, 197, 199, 200, 201, 222, 223, 226, 227, 228, 229 n.13;
The Pilgrim's Regress, 5, 7, 9, 11 n.13, 13-27, 30, 38, 66, 122, 124, 125, 148, 156, 194, 207, 221, 222, 223, 226, 227;
A Preface to 'Paradise Lost', 100, 120 n.4;
'Prelude to Space: An Epithalamium', 99 n.2;
Prince Caspian, 6, 126, 127, 132, 140-8, 149, 161, 167, 191 n.11, 226-7;
The Problem of Pain, 3, 9, 11 ns 3, 13, 101, 120 n.4;
'The Queen of Drum', 5-6, 229 n.8;

'A Reply to Professor Haldane', 47 n.7;
'Science Fiction Cradlesong', 99 n.2;
The Screwtape Letters, 2, 4, 32, 101, 120 n.4;
'Screwtape Proposes a Toast', 120 n.6;
'The Shoddy Lands', 25, 221;
The Silver Chair, 6, 127, 158-65, 167-8, 200, 221, 223, 226;
'Sometimes Fairy Stories May Say Best What's To Be Said', 7, 125;
space trilogy, 4, 5, 9, 128, 226, 227;
Surprised by Joy, 3-4, 11 n.13, 13, 15, 76 n.7, 94, 99 n.12, 123, 229 n.9;
That Hideous Strength, 4, 5, 6, 7, 9, 53, 75, 76 n.7, 76-97, 101, 105, 122, 125, 194, 196, 221, 223, 225, 226;
Till We Have Faces, 4.5, 9-10, 20, 49, 104, 123, 128, 193-220, 221, 223-7 *passim*;
'Unreal Estates', 6;
The Voyage of the 'Dawn Treader', 6, 125, 126-7, 149-57, 160, 167, 175, 178, 221, 223, 224, 226;
'The Weight of Glory', 11 n.13, 224, 229 n.9
Lewis, Warren, 122
Lewis, Wyndham, *The Childermass*, 102
Lindsay, David,
   A Voyage to Arcturus, 8, 29
Lindskoog, Katherine, 191 n.9
Lofting, Hugh,
   Doctor Dolittle in the Moon, 29, 47 n.1

M

MacDonald, George, 121, 123, 125, 156, 175, 215, 222;
  'The Giant's Heart', 159;
  The Great Divorce (as 'George MacDonald'), 103, 107, 116-9 *passim*;
  Phantastes, 3, 94, 103, 191 n.7;
  The Princess and Curdie, 143;
  The Princess and the Goblin, 159
Manlove, C.N., 47 n.9, 64, 76 ns 3, 8, 10-13

Masefield, John, 121;
  The Midnight Folk, 149
Meilaender, Gilbert, 27 n.5, 53, 76 n.9
Meredith, George,
  The Shaving of Shagpat, 167
Milton, John,
  Comus, 192 n.18;
  Paradise Lost, 61, 175, 192 n.25, 222
Mitchison, Naomi,
  The Corn King and the Spring Queen, 193-4
Morris, William,
  The Well at the World's End, 154
Murphy, Brian, preface, 1, 47 ns 2,6, 99 n.6
Myers, Doris, preface, 1

N

Nesbit, Edith,
  'The Aunt and Amabel', 191 n.7;
  'The Cockatoucan', 15;
  The Story of the Amulet, 126, 175, 192 n.4;
  'Whereyouwantogoto', 124
Nichols, Beverley,
  The Stream That Stood Still, 124

O

Orwell, George,
  Nineteen Eighty-Four, 89, 99 n.8, 104
Oury, Scott, 27 n.5

P

Paxton, Fred, 192 n.19
Peake, Mervyn,
  Titus Groan, 159
Pearl, 198
Pliny,
  Natural History, 153
Poe, Edgar Allen,
  'The Fall of the House of Usher', 30
Pope, 53;
  Moral Essay IV, 111
Potter, Beatrix, 130
Purtill, Richard, 99 ns 3, 11

R

Refrigerium, the, 102-03, 104, 118, 120 n.1
Rowling, J.K., 124

S

Schakel, Peter, preface, 1, 168, 192 n.23, 220 ns 2, 3, 6
Shakespeare, William,
  As You Like It, 146;
  Hamlet, 146, 222;
  Henry IV Parts I and II;
  Macbeth, 141-2;
  Richard II, 142;
  The Winter's Tale, 146
Shelley, Mary,
  Frankenstein, 7
Shumaker, Wayne, 47 n.3
Spenser, Edmund,
  The Faerie Queene, 31, 159-60
Spock, Benjamin, 124

Stapledon, Olaf, 29

T
Tao, the, Lewis on, 90
Thisted, V.A.,
   Letters from Hell, 101, 120 n.2
Thomson, James,
   The City of Dreadful Night, 102
Thousand and One Nights, the, 166
Tolkien, J.R.R., 3, 53, 155
'Tom Thumb', 159
Traherne, Thomas, 15

U
Urang, Gunnar, 27 n.1, 99 n.4, 220 n.3

V
Van Der Weele, Steve, 220 n.5
Voyage of Bran, The, 149

W
Walsh, Chad, 27 ns 2, 3, 47 n.4, 99 n.4, 220 n.3
Ward, Michael, 1
Weil, Simone, 15
Wells, H.G., 222;
   The First Men in the Moon, 29, 47 n.1, 101;
   The Time Machine, 30
White, William L., 47 n.7
Williams, Charles, 26, 68, 78, 82, 86-7, 20 n.6, 224;
   All Hallows Eve, 104;
   Descent into Hell, 78;
   He Came Down From Heaven (quoted), 128;
   The Place of the Lion, 92
Wilson, A.N., 2
Wilson, Harold, 80
Wrong, Charles, 220 n.1

Z
Zogby, Edward J, Jr, 27 n.4

Other Titles of Interest

C. S. Lewis

C. S. Lewis: Views From Wake Forest - Essays on C. S. Lewis
Michael Travers, editor

Contains sixteen scholarly presentations from the international C. S. Lewis convention in Wake Forest, NC. Walter Hooper shares his important essay "Editing C. S. Lewis," a chronicle of publishing decisions after Lewis' death in 1963.
"Scholars from a variety of disciplines address a wide range of issues. The happy result is a fresh and expansive view of an author who well deserves this kind of thoughtful attention."
Diana Pavlac Glyer, author of *The Company They Keep*

Why I Believe in Narnia: 33 Essays & Reviews on the Life & Work of C. S. Lewis
By James Como

Chapters range from reviews of critical books, documentaries and movies to evaluations of Lewis' books to biographical analysis.
"A valuable, wide-ranging collection of essays by one of the best informed and most astute commentators on Lewis' work and ideas."
Peter Schakel, author *Imagination & the Arts in C. S. Lewis*

C. S. Lewis & Philosophy as a Way of Life: His Philosophical Thoughts
Adam Barkman

C. S. Lewis is rarely thought of as a "philosopher" per se despite having both studied and taught philosophy for several years at Oxford. Lewis's long journey to Christianity was essentially philosophical – passing through seven different stages. This 624 page book is an invaluable reference for C. S. Lewis scholars and fans alike.

The Hidden Story of Narnia: A Book-By-Book Guide to Lewis' Spiritual Themes
Will Vaus

A book of insightful commentary – Will Vaus points out connections between the *Narnia* books and spiritual and biblical themes in our world, as well as between ideas in the *Narnia* books and C. S. Lewis' other books. Each chapter includes questions for individual use or small group discussion.

George MacDonald

Diary of an Old Soul & The White Page Poems
George MacDonald and Betty Aberlin

The first edition of George MacDonald's book of daily poems included a blank page opposite each page of poems. Readers were invited to write their own reflections on the "white page." MacDonald wrote: "Let your white page be ground, my print be seed, growing to golden ears, that faith and hope may feed." Betty Aberlin responded to MacDonald's invitation with daily poems of her own.
Betty Aberlin's close readings of George MacDonald's verses and her thoughtful responses to them speak clearly of her poetic gifts and spiritual intelligence. Luci Shaw, poet

George MacDonald: Literary Heritage and Heirs
Roderick McGillis, editor

This latest collection of 14 essays sets a new standard that will influence MacDonald studies for many more years. George MacDonald experts are increasingly evaluating his entire corpus within the nineteenth century context.
This comprehensive collection represents the best of contemporary scholarship on George MacDonald. Rolland Hein, author of *George MacDonald: Victorian Mythmaker.*

In the Near Loss of Everything: George MacDonald's Son in America
Dale Wayne Slusser

In the summer of 1887, George MacDonald's son Ronald, newly engaged to artist Louise Blandy, sailed from England to America to teach school. The next summer he returned to England to marry Louise and bring her back to America. On August 27, 1890, Louise died leaving him with an infant daughter. Ronald once described losing a beloved spouse as "the near loss of everything". Dale Wayne Slusser unfolds this poignant story with unpublished letters and photos that give readers a glimpse into the close-knit MacDonald family. Also included is Ronald's essay about his father, *George MacDonald: A Personal Note*, plus a selection from Ronald's 1922 fable, *The Laughing Elf*, about the necessity of both sorrow and joy in life.

A Novel Pulpit: Sermons From George MacDonald's Fiction
David L. Neuhouser

"In MacDonald's novels, the Christian teaching emerges out of the characters and story line, the narrator's comments, and inclusion of sermons given by the fictional preachers. The sermons in the novels are shorter than the ones in collections of MacDonald's sermons and so are perhaps more accessible for some. In any case, they are both stimulating and thought-provoking. This collection of sermons from ten novels serve to bring out the 'freshness and brilliance' of MacDonald's message."
from the author's introduction

Other Titles

To Love Another Person: A Spiritual Journey Through Les Miserables
John Morrison

The powerful story of Jean Valjean's redemption is beloved by readers and theater goers everywhere. In this companion and guide to Victor Hugo's masterpiece, author John Morrison unfolds the spiritual depth and breadth of this classic novel and broadway musical.

The Eye of the Beholder: How to See the World Like a Romantic Poet
Louis Markos

This accessible guide to Romantic poetry focuses almost exclusively on short lyrical poems (the exceptions are Coleridge's *Rime of the Ancient Mariner*, Blake's *Marriage of Heaven and Hell* and Wordsworth's "Preface to Lyrical Ballads"). A detailed bibliographic essay on each poet is provided that cites critical studies of their work.

Through Common Things: Philosophical Reflections on Popular Culture
Adam Barkman

"Barkman presents us with an amazingly wide-ranging collection of philosophical reflections grounded in the everyday things of popular culture – past and present, eastern and western, factual and fictional. Throughout his encounters with often surprising subject-matter (the value of darkness?), he writes clearly and concisely, moving seamlessly between Aristotle and anime, Lord Buddha and Lord Voldemort. . . . This is an informative and entertaining book to read!"
    Doug Blomberg, Professor of Philosophy, Institute for Christian Studies

The Order of Harry Potter: The Literary Skill of the Hogwarts Epic
Colin Manlove

The *Harry Potter* stories work as the best kinds of literature work, with the style both mirroring and commenting on the content. *The Order of Harry Potter* book is about their character, their individuality, and how they work as unique forms of literature. It looks at the ways in which they are like and unlike the fantasy works of the 'Inklings'; at their readability; at their treatment of the topic of imagination; at their skill in organization and the use of language; and at their underlying motifs and themes. In other words, it looks at how the books *exist*, rather than what they are *for*.

For these books not only *mean*, they *are*, and what they are is a construct of style and imagery and brilliant invention. Almost without exception literary criticism of the *Harry Potter* books has concerned what they signify: what are their moral, religious or philosophical meanings. In moving away from such readings Colin Manlove brings the debate back to where it should start, from a discussion of how well the books work. For that, given the millions of their readers who cannot put them down, is the first consideration.

              adapted from the author's preface

About the Author

Colin Manlove is a writer and literary critic, with a particular interest in fantasy works. His monumental work, *Modern Fantasy: Five Studies* (1975), made a comprehensive study of the writers Charles Kingsley, George MacDonald, C. S. Lewis, J. R. R. Tolkien and Mervyn Peake, at  a time when fantasy literature was yet to emerge as a subject worthy of academic treatment. Manlove went on to write and edit various other definitive works on Christian, English, Scottish and modern British fantasy, including *The Impulse of Fantasy Literature* (1982), *Christian Fantasy: From 1200 to the Present* (1992), *The Chronicles of Narnia: The Patterning of a Fantastic World* (1993), *Scottish Fantasy Literature: A Critical Survey* (1994), *The Fantasy Literature of England* (1999), *From Alice to Harry Potter: Children's Fantasy in England* (2003), and *An Anthology of Scottish Fantasy Literature* (1996). His other publications include studies of Shakespeare, 17th and 18th century literature, science fiction and an introductory text for students of literature, entitled *Critical Thinking: A Guide to Interpreting Literary Texts* (1989).

Manlove taught English Literature at Edinburgh University for several years, where he received an honorary D. Litt in recognition of his pioneering research publications. Currently, he is working as a full-time writer and independent scholar, and has just completed a book looking at the *Harry Potter* books as literary works in contrast to previous critical studies in terms of their theology and symbology.

In his spare time Manlove is a collector of minerals, which are displayed all over his house in Edinburgh. He is widowed, with two married sons and four grandchildren.